Imagination and the Imaginary

The concept of the imaginary is pervasive within contemporary thought, yet can be a baffling and often controversial term. In *Imagination and the Imaginary*, Kathleen Lennon explores the links between imagination – regarded as the faculty of creating images or forms – and the imaginary, which links such imagery with affect or emotion and captures the significance which the world carries for us.

Beginning with an examination of contrasting theories of imagination proposed by Hume and Kant, Lennon argues that the imaginary is not something in opposition to the real, but the very faculty through which the world is made real to us. She then turns to the vexed relationship between perception and imagination and, drawing on Kant, Merleau-Ponty and Sartre, explores some fundamental questions, such as whether there is a distinction between the perceived and the imagined; the relationship between imagination and creativity; and the role of the body in perception and imagination. Invoking also Spinoza and Coleridge, Lennon argues that, far from being a realm of illusion, the imaginary world is our most direct mode of perception. She then explores the role the imaginary plays in the formation of the self and the social world.

A unique feature of the volume is that it compares and contrasts a philosophical tradition of thinking about the imagination   running from Kant and Hume to Strawson and John McDowell – with the work of phenomenological, psychoanalytic, poststructuralist and feminist thinkers such as Merleau-Ponty, Sartre, Lacan, Castoriadis, Irigaray, Gatens and Lloyd. This makes *Imagination and the Imaginary* essential reading for students and scholars working in phenomenology, philosophy of perception, social theory, cultural studies and aesthetics.

Kathleen Lennon is Professor of Philosophy in the School of Politics, Philosophy and International Studies at the University of Hull, UK. Her most recent publications include the co-authored books *The World, the Flesh and the Subject* (2005) and *Theorizing Gender* (2002), and the co-edited volume *Embodied Selves* (2013).

Imagination and the Imaginary

Kathleen Lennon

Routledge
Taylor & Francis Group

LONDON AND NEW YORK

First published 2015
by Routledge
2 Park Square, Milton Park, Abingdon, Oxon OX14 4RN

and by Routledge
711 Third Avenue, New York, NY 10017

Routledge is an imprint of the Taylor & Francis Group, an informa business

British Library Cataloguing in Publication Data
A catalogue record for this book is available from the British Library

Library of Congress Cataloging in Publication Data
Lennon, Kathleen.
Imagination and the imaginary / by Kathleen Lennon. -- 1 [edition].
Includes bibliographical references and index.
1. Imagination (Philosophy) 2. Perception (Philosophy) I. Title.
B105.I49L46 2015
128'.3--dc23
2014030570

ISBN: 978-0-415-43092-0 (hbk)
ISBN: 978-1-315-73038-7 (ebk)

Typeset in Sabon
by Taylor & Francis Books

Printed and bound in the United States of America by Publishers Graphics, LLC on sustainably sourced paper.

In memory of Margaret Whitford

In the sensible a certain rhythm of existence is put forward.

Maurice Merleau-Ponty

Contents

Acknowledgements

My interest in the imaginary was first fuelled by my friend Margaret Whitford in her groundbreaking work on the philosophy of Luce Irigaray, expounded initially at meetings of the Society of Women in Philosophy. I have also been much informed by the writings of Genevieve Lloyd and Moira Gatens, particularly by Moira's book *Imaginary Bodies*, and their joint writings on Spinoza since. Susan James has also been very helpful in informing me about Spinoza. In my early days at Oxford I encountered the pioneering work of Gabriele Taylor on the emotions, showing how our emotional life can be assessed, and made sense of; understood and not simply causally explained. This book is a continuation of those concerns. There I was also taught Kant by Peter Strawson, and have myself taught the first *Critique* throughout my academic career. I am grateful to my students for forcing clarity and constant re-evaluation of this text. Strawson's paper 'Imagination and Perception' was also central in informing the thinking of this book. I was lucky to attend the lectures of John McDowell on the perception of moral value. These, together with his later writings, jolted me out of a naturalising slumber, and ultimately led to the questions addressed here. In the last ten years or so I have been much absorbed in phenomenology and, as will be evident from what follows, inspired by the work of Merleau-Ponty. The writings of Galen Johnson have been helpful in this. I owe a great debt to continual conversations with my friend and colleague Paul Gilbert whose breadth of reading, and subtlety of philosophical thought, have set the standard for me. Very special thanks are due to Rhiannon Goldthorpe for her careful and illuminating attention to my reading of Sartre; a reading also informed by the writings of Robert Denoon Cumming. I am also grateful to Ismay Barwell for perceptive interrogation of the ideas informing this book. Mary Warnock's 1976 book *Imagination* was an early model for this one. Comments from an anonymous Routledge reader were very helpful in improving the clarity of the book.

Kathleen Lennon, University of Hull, July 2014

1   The disenchanted world and the world of experience

[handwritten margin note: how do I distinguish the "knowing" the I am who I am]

Imagination and the imaginary

[handwritten margin note: imaginary]

The concept of the imaginary is pervasive within contemporary writing concerning the self, the body and social groupings. The notion of the imaginary which is employed in this way may be broadly characterised as the affectively laden patterns/images/forms, by means of which we experience the world, other people and ourselves. This contemporary usage is distinguished most importantly by its constitutive linkage of imagery with *affect*, the emotions, feelings and desires which mark our engagement with the world. The images are the vehicles for such affect, the way in which it is given form. By means of *[handwritten margin note: vehicle]* these images the emotional contours of the subject's world are revealed. They are the way in which we not only think, but also feel our way around. This use is indebted particularly to the work of Lacan, Castoriadis, and Irigaray.[1] In the important applications by Gatens and Lloyd[2] it is traced back to Spinoza. I will *[handwritten margin note: affect]* return to each of these in the discussions in later chapters, comparing them to the phenomenological writers who form the heart of this book. Sharing the constitutive link of image and affect these sources nonetheless have important differences. For Lacan the Imaginary[3] is the domain of misrecognition and illusion, and it is a stage (moment) of development from which, although it remains in play, we move to the public Symbolic order. For him the Imaginary, initially an Imaginary of the self, is the illusion of a coherent and unified ego, which disguises from us the extent to which we are constituted by the working of the other within us (via the working of language, for example). For the other writers mentioned the imaginary, which extends beyond images of the self, is necessary for experience of any kind. Although we can criticise false and debilitating imaginaries, we cannot draw a sharp distinction between the imaginary and the symbolic, cognition and affect, between what is known and what *[handwritten margin note: OK here I differ]* is imagined. This will be the view defended here.

This book explores the links between such a concept of the imaginary and more traditional conceptions of the imagination, particularly that found in discussions of the relation between imagination and perception, for example in Hume and Kant. For Hume[4] the imagination is the domain of mental images, faint copies of sensory impressions derived from perceptions. Here we have imagination as yielding mental or *inner images*; these images are distinct from sensory images and so *imagination is distinct from perception*, but the images are *copies* of perceptions or re-arrangements of elements which are copied from perception. The imagination then makes *things which are absent* in some way *present*. The imagination is nonetheless needed to supplement perception if we are to take our sensory data to be of spatio-temporal objects. For Kant,[5] however, the imagination is at work in perception in a different way. It is the faculty by which sensory intuitions are given shape or form, without which perceptual experiences are not possible. It is not therefore simply a source of inner copies of sensory experience, but is needed to give shape to such experiences. It is the domain of images, but such images are not only items in our stream of consciousness, they provide the shape of the spatio-temporal world. Images, in this sense, weave together the sensory *present* with what is *past*, the projected *future*, and the spatial *elsewhere*. Thus imagination is that by which there is a world for us. This is the thesis which will be discussed and defended here. It will be suggested, following Kant, that the imagination is required for experiences of the world *and* for the creation of fictions or illusions. It is not, therefore, simply the activity of forming fictional/illusory/unreal/non-actual worlds, as some everyday usages might suggest. In Kant's work on aesthetic judgments there is also an emphasis on the imagination as the domain of *creativity*, the images or forms which we experience not dictated by what we encounter, but remaining answerable to this and detectable by others. This thought will also turn out to be central in what follows.

In this book the concepts of the imagination and the imaginary, which are distilled through the chapters, take their starting point from Kant, but they are then routed through the writings of the phenomenologists. A conception of the imaginary emerges which characterises it not as a domain of illusion posited in opposition to a 'real', but rather as *that by which* the real is made available to us. (Here the real is, simply, the world, the actual, in contrast to the fictional, or illusory.) Central to this is a recognition of the imagination working *within everyday experience*, deriving from the characterisation of such experience provided particularly by Heidegger[6] and Merleau-Ponty.[7] The work of Sartre[8] is also pivotal, although his fundamental distinction between perceiving and imagining consciousness is rejected. The working of the imagination within experience which is suggested is not, however, that of a synthesising transcendent subject delivering order to the world. Rather imagination is a (creative) capacity to experience the world in a certain way, in the form of *images*. This concept of image is much wider than what is sometimes taken to be its standard definition: 'the internal [or external] representation of a sensory object in the absence of a corresponding sensory stimulus'.[9] Instead images are conceived of in this work as the *shapes or forms* in terms of which we experience the world, which weave together the present and absent in a way that requires both invention and discovery, and remain open to possibilities of revision. As Merleau-Ponty points out:

> The word image is in bad repute because we have thoughtlessly believed that the design was a tracing, a copy, a second thing and that the mental image was … belonging among our private bric a brac. But in fact it is nothing of the kind … They are [that] … without which we would never understand the quasi presence and imminent visibility which make up the whole problem of the imaginary.[10]

Such images can be sensory but we also have images of mathematical proofs, universals like love, the state of the country, social difference, the pattern of a life, etc. In some respect the notion of an image is close to the notion of an aspect in Wittgenstein's discussion in the *Philosophical Investigations*,[11] and he himself says 'the concept of an aspect is akin to the concept of an image',[12] clarifying in relation to a puzzle picture: 'I recognise not only that it has shape or colour but also a quite particular organisation'.[13] However, the distinction which this remark might suggest between sensory content and organisational form is not one which will be maintained, for we shall see that to experience colour or shape also requires the imagination. To speak of images in this way, and of the imagination as that which concerns such images, is not to employ a usage quite removed from our everyday one. When we speak of people as imaginative, we do not usually mean that they live in a world of make believe, played out within their interior life. We often mean that they are particularly perceptive, sensitive to the shapes which the world around them can take.

This book therefore outlines what Merleau-Ponty coins 'the imaginary texture of the real'.[14] The imagination is at work in the everyday world which we perceive, the world as it is for us. What is important in linking this concept of the imaginary with that with which we began, the affectively laden patterns which constitute our sense of the world, others and ourselves, is to recognise that the working of the imagination within the world gives that world *an affective texture*. It has a salience and significance for us, suggesting and sometimes demanding the desiring and sometimes fearful responses we make to it. In the discussion in Chapter 4 this feature of images is spelt out by the suggestion that images are *expressive*, such that experiencing in terms of images provides normative anchorage for our desiring, fearful, etc., responses.

The treatment of imagination and the imaginary offered here is, therefore, distinct from at least two other directions of attention found in contemporary writing. There is, of course, much written about the fact that we live in the age of the image. Here, with particular emphasis on visual images, images are conceived of as representations, mostly public. Concern has been expressed that such representations have become increasingly self-referential,[15] following a logic unconstrained by what they, in principle, represent; but able to be mistaken by their consumers to be a transparent copy of something beyond themselves.[16] Much attention is also paid to the interpretation of such images against the background of a poststructuralist theory in which such content is contextual, indeterminate and open to indefinite reworking.[17] This work will not directly address such concerns. Nonetheless the images which are the focus of such attention are a subcategory of images in the wider sense in which that term is used here. Not all images in this wider sense are *re*presentations. Nonetheless, in the account offered our experiences take the form of images, and images offered as representations can reorder the way in which we experience the world (see the discussion of works of art, particularly in Chapter 3). Moreover, the insights of poststructuralism, concerning the openness and indeterminacy of imagery, also have resonances for images in the wider sense adopted here. And such insights accrue to the saliences of our everyday experiences, as well as to the content of images offered as representations.

There is also work on the imagination within contemporary philosophy of mind, as part of its engagement with cognitive processing.[18] One question concerns what is distinctive about thinking in images as opposed to linguistic thinking. Others concern how the creativity of the imagination is to be most appropriately modelled within functionalist accounts of mental processes. Another area of research involves the role of imagination in enabling us to understand others, perhaps by simulating their mental states. These concerns most commonly view the imagination as an inner mental faculty and the images it produces as part of the contents of our subjective conscious experience. Although the account offered in this book must allow for the possibility of mental images it does not take its starting points from images of this kind. These are only one type of image which the imagination makes possible. The questions of this work are therefore distinct from (though not necessarily in opposition to) concerns with the appropriate modelling of inner cognitive processes. What some recent work in philosophy of mind does share with the direction of thought here is, however, a recognition of the interweaving of the cognitive and the emotional,[19] an interweaving which can be characterised by attention to the role which images play in our experiencing of the world.

The disenchanted world

In a much quoted lecture, published in 1922, Max Weber characterised the world which it was the job of the scientist to describe as a world in the 'process of disenchantment'. In such a world

> there are no mysterious incalculable forces that come into play ... one can, in principle, master all things by calculation ... One need no longer have recourse to magical means in order to master [it] or implore the spirits, as did the savage, for whom such mysterious powers existed. Technical means and calculations perform the service.[20]

Such a world view derives from 'the rationalization' and 'intellectualization' which Weber called 'the fate of our times'.[21] Such intellectualisation provides us with a world of facts which we can put to use to increase our technical control of our surroundings. Such scientific work is tied to a conception of progress, progress which is measured in relation to such technical control. For Weber it was not only magical and mysterious forces which have no place in such a scientific world, but also meaning and value. 'If these natural sciences lead to anything in this way, they are apt to make the belief that there is such a thing as the "meaning" of the universe die out at its very roots.'[22] He quotes approvingly Tolstoy's remark, 'Science is meaningless because it gives no answer to our question ... "What shall we do and how shall we live?"'[23] For Weber questions of meaning and value were ones which were settled subjectively, outside of the realm of factual considerations. Once settled, science can provide us with information instrumental to achieving goals set independently of it.

It is often claimed that it is characteristic of modernist thinking to yield such a disenchanted view of nature, and hand in hand with it, to assume that everything in the world is, in principle, able to be made sense of by scientific calculation. John McDowell has remarked how such a conception of nature, 'a hard-won achievement of human thought at a specific time', can now seem 'sheer common sense';[24] standing in contrast to a conception in which 'what we now see as the subject matter of natural science was conceived as filled with meaning, as if all nature was a book of lessons for us'.[25] There are two key features of this scientific approach. One is that the world so characterised is viewed as objective in a very particular sense. Science attempts to characterise the world as if from no particular point within it; attempting to discount for the position of the investigator to give us a view as if 'from nowhere'.[26] Second, nature is conceived of as the realm of law; the realm of detectable empirical regularities which we can uncover and knowledge of which enables our manipulation of it. For a view which McDowell characterises as 'bald naturalism', these features are combined with a third, namely a 'conviction ... that conceptualizations of things as natural, in that sense, exhaust the conceptualizations of things that stand a chance of truth'.[27] This is the framework within which as Merleau-Ponty points out 'If I want to know what light is, surely I should ask a physicist'[28] (rather than, for example, a painter). For bald naturalists any characterisations of the world, not employing the resources of natural science, will be true in virtue of the truth of such scientific claims. Their apparent distinctiveness will be explained away by showing how facts captured in other terms can simply be shown to follow from the truth of facts which the bald naturalist can accommodate.

This disenchanted view of the world has consequences for the conceptions of ourselves, as experiencing subjects, which are somewhat paradoxical.[29] On the one hand the meaning, value and purpose which have been ejected from the world come to be seen as residing within subjects. Only conscious subjects can behave purposively. They are also the *source* of meaning and of value, as Weber makes clear. This seems to set up a contrast between the human subject and the world in which they are placed, a contrast reinforced when such subjects were conceived of as capable of a spontaneity of thought and action, which contrasted with the rule-governed operations of the world exterior to them. With the rise of the bald naturalist view, however, such a contrast between the experiencing subject and the world in which they are placed has been found intolerable. Human subjects are themselves treated as susceptible to scientific

explanations which have the characteristics listed above; their apparent pur-
posiveness and spontaneity capturable within, and reducible to, a structure of
law-like empirical regularities.

The world as experienced

When we turn our attention to our perceptual experience of the world it is clear
that the world we experience is quite different from that offered by scientific
accounts. Certain aspects show up for us, while others are passed over; and what
shows up is interwoven with the lives we lead as we are immersed within our
surroundings. To make this point clear let us think first of the way in which we
experience other bodies. When we encounter the bodies of other people, we are
not perceiving them according to their physiological characteristics. That is
the job of science. Rather we are recognising what Wittgenstein calls a *physiognomy*, a form expressive of character. *(Physiognomy: The face, especially,
viewed as an index of ... character. Also the contour of a country – OED.)*[30]
We perceive the joy or sadness in a face without being able to describe the
position of its features as arrangements in objective space. We could not
describe how much the mouth had gone up and down, or what the position of the
cheek bones were. Such a physiognomy is evident also when we see people
engaged in intentional acts. Again what we perceive are not sets of bodily
movements as they would be detected by a physiologist. Instead we see people
shopping or making tea, taking a rest or engaged in conversation (see the
discussion in Chapters 4 and 7).

   When we turn away from the perception of persons and turn our attention to
other parts of the world, it becomes clear that this also has a physiognomy, in
both a parallel and interdependent way. The *OED* notes that the notion of
physiognomy, used for the character of a face, can also be used for the contours
or character of a landscape. An example might help give something of the
flavour of such parallels. Mitch Rose, discussing people's relations to the land-
scapes which surround them, cites the following directions. They give the
flavour their surroundings have, for the person giving the directions:

> All right now, you know where Miss Banks stays at up there, don't you? ...
> Now go on down Miss Banks place past that big ol bridge where that
> McKinney boy went over and hit looks like you might go in after'm if you
> ain't careful buddy ... keep on 'til you see the Black Eagle post office.
> That's where the snake handlers stay at and Bud says he's skeered to deliver
> the mail down there, where he might put his hand in a mailbox and ther's a
> snake in there ... now, keep on, keep on, pretty soon you come to that
> place where they shot up that boy ...[31]

We might say, drawing a parallel with our perception of people, that the world
we experience has a character. It is just such character of the world that the
disenchanted view of it seems to leave out.

The phenomenological tradition

The character of the experienced world has been carefully articulated within the phenomenological tradition, where both the exclusivity and the primacy of the scientific characterisation of the world are challenged. The goal of such phenomenological descriptions is to enable us to rediscover the world in which we live.[32] Phenomenology's task is the 'disclosure' of such a world; to describe it, not analyse or explain it.[33] The task is to describe the world as lived and experienced by subjects, not as detached observers seeking its laws of making, but as participants for which it forms the 'natural milieu and field of ... thoughts and ... explicit perceptions'.[34] There are a number of key characteristics of our world which the phenomenologists draw our attention to. Our perceptions reveal a world of sensory qualities: colours, noises, and tactile sensations. These are not pure sensations, inner items within an interior subjectivity, the isolated impressions beloved of empiricists, but qualities *of objects*, qualities of what is sensed, not of the sensor. Such sensory qualities are not isolated items. They are part of a whole sensory field in which their (changing) character reflects the character of the whole. The sensory qualities we encounter are qualities of everyday objects which are perceived immediately as 'houses, the sun, mountains'.[35] We do not first encounter an object as science would characterise it and then interpret it 'as a door, as a house'.[36] 'What we "first" hear is never noises or complexes of sounds, but the creaking wagon, the motorcycle. We hear the column on the march, the north wind, the woodpecker tapping, the fire crackling.'[37] The objects which we perceive are objects which are woven into our engagement with the world, objects which hold out possibilities for us: the sun for warming our face or dazzling our eyes. Heidegger characterises this in terms of the world which we initially encounter being a world which is 'ready to hand'. 'In our dealings, we come across equipment for writing, sewing, working, transportation.'[38] 'What we encounter as closest to us ... is the room; and we encounter it not as something between four walls in a geometrical spatial sense, but as equipment for residing.'[39] For Merleau-Ponty, for the normal person, 'the object "speaks" and is significant ... the perceptual field ... a wave of significance'.[40] This is in contrast to patients who have lost the capacity to perceive the world in this way and who have to be taught an interpretation, which still holds no possibilities for them.

Such a world requires a subject who exists within and alongside it; a subject for whom this pattern of significance can show up. The subject for Heidegger (who characterises it as *Dasein*) and Merleau-Ponty is part of the world they experience, not an observer detached from it. Such being-in-the-world is not a matter of the subject simply having a spatial position next to objects within a three-dimensional objective space, a position from which two-way causal encounters result. A subject being in the world alongside objects is not the same as the pencil being on the desk next to the computer. Being in the world requires that the world can show up for subjects in the way described above. To be a subject is to be aware of, have, a world of this kind available to us.

'*Dasein in its familiarity with significance, is the ontical condition for the possibility of discovering entities which are encountered in a world with involvement (readiness-to-hand) as their kind of Being.*'[41] This does not, however, mean that, as subjects of experience, existing within the world we experience, we are the *source* of the significance encountered. (This is a point discussed further in Chapter 4.)

The world which the phenomenologists characterise for us is a world with affective texture. It is, in Heidegger's terms, a world which is 'lit up' for us. The character of such affectivity can be captured by considering Heidegger's discussion of *moods* or *states of mind*.[42] For Heidegger all our encounters with the world are coloured by some mood. Moods are not phenomena purely accompanying our perceptual states. By mood or state of mind Heidegger does not mean an inner state which we project outwards to provide colour to an otherwise neutral environment. Rather the notion of mood for him carries with it an association of the German word which we might characterise as *attunement*. To be in a mood is to be tuned in to the world in a certain kind of way; so that certain kinds of things show up for us and offer possibilities for response: 'it is not just sensing something or staring at it ... it has the character of being affected in some way'.[43] We may, for example, find the world, or parts of it, threatening. In the world, as characterised by the scientist, what Heidegger calls the present-at-hand, nothing, he suggests, could be discovered which mattered to us. There is no room for the feature of, for example, 'being threatening' to appear. Yet such an appearance is what is required if the world is to be one in which we are engaged. Moods as openness to characteristics of the world which matter to us are, for Heidegger, 'prior to cognition and volition'.[44] They are also all-pervasive. We are never not in a mood. Even theoretical contemplation of the world requires a tranquillity without which it is not possible to reflect. Even what seems like 'the pallid, evenly balanced lack of mood, which is often persistent ... is far from nothing at all'.[45] Without moods, that is without openness to aspects of the world which matter to us, we could not grasp what possibilities there are for engagement. None of these possibilities would appear desirable or undesirable. If the world could not appear threatening then we could not grasp the need for flight. Here Heidegger is rejecting a picture in which our needs and desires are prior inner states setting our goals, and the world is a world of neutral facts which we utilise to find ways of fulfilling them. In contrast, our responses arise out of our openness to a world whose affective qualities suggest possibilities to us (Chapter 4).

For the phenomenological writers under discussion here the characteristics of the world as lived are not 'mere' appearances behind which lie the 'real' features of the world which science will discover. For the scientific conception of the world, objects are, what Heidegger terms, present-at-hand; they occupy positions within a three-dimensional space conceived of from no position within it. Their features are captured in ways that remove them from being objects of concern for us. For Merleau-Ponty 'Scientific thinking ... looks on from above, and thinks of the object-in-general'.[46] Such scientific thinking is not

'*Dasein in its familiarity with significance, is the ontical condition for the possibility of discovering entities which are encountered in a world with involvement (readiness-to-hand) as their kind of Being.*'[41] This does not, however, mean that, as subjects of experience, existing within the world we experience, we are the *source* of the significance encountered. (This is a point discussed further in Chapter 4.)

The world which the phenomenologists characterise for us is a world with affective texture. It is, in Heidegger's terms, a world which is 'lit up' for us. The character of such affectivity can be captured by considering Heidegger's discussion of *moods* or *states of mind*.[42] For Heidegger all our encounters with the world are coloured by some mood. Moods are not phenomena purely accompanying our perceptual states. By mood or state of mind Heidegger does not mean an inner state which we project outwards to provide colour to an otherwise neutral environment. Rather the notion of mood for him carries with it an association of the German word which we might characterise as *attunement*. To be in a mood is to be tuned in to the world in a certain kind of way; so that certain kinds of things show up for us and offer possibilities for response: 'it is not just sensing something or staring at it ... it has the character of being affected in some way'.[43] We may, for example, find the world, or parts of it, threatening. In the world, as characterised by the scientist, what Heidegger calls the present-at-hand, nothing, he suggests, could be discovered which mattered to us. There is no room for the feature of, for example, 'being threatening' to appear. Yet such an appearance is what is required if the world is to be one in which we are engaged. Moods as openness to characteristics of the world which matter to us are, for Heidegger, 'prior to cognition and volition'.[44] They are also all-pervasive. We are never not in a mood. Even theoretical contemplation of the world requires a tranquillity without which it is not possible to reflect. Even what seems like 'the pallid, evenly balanced lack of mood, which is often persistent ... is far from nothing at all'.[45] Without moods, that is without openness to aspects of the world which matter to us, we could not grasp what possibilities there are for engagement. None of these possibilities would appear desirable or undesirable. If the world could not appear threatening then we could not grasp the need for flight. Here Heidegger is rejecting a picture in which our needs and desires are prior inner states setting our goals, and the world is a world of neutral facts which we utilise to find ways of fulfilling them. In contrast, our responses arise out of our openness to a world whose affective qualities suggest possibilities to us (Chapter 4).

For the phenomenological writers under discussion here the characteristics of the world as lived are not 'mere' appearances behind which lie the 'real' features of the world which science will discover. For the scientific conception of the world, objects are, what Heidegger terms, present-at-hand; they occupy positions within a three-dimensional space conceived of from no position within it. Their features are captured in ways that remove them from being objects of concern for us. For Merleau-Ponty 'Scientific thinking ... looks on from above, and thinks of the object-in-general'.[46] Such scientific thinking is not

The phenomenological tradition

The character of the experienced world has been carefully articulated within the phenomenological tradition, where both the exclusivity and the primacy of the scientific characterisation of the world are challenged. The goal of such phenomenological descriptions is to enable us to rediscover the world in which we live.[32] Phenomenology's task is the 'disclosure' of such a world; to describe it, not analyse or explain it.[33] The task is to describe the world as lived and experienced by subjects, not as detached observers seeking its laws of making, but as participants for which it forms the 'natural milieu and field of ... thoughts and ... explicit perceptions'.[34] There are a number of key characteristics of our world which the phenomenologists draw our attention to. Our perceptions reveal a world of sensory qualities: colours, noises, and tactile sensations. These are not pure sensations, inner items within an interior subjectivity, the isolated impressions beloved of empiricists, but qualities *of objects*, qualities of what is sensed, not of the sensor. Such sensory qualities are not isolated items. They are part of a whole sensory field in which their (changing) character reflects the character of the whole. The sensory qualities we encounter are qualities of everyday objects which are perceived immediately as 'houses, the sun, mountains'.[35] We do not first encounter an object as science would characterise it and then interpret it 'as a door, as a house'.[36] 'What we "first" hear is never noises or complexes of sounds, but the creaking wagon, the motorcycle. We hear the column on the march, the north wind, the woodpecker tapping, the fire crackling.'[37] The objects which we perceive are objects which are woven into our engagement with the world, objects which hold out possibilities for us: the sun for warming our face or dazzling our eyes. Heidegger characterises this in terms of the world which we initially encounter being a world which is 'ready to hand'. 'In our dealings, we come across equipment for writing, sewing, working, transportation.'[38] 'What we encounter as closest to us ... is the room; and we encounter it not as something between four walls in a geometrical spatial sense, but as equipment for residing.'[39] For Merleau-Ponty, for the normal person, 'the object "speaks" and is significant ... the perceptual field ... a wave of significance'.[40] This is in contrast to patients who have lost the capacity to perceive the world in this way and who have to be taught an interpretation, which still holds no possibilities for them.

Such a world requires a subject who exists within and alongside it; a subject for whom this pattern of significance can show up. The subject for Heidegger (who characterises it as *Dasein*) and Merleau-Ponty is part of the world they experience, not an observer detached from it. Such being-in-the-world is not a matter of the subject simply having a spatial position next to objects within a three-dimensional objective space, a position from which two-way causal encounters result. A subject being in the world alongside objects is not the same as the pencil being on the desk next to the computer. Being in the world requires that the world can show up for subjects in the way described above. To be a subject is to be aware of, have, a world of this kind available to us.

explanations which have the characteristics listed above; their apparent pur-posiveness and spontaneity capturable within, and reducible to, a structure of law-like empirical regularities.

The world as experienced

When we turn our attention to our perceptual experience of the world it is clear that the world we experience is quite different from that offered by scientific accounts. Certain aspects show up for us, while others are passed over; and what shows up is interwoven with the lives we lead as we are immersed within our surroundings. To make this point clear let us think first of the way in which we experience other bodies. When we encounter the bodies of other people, we are not perceiving them according to their physiological characteristics. That is the job of science. Rather we are recognising what Wittgenstein calls a *phy-siognomy*, a form expressive of character. (*Physiognomy: The face, especially, viewed as an index of ... character. Also the contour of a country* – OED.)[30] We perceive the joy or sadness in a face without being able to describe the position of its features as arrangements in objective space. We could not describe how much the mouth had gone up and down, or what the position of the cheek bones were. Such a physiognomy is evident also when we see people engaged in intentional acts. Again what we perceive are not sets of bodily movements as they would be detected by a physiologist. Instead we see people shopping or making tea, taking a rest or engaged in conversation (see the discussion in Chapters 4 and 7).

When we turn away from the perception of persons and turn our attention to other parts of the world, it becomes clear that this also has a physiognomy, in both a parallel and interdependent way. The *OED* notes that the notion of physiognomy, used for the character of a face, can also be used for the contours or character of a landscape. An example might help give something of the flavour of such parallels. Mitch Rose, discussing people's relations to the land-scapes which surround them, cites the following directions. They give the flavour their surroundings have, for the person giving the directions:

> All right now, you know where Miss Banks stays at up there, don't you? ... Now go on down Miss Banks place past that big ol bridge where that McKinney boy went over and hit looks like you might go in after'm if you ain't careful buddy ... keep on 'til you see the Black Eagle post office. That's where the snake handlers stay at and Bud says he's skeered to deliver the mail down there, where he might put his hand in a mailbox and ther's a snake in there ... now, keep on, keep on, pretty soon you come to that place where they shot up that boy ...[31]

We might say, drawing a parallel with our perception of people, that the world we experience has a character. It is just such character of the world that the disenchanted view of it seems to leave out.

scientific world, but also meaning and value. 'If these natural sciences lead to anything in this way, they are apt to make the belief that there is such a thing as the "meaning" of the universe die out at its very roots.'[22] He quotes approvingly Tolstoy's remark, 'Science is meaningless because it gives no answer to our question ... "What shall we do and how shall we live?"'[23] For Weber questions of meaning and value were ones which were settled subjectively, outside of the realm of factual considerations. Once settled, science can provide us with information instrumental to achieving goals set independently of it.

It is often claimed that it is characteristic of modernist thinking to yield such a disenchanted view of nature, and hand in hand with it, to assume that everything in the world is, in principle, able to be made sense of by scientific calculation. John McDowell has remarked how such a conception of nature, 'a hard-won achievement of human thought at a specific time', can now seem 'sheer common sense';[24] standing in contrast to a conception in which 'what we now see as the subject matter of natural science was conceived as filled with meaning, as if all nature was a book of lessons for us'.[25] There are two key features of this scientific approach. One is that the world so characterised is viewed as objective in a very particular sense. Science attempts to characterise the world as if from no particular point within it; attempting to discount for the position of the investigator to give us a view as if 'from nowhere'.[26] Second, nature is conceived of as the realm of law; the realm of detectable empirical regularities which we can uncover and knowledge of which enables our manipulation of it. For a view which McDowell characterises as 'bald naturalism', these features are combined with a third, namely a 'conviction ... that conceptualizations of things as natural, in that sense, exhaust the conceptualizations of things that stand a chance of truth'.[27] This is the framework within which as Merleau-Ponty points out 'If I want to know what light is, surely I should ask a physicist'[28] (rather than, for example, a painter). For bald naturalists any characterisations of the world, not employing the resources of natural science, will be true in virtue of the truth of such scientific claims. Their apparent distinctiveness will be explained away by showing how facts captured in other terms can simply be shown to follow from the truth of facts which the bald naturalist can accommodate.

This disenchanted view of the world has consequences for the conceptions of ourselves, as experiencing subjects, which are somewhat paradoxical.[29] On the one hand the meaning, value and purpose which have been ejected from the world come to be seen as residing within subjects. Only conscious subjects can behave purposively. They are also the *source* of meaning and of value, as Weber makes clear. This seems to set up a contrast between the human subject and the world in which they are placed, a contrast reinforced when such subjects were conceived of as capable of a spontaneity of thought and action, which contrasted with the rule-governed operations of the world exterior to them. With the rise of the bald naturalist view, however, such a contrast between the experiencing subject and the world in which they are placed has been found intolerable. Human subjects are themselves treated as susceptible to scientific of images in the wider sense in which that term is used here. Not all images in this wider sense are *re*presentations. Nonetheless, in the account offered our experiences take the form of images, and images offered as representations can reorder the way in which we experience the world (see the discussion of works of art, particularly in Chapter 3). Moreover, the insights of poststructuralism, concerning the openness and indeterminacy of imagery, also have resonances for images in the wider sense adopted here. And such insights accrue to the saliences of our everyday experiences, as well as to the content of images offered as representations.

There is also work on the imagination within contemporary philosophy of mind, as part of its engagement with cognitive processing.[18] One question concerns what is distinctive about thinking in images as opposed to linguistic thinking. Others concern how the creativity of the imagination is to be most appropriately modelled within functionalist accounts of mental processes. Another area of research involves the role of imagination in enabling us to understand others, perhaps by simulating their mental states. These concerns most commonly view the imagination as an inner mental faculty and the images it produces as part of the contents of our subjective conscious experience. Although the account offered in this book must allow for the possibility of mental images it does not take its starting points from images of this kind. These are only one type of image which the imagination makes possible. The questions of this work are therefore distinct from (though not necessarily in opposition to) concerns with the appropriate modelling of inner cognitive processes. What some recent work in philosophy of mind does share with the direction of thought here is, however, a recognition of the interweaving of the cognitive and the emotional,[19] an interweaving which can be characterised by attention to the role which images play in our experiencing of the world.

The disenchanted world

In a much quoted lecture, published in 1922, Max Weber characterised the world which it was the job of the scientist to describe as a world in the 'process of disenchantment'. In such a world

> there are no mysterious incalculable forces that come into play ... one can, in principle, master all things by calculation ... One need no longer have recourse to magical means in order to master [it] or implore the spirits, as did the savage, for whom such mysterious powers existed. Technical means and calculations perform the service.[20]

Such a world view derives from 'the rationalization' and 'intellectualization' which Weber called 'the fate of our times'.[21] Such intellectualisation provides us with a world of facts which we can put to use to increase our technical control of our surroundings. Such scientific work is tied to a conception of progress, progress which is measured in relation to such technical control. For Weber it was not only magical and mysterious forces which have no place in such a

The word image is in bad repute because we have thoughtlessly believed that the design was a tracing, a copy, a second thing and that the mental image was ... belonging among our private bric a brac. But in fact it is nothing of the kind ... They are [that] ... without which we would never understand the quasi presence and imminent visibility which make up the whole problem of the imaginary.[10]

Such images can be sensory but we also have images of mathematical proofs, universals like love, the state of the country, social difference, the pattern of a life, etc. In some respect the notion of an image is close to the notion of an aspect in Wittgenstein's discussion in the *Philosophical Investigations*,[11] and he himself says 'the concept of an aspect is akin to the concept of an image',[12] clarifying in relation to a puzzle picture: 'I recognise not only that it has shape or colour but also a quite particular organisation'.[13] However, the distinction which this remark might suggest between sensory content and organisational form is not one which will be maintained, for we shall see that to experience colour or shape also requires the imagination. To speak of images in this way, and of the imagination as that which concerns such images, is not to employ a usage quite removed from our everyday one. When we speak of people as imaginative, we do not usually mean that they live in a world of make believe, played out within their interior life. We often mean that they are particularly perceptive, sensitive to the shapes which the world around them can take.

This book therefore outlines what Merleau-Ponty coins 'the imaginary texture of the real'.[14] The imagination is at work in the everyday world which we perceive, the world as it is for us. What is important in linking this concept of the imaginary with that with which we began, the affectively laden patterns which constitute our sense of the world, others and ourselves, is to recognise that the working of the imagination within the world gives that world *an affective texture*. It has a salience and significance for us, suggesting and sometimes demanding the desiring and sometimes fearful responses we make to it. In the discussion in Chapter 4 this feature of images is spelt out by the suggestion that images are *expressive*, such that experiencing in terms of images provides normative anchorage for our desiring, fearful, etc., responses.

The treatment of imagination and the imaginary offered here is, therefore, distinct from at least two other directions of attention found in contemporary writing. There is, of course, much written about the fact that we live in the age of the image. Here, with particular emphasis on visual images, images are conceived of as representations, mostly public. Concern has been expressed that such representations have become increasingly self-referential,[15] following a logic unconstrained by what they, in principle, represent; but able to be mistaken by their consumers to be a transparent copy of something beyond themselves.[16] Much attention is also paid to the interpretation of such images against the background of a poststructuralist theory in which such content is contextual, indeterminate and open to indefinite reworking.[17] This work will not directly address such concerns. Nonetheless the images which are the focus of such attention are a subcategory imagination as yielding mental or *inner images*; these images are distinct from sensory images and so *imagination is distinct from perception*, but the images are *copies* of perceptions or re-arrangements of elements which are copied from perception. The imagination then makes *things which are absent* in some way *present*. The imagination is nonetheless needed to supplement perception if we are to take our sensory data to be of spatio-temporal objects. For Kant,[5] however, the imagination is at work in perception in a different way. It is the faculty by which sensory intuitions are given shape or form, without which perceptual experiences are not possible. It is not therefore simply a source of inner copies of sensory experience, but is needed to give shape to such experiences. It is the domain of images, but such images are not only items in our stream of consciousness, they provide the shape of the spatio-temporal world. Images, in this sense, weave together the sensory *present* with what is *past*, the projected *future*, and the spatial *elsewhere*. Thus imagination is that by which there is a world for us. This is the thesis which will be discussed and defended here. It will be suggested, following Kant, that the imagination is required for experiences of the world *and* for the creation of fictions or illusions. It is not, therefore, simply the activity of forming fictional/illusory/unreal/non-actual worlds, as some everyday usages might suggest. In Kant's work on aesthetic judgments there is also an emphasis on the imagination as the domain of *creativity*, the images or forms which we experience not dictated by what we encounter, but remaining answerable to this and detectable by others. This thought will also turn out to be central in what follows.

In this book the concepts of the imagination and the imaginary, which are distilled through the chapters, take their starting point from Kant, but they are then routed through the writings of the phenomenologists. A conception of the imaginary emerges which characterises it not as a domain of illusion posited in opposition to a 'real', but rather as *that by which* the real is made available to us. (Here the real is, simply, the world, the actual, in contrast to the fictional, or illusory.) Central to this is a recognition of the imagination working *within everyday experience*, deriving from the characterisation of such experience provided particularly by Heidegger[6] and Merleau-Ponty.[7] The work of Sartre[8] is also pivotal, although his fundamental distinction between perceiving and imagining consciousness is rejected. The working of the imagination within experience which is suggested is not, however, that of a synthesising transcendent subject delivering order to the world. Rather imagination is a (creative) capacity to experience the world in a certain way, in the form of *images*. This concept of image is much wider than what is sometimes taken to be its standard definition: 'the internal [or external] representation of a sensory object in the absence of a corresponding sensory stimulus'.[9] Instead images are conceived of in this work as the *shapes or forms* in terms of which we experience the world, which weave together the present and absent in a way that requires both invention and discovery, and remain open to possibilities of revision. As Merleau-Ponty points out:

1 The disenchanted world and the world of experience

[handwritten margin note: how do I distinguish the knowing who I am who I am]

Imagination and the imaginary

[handwritten margin note: imaginary]

The concept of the imaginary is pervasive within contemporary writing concerning the self, the body and social groupings. The notion of the imaginary which is employed in this way may be broadly characterised as the affectively laden patterns/images/forms, by means of which we experience the world, other people and ourselves. This contemporary usage is distinguished most importantly by its constitutive linkage of imagery with *affect,* the emotions, feelings and desires which mark our engagement with the world. The images are the vehicles for such affect, the way in which it is given form. By means of these images the emotional contours of the subject's world are revealed. They are the way in which we not only think, but also feel our way around. This use is indebted particularly to the work of Lacan, Castoriadis, and Irigaray.[1] In the important applications by Gatens and Lloyd[2] it is traced back to Spinoza. I will return to each of these in the discussions in later chapters, comparing them to the phenomenological writers who form the heart of this book. Sharing the constitutive link of image and affect these sources nonetheless have important differences. For Lacan the Imaginary[3] is the domain of misrecognition and illusion, and it is a stage (moment) of development from which, although it remains in play, we move to the public Symbolic order. For him the Imaginary, initially an Imaginary of the self, is the illusion of a coherent and unified ego, which disguises from us the extent to which we are constituted by the working of the other within us (via the working of language, for example). For the other writers mentioned the imaginary, which extends beyond images of the self, is necessary for experience of any kind. Although we can criticise false and debilitating imaginaries, we cannot draw a sharp distinction between the imaginary and the symbolic, cognition and affect, between what is known and what is imagined. This will be the view defended here.

[handwritten margin notes: vehicle; affect; ok – here I differ!]

This book explores the links between such a concept of the imaginary and more traditional conceptions of the imagination, particularly that found in discussions of the relation between imagination and perception, for example in Hume and Kant. For Hume[4] the imagination is the domain of mental images, faint copies of sensory impressions derived from perceptions. Here we have rejected by these writers but it is viewed as a very particular intellectual achievement. It is one which must, however, have its starting point in the world of everyday experience and proceed by abstraction from that world. The perceived world, for writers such as Heidegger and Merleau-Ponty, is a necessary precondition for the construction of a scientific world view which consciously abstracts from its particularity and perspectivity. 'The entire universe of science is constructed upon the lived world, and if we wish to think science rigorously ... we must first awaken that experience of the world of which science is the second order expression.'[47] What is rejected is a suggestion that it is to the scientific world that we must look for an exclusive account of Nature. For Heidegger:

> Nature is itself an entity which is encountered ... and which can be discovered in various ways and at various stages.[48]
>
> 'Nature' is not to be understood as that which is just present-at-hand ... The wood is a forest of timber, the mountain a quarry of rock; the river is water-power, the wind is wind 'in the sails' ... If its kind of Being as ready-to-hand is disregarded, this Nature itself can be discovered and defined simply in its pure presence-at-hand. But when this happens, the Nature which 'stirs and strives', which assails us and enthrals us as a landscape, remains hidden. The botanist's plants are not the flowers of the hedgerow.[49]

'When we move from the Nature of the hedgerow to the botanist's chart', Heidegger argues, 'we have not simply removed a "subjectivistic" way of taking an entity which "in itself" is otherwise.'[50] 'For hedgerows are *not* subjective in this sense, and in removing them from a Nature scientifically rendered, we are, perhaps, missing "the 'Reality'" of the world at its most Real.'[51]

We may feel that in his characterisation of Nature, Heidegger himself is too instrumentalist. For it is Nature put to work for our projects, rather than, as Levinas would point out, simply enjoyed in the moment (the sun on my face).[52] We may also begin to wonder whether the characterisation of the scientific world as a disenchanted one, which he is drawing on here, and which was the starting point of this chapter, is itself an accurate one. The botanist's chart may itself be an appropriate source of wonder. What we can agree on, however, is that if we follow the bald naturalist line of restricting the features of Nature to those that can be accommodated within a scientific description, then we lose sight of the very characteristics of our environment which can make sense of our engagements with it.

Reason constituting perception

In the writings of John McDowell we find an attack on the exclusivity of the disenchanted view of nature which has many parallels with the views put forward by the phenomenologists. McDowell, however, is motivated less by the desire to provide a description of the lived experience of the world, and more by the need to find room within nature for creatures who have a capacity for spontaneity. Such a capacity is characterised, not simply in terms of an escape from the realm of deterministic laws, but more, in a way that explicitly echoes Kant, by our susceptibility to the workings of reason. We are the kind of creatures whose states bear relations to each other, to the world and to our behaviour of a reason-giving kind. That is, they are related not (or not only) by empirical law-like regularities, but by relations of justification, normative relations. Here McDowell is drawing a distinction between two kinds of intelligibility,

> the kind that is sought by, (as we call it), natural science … and the kind we find in something when we place it in relation to other occupants of 'the logical space of reasons' … the kind of intelligibility that is proper to meaning.[53]

McDowell is quite clear that such rationalising relations hold between us and our world: 'the world we experience … is not external … to the kind of intelligibility that is proper to meaning', and this is not possible if this world is exhausted by a disenchanted characterisation of it. McDowell, nonetheless, is not suggesting that we return to a conception of the natural world in which the 'movements of the planets, or the fall of a sparrow'[54] are themselves seen as purposive, in a way that is wholly independent of us. It is the world-as-experienced-by-us, which is susceptible to the kind of intelligibility that is proper to meaning, for such susceptibility is a perspectival feature, which, in a way that parallels Heidegger, requires experiencing subjects for its disclosure.

For McDowell there is an internal, rationalising or justificatory link between characteristics of the world and appropriate responses to them. Getting clear about the nature of the link between the perceptions and the responses which they rationalise requires getting clearer about *what is involved in experiencing the world in a reason-constituting way.* Such a notion informs both *Mind and World* and the earlier work on the perception of value, collected in *Mind, Value and Reality.* The world we experience provides us with reasons for our beliefs and judgments and also for our desires, emotions, and intentional and expressive responses to it. The notion of there being a special 'reason constituting conception of a situation'[55] is introduced by McDowell in his work on the perception of value. Values are features of our world which, once grasped, provide us with reasons for responses. Certain features of the world show that certain responses to it are appropriate, or in some cases, show them to be required. We do not perceive some neutral state of affairs, we instead perceive a world which is salient to us, and such 'perception of saliences'[56] yields, without the need for additional motivational states, our reasons for responding in certain ways, a response appropriate to, *merited* by, such characteristics of world. Upbraiding someone for their behaviour we might say 'You don't know what it means that someone is shy and sensitive'.[57] Here we are drawing attention to features of a situation, which if they were grasped, would suggest behaviour of a different kind. And to attempt to change behaviour we try and initiate someone into the *way of seeing* the situation which would prompt reform. (McDowell compares our strategy here to 'what we might do and say to someone who says "Jazz sounds to me like a mess"'.[58]) It is not only moral properties which provide reasons of this kind. McDowell discusses the example of fear: 'we make sense of fear by seeing it as a response to objects that merit such a response',[59] or of laughter by pointing out characteristics of a situation that make it funny.[60] The reason-constituting perception, to which McDowell draws attention in his account of value, is at the heart of the account of perception which he offers in *Mind and World*.[61] In these lectures McDowell is concerned to articulate the way in which our sensory experience can provide us with justification for our knowledge claims about the world. What links the account in *Mind and World* to the earlier work on value is a view of the world as perceived, which sees it as constituting reasons for our responses, cognitive, affective and intentional. This is at the heart of McDowell's picture of how *spontaneity* is at work in experience.[62]

McDowell is anxious that his commitment to a re-enchanted world should not be seen as requiring anything magical or mysterious, anything supernatural. He is also anxious that, in insisting on our sensitivity to reason-giving relations, we should not conceive of ourselves as somehow split between existence within a natural realm and a foot in a Kantian noumenal realm, which is the source of our spontaneity. He therefore insists that we should not allow the term 'nature' to be appropriated by 'bald naturalists'. It is simply a part of our nature, he insists, that we can be initiated into the space of reasons by upbringing. By such an initiation we are given, what McDowell terms, second nature; an ability to 'act in a world in which [we] find more than what is open to view from ... the natural sciences ... And there is nothing against bringing this richer reality under the rubric of nature too'.[63]

Imaginary worlds

This chapter has been characterising the world as experienced by subjects located within and alongside it. This is not the disenchanted world, supposedly offered by science, but an, at least 'partially, reenchanted world'. The meaning and value, which our modernist accounts of the world claim to have removed, remains in the enchantment of everyday experience. Such a world matters to us. It has a salience and significance which renders intelligible, makes sense of our responses to it. (In the broadest sense of reason it provides reason for those responses.) What this book suggests is that such a world can be perspicuously characterised as an imaginary world; not in the sense of a world of illusions or projected fantasies, but a world in which the imagination is at work, creating/disclosing forms, expressive of possibilities for living affectively and effectively within it. This suggestion is what the following chapters unpack.

One question which will arise is whether we can defend the claim that the imaginary is a texture of the *real*, something *disclosed*[64] to us in the perceptual encounter, especially once we recognise the multiplicity of imaginaries and their anchorage in individual and social lives (see Chapter 5). One sense of being a realist requires that the world we perceive *exceeds* any possible perceptions we may have of it, and any images in terms of which we may experience it. That sense of realism is echoed here. However many ways we have of perceiving the world, they can never exhaust what we are presented with. Despite the modernist picture, the world can never be fully intelligible to us. The variety of salience which the world can bear opens up different possibilities of existence within it. But the range of these is not something we could hope to capture. The dimension of creativity suggested by the claim that our world is an imaginary world allows for the possibility of it being imagined in different ways, being open to alternative visions; 'interminable reinterpretations to which it is legitimately susceptible'.[65] These are visions which can be invoked by artists and political revolutionaries, the validity of whose imaginary creations requires the possibility of bringing others to share them.

A second strand to realism requires an accountability of the images we invoke to a world whose existence has some independence from us, so that the notion of *disclosure* is an appropriate one. The visions of the world we invoke, as Merleau-Ponty points out in the quote above, must be ones to which it is legitimately susceptible. The possibility of such accountability and the route to its assessment, is anchored in this work in a position found in Kant's account of Beauty; and invoked in Wittgenstein's account of rule following (see Chapter 2). Legitimate visions are ones which others can not only be brought causally to share, but ones which they can recognise are appropriate. Publicly recognisable legitimacy is necessary if our imaginary forms are to be disclosive.

Once we have recognised the workings of imagination in perception, then the scientific world, which was offered as an implied contrast, can be seen, not as lacking an imaginary, but as simply carrying imaginaries of its own. As Bruno Latour has argued, 'modern attempts to disenchant nature ... [simply] recreate a new kind of enchantment'.[66] Science continually reshapes the image we have of the world we inhabit. And as many writers have pointed out, 'learning a scientific theory ... one acquires a repertoire ... for seeing, imagining, and manipulating the world in new ways'.[67]

Notes

1 Lacan, Jacques, 2006 [1966], *Ecrits*, trans. Bruce Fink, Norton, New York; Castoriadis, Cornelius, 1998 [1987], *The Imaginary Institution of Society*, trans. Kathleen Blamey, MIT Press, Cambridge MA; Irigaray, Luce, 1985, *Speculum of the Other Woman*, trans. G. Gill, Cornell University Press, Ithaca NY; 1985, *This Sex Which Is Not One*, trans. C. Porter and C. Burke, Cornell University Press, Ithaca NY. For an illuminating discussion of the imaginary see M. Whitford, 1991, *Luce Irigaray*, Routledge, London and New York, ch. 3.
2 Gatens, Moira and Lloyd, Genevieve, 1999, *Collective Imaginings: Spinoza, Past and Present*, Routledge, London and New York; Gatens, M., 1996, *Imaginary Bodies: Ethics, Power and Corporeality*, Routledge, London and New York.
3 Following convention I shall use upper case for the 'I' only when directly referencing the Lacanian Imaginary.
4 Hume, D., 1964 [1748], *A Treatise of Human Nature*, Everyman, London and New York.

5 Kant, I., 1970 [1781, 1787], *Critique of Pure Reason*, trans. N. Kemp Smith, Macmillan, London; 2007 [1790], *Critique of Judgement*, trans. J. C. Meredith, Oxford University Press.

6 Heidegger, M., 1962, *Being and Time*, trans. E. Macquarrie and J. Robinson, Blackwell, Oxford.

7 Merleau-Ponty, M., 2012, *Phenomenology of Perception*, trans. Donald A. Landes, Routledge, London and New York.

8 Sartre, J.-P., 1958, *Being and Nothingness: An Essay on Phenomenological Ontology*, trans. H. Barnes, Methuen, London.

9 Brann, E. T. H., 1991, *The World of the Imagination*, Rowman & Littlefield, Lanham MD, p. 13.

10 Merleau-Ponty, M., 1993, 'Eye and Mind', in Galen A. Johnson, ed., *The Merleau-Ponty Aesthetics Reader*, Northwestern University Press, Evanston IL, p. 126.

11 Wittgenstein, L., 1968, *Philosophical Investigations*, Blackwell, Oxford.

12 *Philosophical Investigations* 213.

13 Ibid., 196.

14 'Eye and Mind' 126.

15 Kearney, R., 1988, *The Wake of Imagination,* Routledge, London and New York.

16 Debord, Guy, 1995 [1967], *The Society of the Spectacle*, Zone Books, New York.

17 Derrida, Jacques, 1978, *Writing and Difference*, trans. Alan Bass, University of Chicago Press; Butler, Judith, 1990, *Gender Trouble*, Routledge, New York and London.

18 For a summary see entries at: http://plato.stanford.edu/entries/imagination/#Rec CogSocPsyWorIma and www.imagery-imagination.com/

19 Damasio, A. R., 1997, *Descartes' Error*, Grosset/Putnam, New York; 1999, *The Feeling of What Happens*, Harcourt, New York.

20 Weber, Max, 1948, *Essays in Sociology*, trans. and edited by H. H. Gerth and C. Wright Mills, Routledge and Kegan Paul, London, p. 139.

21 Ibid., 155.

22 Ibid., 142.

23 Ibid., 143.

24 McDowell, J., 1996, *Mind and World*, Harvard University Press, Cambridge MA, p. 70.

25 Ibid., 71.

26 McDowell, J., 1998, *Mind, Value and Reality*, Harvard University Press, Cambridge MA, p. 181.

27 Smith, N., ed., 2002, *Reading McDowell on Mind and World*, Routledge, London and New York, p. 297.

28 Merleau-Ponty, M., 2004, trans. O. Davis, *The World of Perception*, Routledge, London and New York, p. 32.

29 Taylor, C., 1975, *Hegel*, Cambridge University Press, p. 1.

30 Kenny, A., ed., 2005, *The Wittgenstein Reader*, Blackwell, Oxford, p. 221.

31 Quoted in M. Rose, 2006, 'Gathering Dreams of Presence', *Environment and Planning* 24, p. 548.

32 *The World of Perception* 32.

33 *Phenomenology of Perception* lxxii.

34 Ibid., lxxiv.

35 Ibid., 16.

36 *Being and Time* 190.

37 Ibid., 207.

38 Ibid., 97.

39 Ibid., 98.

40 *Phenomenology of Perception* 131.

41 *Being and Time* 120.

42   The exposition here is close to that in the co-authored book *The World the Flesh and the Subject*, Paul Gilbert and Kathleen Lennon, Edinburgh University Press, Edinburgh, 2005, chapters 1 and 5. The discussion of moods is particularly indebted to Paul Gilbert.

43   *Being and Time* 176 H137.

44   Ibid., 175 H136.

45   Ibid., 173 H134.

46   'Eye and Mind' 122.

47   *Phenomenology of Perception* lxxii.

48   *Being and Time* 92.

49   Ibid., 100.

50   Ibid., 141.

51   Ibid., 141.

52   For example Levinas, Emmanuel, 1969, *Totality and Infinity: An Essay in Exteriority*, trans. Alphonso Lingis, Duquesne University Press, Pittsburgh PA, pp. 149–150. I am indebted to Antony Wilde for discussions on this matter. See Wilde, A., 2013, 'Levinas: Subjectivity, Affectivity and Desire', Ph.D. thesis, University of Hull, chapter 2.

53   *Mind and World* 70–71.

54   Ibid., 72.

55   *Mind, Value and Reality* 86.

56   Ibid., 70.

57   Ibid., 85.

58   Ibid., 85.

59   Ibid., 144.

60   Ibid., 158–161.

61   *Mind and World.*

62   There are different strands which go to make up the exercise of spontaneity for McDowell, and it is worth highlighting them, to unpick what is involved in perception being reason-constituting. The first strand requires the experienced world to have a certain shape or form. He accuses Hume of offering us 'nature as an ineffable lump, devoid of structure or order … [whereas] we have to suppose the world has an intelligible structure [if it is to be] a world at all'. Here McDowell's use of 'world' echoes that of Heidegger, for a world is something which can show up for the subjects within it. The second strand, in McDowell's account, says more about the kind of shape or form which he is concerned with. Exercising spontaneity involves the detection of a meaning or significance in the world we perceive, which provides *an intelligible link* between it and our responses to it. 'What we want here is a style of explanation that makes sense of what is explained (in so far as sense can be made of it).' The third strand requires that we can reflectively re-evaluate the shape we appear to find in experience and subject it to reflective scrutiny. It is an important question whether it would be possible to find instances of the first and second of these strands without the third. This has bearing on McDowell's discussion of the experience of animals, which I will not discuss here.

63   *Mind and World* 192.

64   The notion of disclosure is a Heideggerian one, see especially M. Heidegger, *Poetry, Language, Thought*, trans. A. Hofstadter, Harper and Row, New York, 1971.

65   *Eye and Mind* 139.

66   Latour, B., 1993, *We Have Never Been Modern*, trans. C. Porter, Harvester, Brighton, p. 23.

67   Rouse, J., 2005, 'Merleau-Ponty's Existential Conception of Science', in *The Cambridge Companion to Merleau-Ponty*, eds T. Carman and M. Hansen, Cambridge University Press.

2 Imagination and perception
The productive and reproductive imagination

The account of the imagination, and its transposition into the concept of the imaginary, which I wish to develop in this book, begins with Kant's work on the *productive* imagination. Kant will therefore be the main focus of this chapter. But Kant's own position itself needs placing in conversation with Hume's account of the *reproductive* imagination. Although there are key problems with Hume's account, which many commentators have discussed, nonetheless, as Strawson points out,[1] he saw the imagination as playing a key role in perception, which is the focus of our attention. (Nonetheless, apologies may be in order. As a stepping stone to our focus on Kant, the richness of Hume's account is not done justice to here.[2])

Hume: the reproductive and associative imagination

For Hume the imagination consists in the possession of mental images, faint copies of perceptions, conjured up in the absence of, and as an inadequate replacement for, the perceptual world. Here images are items in a private mental realm, *copies* of something presented to our senses. Hume offers an account of the imagination which, it will be argued, is not adequate to its role in perception. Nonetheless, on his account, the imagination is central to our perceptual experience and attention to it helps sharpen our sense of what work we might need the imagination to do. The origin of all our experiences, for Hume, lies in what he terms *impressions*, 'sensations, passions and emotions, as they make their first appearance in the soul'.[3] Perceptual sensations arise first, and on reflection, generate feelings of pleasure or pain. Both are impressions. Such originary impressions are immediately present to us, but leave traces, faint images of themselves, *ideas*, which are available for recollection in memory or imagination. In memory the images are exact, but fainter, copies of the original sensory experiences; but in imagination the simple components of complex impressions may be arranged in ways the originating experience did not present. Nonetheless the components of imaginary ideas are all copies of components of sensory impressions. 'I can imagine to myself such a city as the New Jerusalem, whose pavement is gold, and walls are rubies, though I never saw any such',[4] but the parts of this imaginary picture all resemble parts of original sensory impressions from which they derive and which they 'exactly represent'.[5] In this way the imagination is simply a copy or reproduction of originary experiences. The difference between impressions and ideas of memory or imagination is simply that of 'force and liveliness'. Moreover, memory, which must correspond 'in order and form with the original', is itself 'more lively and strong'[6] than the imagination. The imagination is at liberty 'to transpose and change its ideas', into 'winged horses, fiery dragons and monstrous giants',[7] but is claimed, nonetheless, to be less vivacious.

The separation and reunification of simple ideas which are found in the imagination are not simply the workings of chance. Nor are they due to the activity of a conscious subject. It is rather the consequence of

> some bond of union among them, [the ideas] some associating quality, by which one idea naturally introduces another ... The qualities from which this association arises, and by which the mind is, after this manner, conveyed from one idea to another are three, viz.: resemblance, contiguity in time or place, and cause and effect.[8]

These principles of association are simply those which we empirically observe and are viewed by Hume as a kind of 'attraction' between the discrete sensory items.

Here we have Hume's account of the imagination. It is the domain of inner entities, faint copies of original perceptions, linked together by laws of association. Running together the imagination and fancy, he regards the contents of the imagination as fictions or illusions. Given such an account of the imagination, it is somewhat remarkable how central it becomes to his account of perception. This imagination is central to his account of the bringing of individual instances under general concepts, to the taking of our perceptions to be of spatio-temporally continuous objects, and to the taking of ourselves to be single continuous entities. (It is also required to explain the errors we make in taking ourselves to perceive necessary connections between cause and effect and in taking the world to contain evaluative properties.)

For Hume, what we are faced with in present perception is individual sensory items. All ideas are therefore initially ideas of particulars. To bring such sensory items under general concepts the word applied to the individual impression becomes associated with further items of a similar kind; because, it seems, the word stimulates the imagination to produce, actually or potentially, images of such further items. So we need the imagination to see a cat as a cat or a shower of rain as a shower of rain.

The imagination is also essential to our taking certain of our impressions to be impressions of continuous objects, which preserve their identity through time and changes in some of their sensory properties, so it is needed to see the cat walking around in front of me now as the cat I have seen many times before. Sensory impressions for Hume are momentary and continually changing. However, when such changes are small we take ourselves to be perceiving a continuous thing. The imagination, because of the resemblance between the distinct impressions, makes us 'attribute to them a distinct and continuous existence'.[9] It is not exactly clear what the imagination is assumed to be doing here. For the imagination is, for Hume, simply a storehouse of images of different degrees of vivacity, linked together by rules of association. Within this picture we can only assume that when faced with a sensory impression the imagination provides us with actual or potential images of the object, associated with the current impression by resemblance. This provides us with what can mistakenly seem to be one continuous impression (though, implausibly, here the perception of a continuous object seems to be construed as the mistaken belief in a continuous impression). And such a move is the basis of our belief in an external world. The operation of the imagination in this way is fundamental to our human nature. For Hume the resultant belief, though based on fancy, is unavoidable. This is a point on which he expresses unease: 'I cannot conceive how such trivial qualities of the fancy, conducted by such false suppositions, can ever lead to any solid and rational system'.[10]

One major problem with the Humean picture is the fact that it makes our judgments concerning the external world and ourselves, errors, the product of fictions and illusions. But there are other key difficulties. One, of course, concerns the nature of the subject. What exactly is attributing to objects a distinct and continuous existence? In the account which Hume offers of the self 'the identity which we ascribe to the mind of man is only a fictitious one, and ... must proceed from a like operation of the imagination upon like objects'.[11] The imagination unites, via causal and associative processes, distinct ideas and impressions into an imaginary unity of a self, when such ideas are linked by resemblance (of succeeding impressions) and relations of cause and effect.[12] But if personal identity is constituted solely by a bundle of changing impressions and ideas, exactly what is aware of such a bundle, or applies general concepts, or mistakes discontinuity and attributes continuity? Even if we assume each momentary impression comes tagged in some way with consciousness, given that the application of concepts and awareness of objects requires that each momentary impression is placed in relation to, what Kant would call, a manifold of such impressions, what is it that is aware of such a manifold of the present and absent? Merleau-Ponty puts the problem in the following way.

> Perception [for the empiricist] is constructed with states of consciousness as a house is built with stones, and a mental chemistry is imagined which fuses these materials into a compact whole ... [but] this ... describes nothing but *blind processes* ... because there is *nobody who sees* at the centre of this mass of sensations and memories, nobody who could experience the harmony between the given and the evoked.[13]

There is a further and related point here. Hume talks of the imagination *uniting* attributes which bear relations of resemblance, contiguity or cause and effect, to *ascribe* identity across discontinuity. Yet this suggests that the imagination is active in a way his picture cannot allow. For the imagination, for him, is simply a collection of images, linked together by laws of association, without it, of course, being clear to whom the associative regularities are visible.

Hume writes as if each sensory impression was a discrete and immediately present entity. Such entities become associated with each other within the imagination. But, as Kant points out, prior to such laws of association being able to get off the ground such impressions have to be recognised. Merleau-Ponty makes a similar point: 'the unity of the thing in perception is not constructed through association, but rather [is] the condition of association'.[14] Before impressions can be associated they must be placed on the same footing, understood in the light of each other. He points out that

> Association ... never works as an autonomous force; ... it operates only in virtue of the sense it has caught in the context of a previous ... experience; it is efficacious to the extent that the subject recognises it and grasps it in the ... physiognomy of the past.[15]

Thus Hume's theory assumes what it needs to explain, 'the imposing of sense onto the sensible chaos'.[16] Hume takes for granted that our sensory impressions arrive marked with meaning. Mary Warnock seems right here when she says[17] that for Hume I need the imagination to associate this cat I am experiencing with other actual and potential cats. But no account is offered of my grasping the incoming sensory data in a catlike way, which would indicate the aspect under which other items are to be associated as similar. In fact, the account of sensory impressions offered is such that they could not carry significance or meaning: 'Pure sensation will be the undergoing of an undifferentiated instantaneous and punctual "jolt"'.[18] As such it corresponds to nothing in our experience. For our experience is not of individual sensory moments, linked by associative laws, but of: 'figures on a background ... in the middle of some other thing ... An isolated perceptual given ... inconceivable'.[19]

Hume's picture makes the imagination foundational to our ability to perceive continuous objects and bring the manifold of sensory data under concepts. That is, for him, the imagination is required even to yield the world as characterised by the scientist. This, as we have seen, was a source of unease to him, for, on his account, even to get to a world of continuous objects, linked by spatio-temporal and causal relations, we need to rely on fancy and illusion. If we accept the arguments offered above, however, Hume's account is not sufficient to accommodate even such a world. By limiting the components of his picture to discrete sensory impressions and their copies as ideas, and offering us an imagination which is only reproductive and associative, his resources are inadequate even to this task. What he did recognise, however, was that immediate and atomistic sensory data are insufficient to accommodate the features of everyday perception. As Strawson comments: 'the mind looks further than what immediately appears to it, its conclusions can never be put to the account of the senses'.[20] To accommodate this insight, however, we need an account of the imagination of a different kind. We need an account of the imagination which is not only reproductive and associative of images but productive of them. And for this we must turn to Kant.

Kant: the productive imagination in the *Critique of Pure Reason*

What motivated Hume to incorporate imagination into his account of perception was a recognition that our perceptual experience contains more than what, in a certain sense, 'meets the eye'. It is suffused with what, in this book, will be termed *the absent present*. Kant[21] also sought to accommodate this insight, and alongside it a recognition that our experiences have an order or form, an organisation that distinguishes them from the mush of brute sensory data. To accommodate this he added to the notion of the reproductive imagination what he termed the *productive* imagination. The productive imagination was an *active* faculty, for Kant, central to the *synthesis* which was necessary for us to have perceptual experiences at all. For Kant our perceptual experience is never an awareness of momentary, brute sensory data. It is always an awareness of, what he terms, a *manifold* of intuitions, always and already organised/shaped by the application of a concept. Although we cannot disentangle them phenomenologically, all experiences involve *both* intuitions and concepts. Empirical intuitions are the sensory data which we passively receive, but without the shaping provided by concepts they are 'less even than a dream to us'. Concepts are either pure or empirical. Pure concepts are ones provided by the understanding and ones which we know *a priori* will find application in any world we can have experience of. Empirical concepts are anchored in experience, but themselves require more than Humean processes of association to apply, for they too provide rules in terms of which mere sensory inputs are organised. Concepts without application to intuitions are, in Kant's terms, empty, mere logical forms, without content. What we experience, in perception, is a world of phenomena in which the intuitive and the conceptual elements are both in play.

What, then, does this have to do with the imagination? The first step is to recognise that any application of a concept requires a manifold, or multiplicity of experience, for it is a way of ordering or giving shape to such a manifold. This shaping of a manifold is what Kant refers to as synthesis. The activity of synthesis is the distinctive activity of the productive imagination.[22]

> What is first given to us is appearance. When combined with consciousness it is called perception. Now, since every appearance contains a manifold, and since different perceptions therefore occur in the mind separately and singly, combination of them such as they cannot have in sense, is demanded. There therefore must exist in us an active faculty for the synthesis of this manifold. To this faculty I give the name imagination ... imagination has to bring the manifold of intuition into the form of an image.[23]

Here Kant is using the concept of image in a broad sense and not just to denote visual images. Images are the shape or form given to a sensory manifold by the imagination. Kant attaches to this passage an interesting footnote which marks his difference from those who

> have hitherto failed to realise that imagination is a necessary ingredient in perception itself. This is due partly to the fact that the faculty has been limited to reproduction, partly to the belief that the senses not only supply impressions but also combine them so as to generate images of objects, [but] for that purpose something more than the mere receptivity of impressions is undoubtedly required, namely a function for the synthesis of them.[24]

The Kantian account, which stresses that in perceptual experience we have *synthesised* sensory data, is important in drawing our attention to the 'seeing as' structure of perception, which is one stressed by a multitude of writers. Strawson illuminatingly compares the Kantian discussion with Wittgenstein's.[25] Sartre anchors his own account of the imaginary (see following chapter) in the way in which we can see doodles as animals, clouds as castles, and 'the fat and painted cheeks, black hair and female body' of the impersonator Franconay as Maurice Chevalier.[26] In the Kantian account, the imagination is at work, not only when a child treats a broom as a horse, but when she perceives a horse as a horse also.[27] In each case a multiplicity of sensations is organised into a shape or form which enables us to experience it *as* something. In Michael Young's terms our perceptual experience involves a 'construing as', and such construal requires the imagination.[28] It is in this respect that Strawson emphasises the continuity in the workings of imagination from

> seeing a cloud as a camel or a ... formation of stalagmites as a dragon ... to the first application of the word 'astringent' to a remark ... to a ... scientist seeing a pattern in phenomena which has never been seen before ... to Blake seeing eternity in a grain of sand and heaven in a wild flower.[29]

Strawson is unpacking Kant's productive imagination in terms of the 'seeing as' structure of perception, as the formation/detection (both) of a shape or form, an image in the widest sense, in the multiplicity of intuitions which are available to us.

For Kant perception requires synthesis and synthesis requires the workings of both the productive and the reproductive imagination. In the Transcendental Deduction, A edition,[30] he identifies three moments in the process of synthesis: apprehension of a manifold in intuition, reproduction in imagination, and recognition in a concept. The apprehension of a manifold requires that a multiplicity of intuitions 'must be run through and held together',[31] so that the momentary present can be linked to what is not immediately presented to us. This, itself, requires the operation of the *reproductive* imagination, in which access to previous images becomes available to us. 'When I seek to draw a line in thought ... the various manifold representations that are involved must be apprehended by me in thought one after the other ... but if I drop out of thought the preceding representations (the first part of the line ...) and did not reproduce them while advancing to those that follow, a complete representation could never be obtained.'[32] The reproduction involved here is, I think, best understood through Strawson's discussion. He discusses what is involved in perceiving a dog. 'To perceive something as a dog, when silent and stationary, is to see it as a possible mover and barker.'[33] We should not, however, interpret this as requiring us to conjure up inner mental images of the dog moving or barking. Most of the time, we do not do that. Rather, the possible moving and barking is *alive in* the immediate and present perception of the dog.

In the final moment of synthesis the *productive* imagination is put to work to weave this multiplicity into a whole, such that concepts can be applied to it. This is the stage at which something like identification of what is presented to us occurs. It is the taking up of the intuited manifold into a form or order. These *moments* of synthesis are analytic rather than empirical temporal moments, and they are not separately articulated in the second edition. They are not separable from each other. The aspects of the manifold which are held together and run through, and those which are reproduced, depend on the overall unity or image in relation to which they are being placed. Indeed this was just Kant's objection to Hume.

The imagination, in both its productive and reproductive aspects, is required, then, to unify a manifold of sensory intuitions in such a way that we can experience of them. For Kant our sensibility is necessarily spatio-temporal. The temporal present is held together with the past and with future possibilities. A parallel process happens with space. On observing a house and viewing the front, I experience it as having a back and sides. But, as with the dog, such a possibility is part of the character of our present experience, rather than requiring additional inner images which we create. The back and sides of the house, its past and its future possibilities are *alive* in our perception of it. This capacity, *the making of the absent present*, is what, in Fiona Hughes' words[34] 'makes possible our transcendence of the mere moment or present' and 'sets us in relation to something other than ourselves'. The reproductive imagination keeps absent experiences in play and the productive imagination unites this manifold of the present and absent into a unity, a synthesised image. In the *Critique of Pure Reason* Kant is at pains to stress that the synthesising activities of the productive imagination are constrained by the *a priori* categories whose application is necessary if we are to have experience at all, and in particular, if this experience is to be experience of a world of objects. The justification for individual categories will not be discussed here, but they provide rules by which the productive imagination is bound (and which, for many authors,[35] excludes any element of creativity from the activities of the productive imagination, as described in the first *Critique*, a point which will be reconsidered in the discussion of the Schematism, below). Synthesis, then, is the work done by an active, productive imagination, unifying intuitions into the form of images. It also requires the reproductive imagination to provide the 'absent present' of a synthesisable manifold. The categories capture the most general forms/rules in terms of which such syntheses must be undertaken.

The most general transcendental condition of experience, in the context of which the categories find their justification, is *the unity of apperception*, the identity of the self, throughout the manifold of which it is conscious, 'for they [sensory intuitions] can represent something only in so far as they belong, with all others to one consciousness'.[36] The insistence on the condition of a unified consciousness, for the possibility of experience, addresses a problem found with Hume's account. For if a manifold of impressions exist separately from each other, linked only by blind causal regularities, then there is nothing to be aware of such a manifold, holding them together in a single act. For Kant such a unified consciousness is one of which we are, at least implicitly, aware. Such unity of apperception is necessarily interdependent, for Kant, with a synthesis of the manifold of intuitions into *objects*. We can perhaps be helped here, in grasping what syntheses into objects amount to, by Heidegger's description of it as a form given to experience, such that it can 'stand against' the subject *as* an object. Here the imagination is central: 'in providing a foundation for the possibility of the standing over against [me], the synthesis of the power of the imagination fulfils a crucial function'.[37] For Kant, then, for perception to be possible, we require both a unity of consciousness and a world of objects. Both of these require syntheses of the manifold of intuitions by an active imagination.

Imagination and the Schematism

It is central to Kant's account of experience that it has a duality of components: sensibility (sensory data) and understanding (for him, concepts). The role he gives to the imagination is as a mediator between these elements. It is required to bring sensible intuitions under the concepts provided by the understanding (pure *a priori* concepts) or, in the case of empirical concepts, derived via the rules which the understanding provides. Such a mediating role is given particular scrutiny in the section of the first *Critique* called the Schematism. Kant presents the question which the Schematism is to address as 'How, then, is the subsumption of intuitions under pure concepts, the application of a category to appearances, possible?'[38] He makes two moves to answer this question. First that such subsumption requires a schema and second that it requires a transcendental determination of time. I shall address them in turn.

Initially Kant suggests that the question of application or subsumption is an issue only for pure concepts, not for scientific ones (on the basis, it seems, that those concepts are somehow abstracted from sensibility and therefore the question of how they apply to sensibility does not arise). But later he makes clear that all concepts, including empirical ones, require schemas for their application. Empirical concepts do not, however, have the additional problem of being brought into relation to a temporal sensibility, which the pure concepts have. What, then, are schema? Kant insists that they are a product of the imagination. But he distinguishes them from images, which, at this point, he is thinking of as sensory items. (Sensory images here, perhaps, the look of things, or secondarily copies which we make of the look of things.[39]) Schema, in contrast, are something required for the making of images, as they are required for 'unity in the determination of sensibility'.[40] He gives the following examples:

> If five points be set alongside one another, thus . . . . . I have an image of the number five. But if, on the other hand, I think only number in general, this thought is rather the representation of a method whereby a multiplicity ... may be represented in an image in conformity with a certain concept ... This representation of a universal procedure of imagination in providing an image for a concept, I entitle the schema of this concept ... It is a rule of synthesis of the imagination.[41]

Such rules are also needed, he makes clear, for empirical concepts:

> Still less is an object of experience or its image ever adequate to the empirical concept; for this latter always stands in immediate relation to the schema of imagination, as a rule for the determination of our intuition ... in accordance with some specific universal concept. The concept 'dog' signifies a rule according to which my imagination can delineate the figure of a four footed animal in a general manner, without limitation to a single determinate figure such as experience, or any possible image that I can represent, *in concreto*, actually presents.[42]

He goes on to clarify the difference of images, in this sense, and schema as:

> the image is a product of the empirical faculty of reproductive imagination; the schema of sensible concepts ... is a product and, as it were, a monogram, of pure *a priori* imagination, through which and in accordance with which images themselves first become possible.[43]

What becomes clear from this is that the process of schematisation, which is necessary for the application of concepts, is a procedure. In a very famous passage he describes it as 'an art concealed in the depths of the human soul, whose real mode of activity nature is hardly likely ever to allow us to discover'.[44] Why is such a procedure necessary? Why does a concept not simply dictate its own method of application? To make sense of Kant, here, we can draw a comparison with Wittgenstein's discussions of rule following.[45] A concept provides a rule, but the rule itself does not dictate how it is to be applied. Application requires something like a perceptual skill. The skill is that of seeing how a manifold could be viewed as conforming to the rule. It is the skill of being able to produce/detect an order or a shape in the multiplicity of the given, which can be seen as the application of the rule. Both production and detection are involved for Kant, as the manifold which is synthesised by means of schema must be one which is susceptible to such forms. Add five, the rule tells us. The skill comes in being able to appreciate what would count as adding five. The art, which Kant sees as hidden in the human soul, is *the art of being able to detect in the manifold a unity* which, in some sense, conforms to the unity required by the rule the concept provides. This is the art which is the special job of the productive imagination, as it mediates the sensibility and the understanding. If asked to illustrate the number five we may produce five dots. This requires the work of the reproductive imagination, creating a particular image. But the sensory image does not provide us with the means of applying the concept. It is simply an exemplar of it. However the possibility of providing such an exemplar itself requires a capacity to detect in that manifold a structure/schema which brings it into relation with the concept 'five'. As Eva Schaper points out, the imagination here yields something which has the character of a *gestalt*.[46] **The art of the imagination is the recognition of a possibility or possibilities of unification in the sensory manifold.**

For Kant, the schematising function of the imagination requires particular attention when it comes to the application of the pure concepts of the understanding. In the transcendental deduction Kant has argued that such categories must necessarily find application if we are to have experience. They operate within the context of the overarching condition of the unity of apperception; the condition that experiences constitute the experiences of a single subject; which itself is interdependent with experiences being that of objects, in some sense separated from, standing against, such a subject. Yet the categories as Kant has offered them are, he admits, 'mere logical forms' and it becomes particularly urgent for him to consider how these might find application. Now, given the structure of the *Critique*, and the arguments earlier in the Aesthetic, that all sensory experience must conform to the forms of space and time, it might seem as if the job of the imagination here is to apply the categories to intuitions which are already spatio-temporal. But what becomes clear from his discussion is that what is at issue is not simply the *application* of categories to a temporal series (Kant concentrates, in the Schematism, primarily on time), but the actual *determination* of it. In this discussion it becomes clear that the imagination is constitutively central to this determination of time. The categories, Kant says, when applied (schematised),

> are nothing but a priori determinations of time in accordance with rules. These rules relate the order of the categories to the time series, the time content, the time-order, and lastly to the scope of time, in respect of all possible objects.[47]

The awareness of our experiences as those of a single subject *is* awareness of time, in which a manifold of distinct experiences are taken as *manifestations of a structure of past, present and future*. This requires the workings of both the reproductive and productive imagination. The reproductive imagination keeps the manifold of intuitions in play and the productive imagination synthesises it into a time series, by applying the categories to this manifold.[48] The imagination is, therefore, what makes temporal consciousness possible.

The art of the imagination is both constitution and detection of schema. The function of imagination in perception is *to bring the manifold into shape as a perceptual image*. We are shown via his transcendental arguments that if our experience is to be of an objective spatial temporal world then the shape which the imagination bestows/takes up will be that formalised by the *a priori* categories. What about empirical concepts which are not necessary in the same way? Does the spontaneity of the imagination allow it not only to be active, but also *creative* in the empirical patterning found in our experience? Do the rules for finding order determine our concepts, or is there some room for play, for alternative shapes and forms? Kant is not explicit on this point. In the first *Critique* the imagination is active but not explicitly creative. It is, however, arguable that, for the possibility of certain ways of organising the world to be grasped, acts of creativity are involved. And, reflecting on Kant's account in the Schematism, it seems that the imagination's productions of schema are just such creative acts. (See also the discussion of the *advent*, in Chapter 5 below.) For Kant's own exploration of creativity, however, we need to turn to the *Critique of Judgement*.[49]

The productive imagination in the *Critique of Judgement*

In Kant's account of the productive imagination, in the *Critique of Pure Reason*, he stresses its synthesising powers. But the way the synthesis is produced, and the consequent form which the world takes for us, is constrained by the categories, *universal* rules to which all perceptual content must conform. Consequently there is a question mark over how much room the imagination has for the exercise of creativity. However, in Kant's account of beauty in the *Critique of Judgement*,[50] we have an account of the productive imagination operating without the application of determining rules. It is to this account that we will now turn.

In this text Kant returns to the question of the possibility of judgment, which had formed a focus of the Schematism. Judgment in general, for him, is the faculty for thinking the universal within the particular. In his previous discussion he had viewed this process as a process of subsumption. The particular instance is brought under a concept which we hold prior to our encounter with the concrete. In this process the concepts provide the rules for the imagination, guiding the process of synthesis. In this later work, however, he pays attention to a different category of judgment, what he terms reflective judgment. In such judgments the imagination is *searching* for a form. It is within this context that he gives his account of the appreciation of beauty. Judgments of taste are not cognitive judgments. Perceptions of beautiful objects, Kant recognises, are connected to *feelings* of pleasure. Feelings for him are subjective and non-cognitive. Nonetheless such subjective feelings are the ground of aesthetic judgments of beauty which appear to make claims of universal validity. How can this be so?

Well, for him, the feeling of pleasure is the experiencing of the harmonious relation between the manifold of sense and our understanding. Such a feeling is different from that of both pleasurable sensations and the esteem we feel for the morally good. It has a quality of disinterestedness linked to the recognition of *its potential validity for others*. The harmony here is due to the work of the imagination, exercising its freedom in detecting, in what is presented, something which is intelligible to us. Fiona Hughes describes this in the following way: 'the beautiful marks a moment when the senses [I think this should be the imagination] make sense of something in the world'.[51] The beautiful thing is one in which the imagination can creatively weave a form that displays 'the harmonious interplay of understanding and imagination'.[52] (Kant stresses here that the source of the beauty is form; colour, taste, smell, texture are excluded. We do not need to follow him in this.) Although the feeling of pleasure which constitutes the detection of such harmony is subjective, it makes demands of a universal kind. For, if the imagination has done its job properly, and given Kant's humanist assumption that the demands of human understanding are universally shared, then when this form is made evident to others, they should also experience the same feeling. This is not just a claim about a causal regularity: the same objects causing the same feelings because we are made the same way, as some writers[53] seem to suggest. Once the harmony has been made manifest, then everyone would be justified in sharing the feeling, and indeed *should* do so. Failure to have the feelings is failure to detect the harmony. As Kant remarks, 'the assertion is not that every one *will* fall in with our judgement, but rather that every one *ought* to agree with it'.[54] Here Kant is giving a particular version of the notion of a *sensus communis*, at a time[55] when taste was thought of as a special non-rational way of knowing, which nonetheless made universal demands. For Kant this common sense was a public sense, in which the subjective feelings were subject to critical scrutiny by others.[56]

Whatever we may think about this as an account of aesthetic beauty, Kant has given us a model of the way in which the imagination can work, creatively (and without concepts), which can have a more general application. It is one in which the activity of synthesis is put together, as Merleau-Ponty later stresses, with a *receptivity*, in a giving over of the subject to the world; but also of *an accountability to that world*, delivered by the necessity of others recognising the appropriateness of the images/forms, which we imaginatively both create and detect. It provides a model which can be applied in a more general way to our relations to the world, and not only to an aesthetic sensibility narrowly defined as concerned with questions of beauty. Kant argues that the imagination

> must, in the judgment of taste, be regarded in its freedom ... it is not taken as reproductive, as in its subjection to the laws of association, but as productive and exerting an activity of its own (as originator of arbitrary forms of possible intuitions).[57]

But 'a given object, through the intervention of sense, sets the imagination at work in arranging the manifold, and the imagination'.[58] We have seen already, in the discussion of the Schematism, that in bringing of manifold under concepts, the imagination grasps the way in which sensory intuitions *can yield* an appropriate form.

David Bell, among others,[59] argues that the discussion of the imagination in the first *Critique* requires just the schematising which Kant spells out in the *Critique of Judgement*. For the art of the imagination is grasping possible ways in which the manifold can be brought to conform to rules. Kant, however, assumes, at that earlier point, that there is no *range* of possibilities here. It is as if the *a priori* concepts, determining space and time and providing rules for the formation of empirical concepts, not only constrain but determine the possible ways in which the manifold of sense can be synthesised. This seems to leave the imagination no room for creativity. Kant, in this earlier work, was concerned with scientific discourses providing accounts of the workings of nature to generate law-like and mechanical regularities. In this project he did not consider there could be multiple possibilities. Now we are less certain that even scientific methods determine single models. Moreover, we order the manifold for many different purposes. In this ordering the framework of the third *Critique* offers an account of a less determining kind.

The productive imagination in this later work of Kant allows a *creative* apprehension of the form of the sensible, recognising a unity within a multiplicity. He argues here that we employ our creative imagination in *seeking* a form in the sensible world, whose validity depends on it being recognisable by others. The form which we apprehend in the sensory manifold must be a *possible form* for the world to take. It must, if we accept the arguments of the first *Critique*, be constrained by the categories. Its legitimacy as a possible form, as the third *Critique* stresses, requires that it must be available to the apprehension and recognition of others. It is something we creatively, collectively and individually apprehend. Such a dimension of creativity, if attached to an account of perception in general, allows for the possibility of our world being imagined in different ways, formed into a variety of images; 'interminable reinterpretations to which it is legitimately susceptible'.[60]

Conclusion

In this chapter, following a trajectory from Hume to Kant, it has been suggested that our perceptual encounters with the world require the workings of both the reproductive and productive imagination. The reproductive imagination is required to keep a manifold of sensory intuitions in play at each perceptual moment and the productive imagination to find in this manifold a form which yields a sensory image. Fiona Hughes has drawn attention to and challenged what she calls the widespread *impositionist* interpretation[61] of Kant's account. According to this model the imagination *simply imposes* forms on an indeterminate given, in accordance with rules derived from the understanding.

For Hughes such a picture of perception needs to be replaced with a picture of a relational encounter, which requires that the world encountered is one which is *apt for* the forms which we both seek out and impose upon it. We will follow this reading. In his discussion of synthesis Kant stresses that the manifold which is encountered must be one which is *synthesisable*. And in the *Critique of Judgement* the *a priori* principle which renders judgment possible is that nature is *susceptible* to our faculties, 'a principle without which understanding could not feel itself *at home* in nature'.[62] Following Hughes' reading here allows us to claim, following Kant, that the imaginary texture which is the product of the synthesising activities of the productive imagination is indeed a texture *of the real*. For nature must be susceptible to such images for them to be projectibly detectable by ourselves and others. So the imagination delivers such an imaginary texture and remains *the condition of there being a real for us*. For, as Kant stressed from the beginning of the first critique, an unsynthesised mush of sensory impressions is not something which could form the content of perceptual experience.

There is also a more general question of the extent to which, in appropriating Kant's account of the imagination, we also need to accept the *transcendental idealist* framework in which it is placed. What haunts Kant's account of the imagination and makes it problematic for many, amongst whom I count myself, is that it seems to offer a picture of a noumenal subject confronting a noumenal world, which becomes formed according to its subjective conditions of thought and sensibility. The imagination can then appear as a faculty of just such a noumenal subject. (A quite contrary danger, which Kant himself seemed to be aware of in rewriting for the second edition of *The Critique of Pure Reason*, is that the description of the three moments of synthesis found in the first edition is read as a characterisation of an empirical process of sensory processing of empirical subjects.) In the following chapters we will explore the possibilities of rejecting accounts of the imagination presupposing a noumenal subject, while retaining the fundamental Kantian insight that the imagination is what yields the texture of the real, and remains the condition of there being a real for us.

What is retained is sympathy for Kant's transcendental project, an argument for the necessity of imagination that is transcendental, rather than idealist. Kant's articulation and defence of the unity of apperception and the role of the categories is transcendental. He argues for these conditions as necessary components of any experience which can be taken as that of an objective world. This is a project which argues *a priori* for necessary interweavings between our experiencing of a world of objects and our experience being that of a unified consciousness. It argues that our phenomenal experience of the world will necessarily (in the transcendental sense, as a condition of our having perceptual experiences at all) bear the marks *as of* productive and reproductive synthesis, if it is to be unified in that way. Moreover, this requires that, as subjects of experience, we must be able to grasp and *take up* a sensory manifold *as sensory* images; sensory material synthesised in the way Kant describes. That is what it means to have an imagination. These transcendental arguments are, I would suggest, independent of idealist or empirical ones. But they are transcendental arguments which put the imagination at the centre of perceptual experience.

Taking up a sensory manifold in terms of images is not an individualist matter. As becomes clear, below, we are initiated into ways of seeing by an upbringing within a social context, which Kant did not address. For Merleau-Ponty, whose writings we will consider in the following chapters, the grasping of the sensory manifold as an image requires a bodily immersion within it, which Kant also failed to theorise. This will also be addressed in the following chapters.

Notes

1 Strawson, P., 1974, 'Imagination and Perception', in P. Strawson, *Freedom and Resentment*, Methuen, London.
2 For further discussion see Jan Wilbanks, 1968, *Hume's Theory of the Imagination*, M. Nijhoff, The Hague; Annette Baier, 1991, *A Progress of Sentiments*, Harvard University Press, Cambridge MA and London.
3 Hume, D. 1964 [1748], *A Treatise of Human Nature,* Everyman, London and New York, p. 11.
4 Ibid., 13.
5 Ibid., 14.
6 Ibid., 18.
7 Ibid., 18–19.
8 Ibid., 19.
9 Ibid., 189.
10 Ibid., 209.
11 Ibid., 245.
12 Ibid., 246–247.
13 Merleau-Ponty, M., 2012, *Phenomenology of Perception*, trans. Donald A. Landes, Routledge, London and New York, p. 23.
14 Ibid., 17.
15 Ibid., 19.
16 Ibid., 20.
17 Warnock, M., 1976, *Imagination,* Faber, London, p. 19.
18 *Phenomenology of Perception* 3.
19 *Phenomenology of Perception* 4.
20 Strawson, P., 1974, 'Imagination and Perception', in P. Strawson, *Freedom and Resentment*, Methuen, London, p. 24.
21 Kant, I., 1929 [1781, 1787], *Critique of Pure Reason*, trans. N. Kemp Smith, Macmillan, London.
22 A 120 Kemp Smith 144.
23 Ibid.
24 A 120 Kemp Smith 144 f/n.
25 'Imagination and Perception'.
26 Sartre, J.-P., 2004, *The Imaginary, A Phenomenological Psychology of the Imagination*, trans. J. Webber, Routledge, London, p. 25ff.
27 Guyer, Paul, 2004, 'Kant, Immanuel (1724–1804)', *Routledge Encyclopedia of Philosophy online*, www.rep.routledge.com/
28 Young, J. M., 1988, 'Kant's View of Imagination', *Kant Studien* 79, pp. 140–164.
29 'Imagination and Perception' 95.
30 A 96 Kemp Smith 129.

31 A 99 Kemp Smith 131.

32 A 102 Kemp Smith 133.

33 'Imagination and Perception' 89.

34 Hughes, Fiona, 2007, *Kant's Aesthetic Epistemology*, Edinburgh University Press, Edinburgh, p. 147.

35 Makkreel, R. A., 1990, *Imagination and Interpretation in Kant*, University of Chicago Press, Chicago and London.

36 A 116/7 Kemp Smith 142.

37 Weatherston, M., 2002, *Heidegger's Interpretation of Kant*, Palgrave, New York, p. 112.

38 A 138 Kemp Smith 180.

39 *Heidegger's Interpretation of Kant* 168.

40 A 141 Kemp Smith 182.

41 Ibid.

42 Ibid.

43 A 142 Kemp Smith 183.

44 Ibid.

45 Wittgenstein, L. 1968, *Philosophical Investigations*, Blackwell, Oxford, see discussion in D. Bell, 1987, 'The Art of Judgment', *Mind* 96, pp. 221–244.

46 Schaper, E., 1964, 'Kant's Schematism Reconsidered', *The Review of Metaphysics* 18, no. 2, p. 290.

47 'It is evident, therefore, that the schematism of understanding, effected by means of the transcendental synthesis of imagination, is simply the unity of all the manifold of intuition in inner sense, and so indirectly the unity of apperception, which, as a function, corresponds to the receptivity of inner sense' (A145). The way in which the transcendental demand of a unity of apperception is realised for us, is by the unifying of the manifold of *inner sense* (something like our stream of consciousness) in time.

48 Kant's recognition of the role of the imagination in making possible a temporal consciousness was the centre of Heidegger's most sustained engagement with him. See, M. Heidegger, 1962, *Kant and the Problem of Metaphysics*, trans. J. S. Churchill, Indiana University Press, Bloomington. I will not discuss the complexity of Heidegger's readings here. There are some key differences between the two writers. For Heidegger temporality is the ontological (transcendental?), originary, form of experience. This he *identifies* with an imagination which is the *root of both* sensibility and understanding. The stages of syntheses are then the disclosure of different moments (past, present and future) of this originary temporality. For Kant sensibility is tied to a receptivity, which is initially independent of the workings of the imagination, and the transcendental conditions for objective thought are *a priori* and have their source in the understanding. It is when applied to sensibility that they yield a consciousness that is temporal (and spatial).

49 We also need to turn to the discussion in *The Critique of Judgement* to find recognition of the possibility that the manifold could be unified by the imagination, without the application to it of a concept. The function of the imagination is to bring the manifold into shape as a perceptual image, but we might ask whether such an image necessarily requires conceptualisation. Kant in the first *Critique* clearly thinks this is required, and indeed characterises experience as requiring both intuition and concept. A similar position is taken in contemporary writing by John McDowell. See, Schear, J. S., ed., 2013, *Mind, Reason, and Being-in-the-World: The McDowell–Dreyfus Debate*, Routledge, London and New York. For others, however, the syntheses of the imagination may be less demanding than syntheses involving concepts. The world may be brought to order, without that process being dictated by the need to apply a concept to it. Michael Young (Young, 'Kant's View of Imagination', 150–153) suggests that cats can construe their perceptions as

things, and yet cannot apply concepts. For Sarah Gibbons (Gibbons, S., 1994, *Kant's Theory of the Imagination*, Clarendon Press, Oxford, p. 8 and passim), the imaginative synthesis yields a pre-conceptual order which then makes possible the further step of applying concepts. Allison also warns of the dangers of over intellectualising the Kantian imagination: 'the task of the imagination is to synthesise, and of the understanding to bring this synthesis to concepts' (Allison, H. E., 2004, *Kant's Transcendental Idealism*, Yale University Press, New Haven CT, p. 188). Allison endorses Young in suggesting that 'the imagination remains "blind" in the sense that its rule governed interpretive activity is not self consciously performed, which is why it does not amount to cognition "in the proper sense"' (ibid., 189). The plausibility of this depends on what we are going to call conceptual thinking. For many (see *Mind, Reason, and Being-in-the-World: The McDowell–Dreyfus Debate*), the application of concepts, at least potentially, allows critical reflection and evaluation. Conceptual thinking can be woven into structures of reasoning. But, it is suggested (ibid.), we have pre-conceptual, everyday engagements with the world without such links. And such pre-reflective modes of experiencing the world have become central in the writing of the phenomenological writers who we will go on to discuss in the following chapters. McDowell, however, defending what appears to be Kant's position here, suggests that when we are aware of aspects of experience which we have not conceptually articulated, we are aware of them as possibly articulable; and this gives our experience a different quality from that of animals, even within the context of what appears to be pre-conceptual coping. These are not questions which will be pursued here. What does seem clear is that, however like or unlike the experience of animals is to our own experience, if their world has a shape for them, then, in Kantian terms, it manifests the workings of the productive imagination.

50 Kant, I., 2007 [1790], *Critique of Judgement*, trans. J. C. Meredith, Oxford University Press, Oxford.

51 Hughes, *Kant's Aesthetic Epistemology* 6.

52 Schaper, E., 1992, 'Taste, Sublimity and Genius: The Aesthetics of Nature and Art', in P. Guyer, ed., *The Cambridge Companion to Kant*, Cambridge University Press, Cambridge, p. 373.

53 Cohen, T., and Guyer, P., 1982, *Essays in Kant's Aesthetics*, University of Chicago Press, Chicago, Introduction.

54 *Critique of Judgement* 85.

55 Allison, H. E., 2001, *Kant's Theory of Taste*, Cambridge University Press, Cambridge, Introduction.

56 For him, this allowed the recognition of a purposiveness in nature, beauty as part of its final goal, a purposiveness which would elude us if we only utilised the imagination in line with the categories of the first *Critique*. This teleological aspect of Kant's thought is not one which was adopted by the writers discussed in later chapters, and will not be pursued here.

57 *Critique of Judgement* 86.

58 *Critique of Judgement* 83.

59 Bell, 'The Art of Judgment'.

60 Merleau-Ponty, M., 1993, 'Eye and Mind', in Galen A. Johnson, ed., *The Merleau-Ponty Aesthetics Reader*, Northwestern University Press, Evanston IL, p. 139.

61 Hughes, *Kant's Aesthetic Epistemology*.

62 *Critique of Judgement* 35.

3   Imagination and perception
The absent present and bodily synthesis

In this chapter we turn to the views of Sartre and Merleau-Ponty on the imagination and the imaginary. This is to further explore Kant's claim that the imagination is necessary for perception, that the imaginary provides the texture of the real. While Sartre rejects this claim, Merleau-Ponty supports it, and anchors the imaginary schema (*gestalt* in his terms) of the perceived world in our *bodily* presence within it; the shape of the body echoing the shape of the world. Both writers pay attention to what we shall term the role of the *absent present* to our mode of experiencing the world. And Merleau-Ponty follows the Kant of the third *Critique* in making creativity central to the workings of the imaginary.

In Sartre's work on the imagination we find a bifurcation of imagination and perception and correspondingly a bifurcation of the imaginary and the real. He therefore appears to reject a role for imagination within perception, contrary to the direction of thought which is being defended in this work. Merleau-Ponty rejects the dichotomy, found in Sartre's account, for *failing to accurately characterise and make sense* of the phenomenology of both perception and agency. By means of a critical engagement with Kant, Merleau-Ponty offers an account of perception that incorporates elements of *both* receptivity and spontaneity. These, for Sartre, marked two *different* kinds of intentional directedness, perception and imagination. This difference between the two writers underpins many of the other key differences between them: their conception of freedom, the framework of inter-subjective relations, and the nature of value. There were also disagreements about the role of art, and famously and publicly, disputes, between 1952 and 1956, about Sartre's support of the Communist Party.[1] All of which are linked to their differences concerning the imaginary and the real. On this fundamental issue we will be following Merleau-Ponty, and largely for the reasons he gives, namely that Sartre's dichotomy does not make sense of the phenomenology of perception.

Nonetheless, despite their fundamental differences, what is striking in reading the two authors is the similarity to be found in their phenomenological descriptions of perceptual experience. This is strikingly the case in the use of the metaphor of pregnancy. This is used first by Sartre and becomes pivotal to Merleau-Ponty. Perceptual experience is pregnant, with a past, an elsewhere, and with possibilities for our future, in a way that is captured by both writers. I will suggest that this feature, captured in Sartre's descriptions, sits in tension with an ontology which dichotomises the imaginary and the real. What he offers phenomenologically, along with Merleau-Ponty, is an account of perception in which the imaginary gives us the texture of the real, an insight which is not compatible with them standing in oppositional relations.

Sartre explicitly addressed the question of the imagination. He wrote two books on the subject, the first, *L'Imagination*, in 1936.[2] The second in 1940 was *L'Imaginaire: Psychologie Phenomenologique de l'Imagination* (translated first under the title *The Psychology of Imagination* and later as *The Imaginary*[3]). The account of the imagination developed in this second work then provided the foundation for his account of consciousness in *Being and Nothingness*.[4] Moreover, his later biographical works, on Genet and on Flaubert,[5] were said by him to be a continuation of this work on the imagination (see Chapter 6). In all of these works he draws a sharp distinction between imagination and perception. In the *Phenomenology of Perception*,[6] Merleau-Ponty does not talk directly about the imagination. At this point he does not articulate his disagreements with Sartre by the use of this term. Where he does refer to the imagination in that text, it is usually to capture what we might call fanciful thinking. However, in the *Phenomenology of Perception*, Merleau-Ponty offers an account of perception that builds on the insights of Kant and is in contrast to that offered by Sartre, and the differences between them are ones which, in later texts, he articulates in terms of the imaginary. In these later works he introduces the terms *visible and invisible*,[7] as terms which echo and replace Sartre's sets of distinctions, between the present and the absent, being and nothing, the perceived and the imagined. And in some of these texts the 'invisible' and 'the imaginary' are used interchangeably, concerned as he is to explore 'the quasi-presence and imminent visibility which make up the whole problem of the imaginary'.[8]

Presence and absence: *The Imaginary*

In his early works on the imagination[9] Sartre follows Husserl[10] both in rejecting the empiricist account of the imagination, in which it consists in inner pale copies of perceptions (here we will follow him), and in insisting that imagining was a kind of intentional act distinct from perceiving (here we will disagree). Consequently he provides an account of the imagination which also stands in contrast to Kant, for whom both the productive and the reproductive imagination were engaged in perception, in the conjuring up of mental images, and in the production of and engagement with works of art. For Sartre, in both perceiving Pierre and imagining him I am engaged in intentional acts directed in some way at Pierre. But they are intentional acts of quite different kinds: 'consciousness is related [to Pierre] in two different ways'.[11] Nonetheless, 'the imagining consciousness that I have of Pierre is not a consciousness of an image of Pierre'.[12] In perception, something is *present* to us, something which is in excess of any aspects we may grasp of it, and to which we can return for further information. There is, he says, 'a kind of *overflowing* in the world of "things" ... to exhaust the richness of my current perception would take an infinite time'.[13] If my friend Pierre is in front of me I can check what shirt he is wearing, etc. In contrast, if I imagine Pierre, then Pierre is *absent*, and any characteristics of this imagined Pierre are ones which I have bestowed. Pierre, as imagined, has an 'essential poverty',[14] for it is the intentional act of consciousness which constitutes what features he has. 'A perceptual consciousness appears to itself as *passive* ... an imaging consciousness [has] a *spontaneity* that produces and conserves the object as imaged'[15] [my emphasis].

For Sartre the act of consciousness involved in imagining is *a negation of the real* and the constitution of an *irreal* image, whose distinctive mark is its *absence*. This activity takes place in a range of settings; when we imagine a friend who is away from us; when we see a doodle or a cloud as a castle; when we recognise a character in the actions of a performer; when we take a photograph or a portrait to be a portrait of someone or something; when we produce or engage with art works in general: 'mental images, caricatures, photos are so many species of the same genus'.[16]

Insofar as they involve an imaging consciousness each of these contexts involves a double act of negation. First I negate the positive features of perception and focus instead on what is not perceived. Pierre is not in the cafe. Second I constitute, via an act of imagination, an image of Pierre which is also marked by negation, for it has the characteristic of not being real. 'In this sense one can say that the image has wrapped within it a certain nothingness ... it gives its object as not being.'[17] There are parallel acts in the other cases when the imagination is at work. Faced with a photo of Pierre what I *perceive* is 'a paper rectangle of a special quality and colour'.[18] But if I see it as a photo of Pierre I engage in an act of imaging: 'the piece of card is animated ... if I see Pierre in the photo it is because I put him there'.[19] When I make of a doodle the face of a creature, what is perceived is a set of material marks. But I *surpass* such perception by imagining in those marks the face. Here I have gone beyond what is present to create an image which is *not present*. In so doing I use the material of the ink marks as the grounding of my image, but the image itself is something constituted by my acts and, for Sartre, works by negating its ground and replacing it with an image whose constitutive character is its irreality: 'draw a little man on bended knees with arms raised in the air: you will project on his face an indignant amazement, but you will not *see* it there: it is there in a latent state, like an electric charge'.[20] When I take a portrait to be of Charles VIII, 'the dead Charles VIII is there. It is he we see not the picture, and yet we posit him as not being there: we have only reached him "as imaged" ... by the intermediary "of the picture".'[21] I cannot as part of the same act of consciousness both perceive the lines and colours *and* grasp the picture as a portrait; for the second is an act of imagining consciousness which negates the present perception.

Sartre discusses the performance artist Franconay, 'a small stout brunette woman', who is imitating Maurice Chevalier. In this performance I have two options: 'to see Maurice Chevalier as imaged, or a small woman pulling faces'.[22] There is also a third state. I can make a judgment that the woman is imitating Chevalier. But to judge thus is not to imagine Chevalier through the medium of the woman's body. For that to happen 'that black hair we did not see as black; that body we did not perceive as a female body, we did not see those prominent curves'.[23] The absent Chevalier comes, Sartre suggests, *to possess* the body in front of us. (It is hard to fault the phenomenology here.) Nonetheless, for Sartre, I am aware that I am spontaneously and at each moment creating this image. (This seems less accurate.) Again Sartre warns us against treating the image itself as a thing. I am conscious, he says, not of an image but of an object as imaged: 'the image represents a certain type of consciousness, absolutely independent of the perceptual type and, correlatively a sui generis type of existence for its objects'.[24]

In each of these cases there is something perceived which serves as what Sartre calls the *analogon* of the image which is created; the perceptual ground which is surpassed in the creation of the image. The image itself does not, however, exist as a thing, like the objects which ground it; for it exists only as constituted by the intentional act of the consciousness which posits it. Something like an analogon seems required for Sartre to make the distinction, for him, between imagining and conceiving; for we can think about Chevalier and make judgments about him, without imagining him. Imaging consciousness requires *something like perception*, for Sartre, what he calls *quasi observation*: 'its contents retain, like a phantom … a sensible opacity'.[25] For this we seem to require something like a sensory matter, which we surpass with an imagining form. Sartre applies this analysis to works of art in general. When an artist creates a work of art she utilises paint or lines or clay or sounds as the perceptual ground which enable her audience to create the work of art as an image which is not present, but which imagining consciousness brings into being. He claims 'the work of art is an irreality'.[26] The painter does not give us an image. He simply constitutes 'a material analogon such that anyone can grasp that image if only they gaze at the analogon'.[27] Talking of the reds in a Matisse painting, he says:

> one grasps it … as making up part of an irreal whole, one can genuinely enjoy the red only in grasping it as red of the rug, and therefore as irreal … the painting … functions as an analogon … what is manifested through it is an irreal ensemble of new things.[28]

These new things are grasped through imagining consciousness. The same analysis is applied to fiction, poetry and drama, with the words or the body providing the analogon for imaginary people and worlds. In the case of mental imaging it is not quite clear what constitutes the analogon. In his discussion of different cases of imagining Sartre recognises that the matter which grounds our imagining can become more and more perfunctory. In mental imaging the analogon seems to be provided by scraps of knowledge and residual feelings which past perceptual experiences have left us with. But in each case they serve only as that through which consciousness posits its imaginary, and therefore irreal, objects.

Sartre, therefore, distinguishes images from perceptions and thus rejects any account of perceptual experience that makes it 'an amalgam of sensations and images'[29] (of which Kant's view would be an example). For 'imaging consciousness is accompanied ... by an annihilation of perceptual consciousness, and reciprocally'.[30] The act involved in perceiving a horse as a horse and the act involved in taking a hobby horse to be a horse are therefore distinct for him. The role of consciousness in perception is to provide a space in which the thing can be posited as opposed to the seer, in its reality, its positivity; a positivity which is then passively received. And, in contrast, the act of imagining requires a negation of such positivity, and the creation of an image. Imagination is therefore the realm of activity/spontaneity.

How then does Sartre accommodate the features of perception which he characterises as our perceiving 'more and otherwise' than we see,[31] that others invoke the work of imagination to explain? These are features of perception such as 'it is understood that this ashtray before me has an underneath, that it rests by means of this underneath on the table, that this underneath is white porcelain etc.'[32] This is referred to by more recent writers as the characteristic of *perceptual presence*:

> Consider as an example a perceptual experience such as that you might enjoy if you were to hold a bottle in your hand with eyes closed. *You have a sense of the presence* of the whole bottle, even though you only make contact with the bottle at a few *isolated points* ... crucially, your sense of the presence of the bottle is a sense of its *perceptual* presence. That is, you do not merely think or infer that there is a bottle present, in the way, say, that you think or infer that there is a room next door. The presence of the bottle is not inferred or surmised. It is experienced.[33]
>
> (first emphasis added)

We see an apple, for example, as 'not only having a red surface but as white inside'.[34]

For Sartre, however, what is involved in such perception is radically dishomogeneous with imagination. For him these features of perceptual experience do not require the imagination. Contrary to the formulation above, he puts down such characteristics of experience to unformulated *knowledge* concerning the objects; awareness of possibilities concerning it, possibilities were we to shift perspective:

> For example, the arabesques of a tapestry that I am gazing at are only partly given to my intuition, the legs of the armchair in front of the window hide certain curves. I, nevertheless, grasp these hidden arabesques as presently existing, as veiled and not at all absent. I perceive their hidden beginnings and endings ... as being continued behind the legs of the armchair.[35]

Such knowledge *can* lead us to the formulation of images. I can imagine the tapestry extending behind the cupboard. But this requires a distinct and what he calls an 'inverse act'[36] from *perceiving it as continuous*. In perception 'the hidden arabesques ... constitute a quality of the visible arabesques – namely that ... they continue without interruption'. But, when I imagine them, they appear as isolated, autonomous objects. Perception can therefore provide us with the beginning of an infinity of imaginings; but only at the price of the 'annihilation of perceptual consciousness'.[37] 'Thus the imaginative act is at once constituting, isolating and annihilating.'[38]

The apparent presence in perception of characteristics not immediately in view applies, of course, not just to spatial qualities but also to temporal ones. In his treatment of the temporal quality of our experience Sartre makes a parallel move. The structure of 'retention' and 'protention' articulated by Husserl and illustrated in relation to the recognition of a melody[39] are, for Sartre, characteristics of the actual: 'the successive notes of a melody are grasped by appropriate retentions as that which make the note presently heard precisely what it is'.[40] The retention is a character of present experience constituted by the *knowledge* of it being after a certain quality. The protention, a quality of 'being before' which the experience has in virtue of an *expectation* of a future quality: 'retention and protention constitute, in every way, the sense of the present visual impression'.[41] They do not require the imagination. This allows him to draw at some points a sharp distinction between memory and imagination. In memory I direct my attention towards a past but real event. Whereas when I imagine, 'I grasp nothing'.[42] Consequently 'the imaging consciousness of Pierre in Berlin ... is much closer to that of the centaur ... than to the memory of Pierre as he was the day he left'.[43] (At other points, though, he seems to regard memory as creating an imaginative reconstruction of the past, in the present.[44])

It is in imaging consciousness that Sartre sees the workings of spontaneity, and therefore the ground for his account of freedom. It is also spontaneous, imaginary transformations that serve as the source of the significance, affectivity and value, found in everyday experience. These themes are further spelt out in his later work, *Being and Nothingness*.

Being and Nothingness

In the final chapter of *The Imaginary* Sartre sums up the distinctive features of imagining consciousness and makes the claim that the possibility of exercising itself in this way is an essential feature of consciousness per se. This is because 'to posit an image is ... to hold the real at a distance, to be freed from it, in a word to deny it'.[45] On such a denial rests the possibility of our freedom: 'it is because we are transcendentally free that we can imagine'.[46] At any point we can *surpass* the real into an imagined future which we ourselves posit and which the real does not determine. Such a denial has certain key features. It is a standing back from the world to posit certain possibilities which are not found within it. Such a standing back, however, requires a grounding, an anchorage in the real which it is surpassing. Imagining is only possible from a situation within the world, a point of view onto reality, *from which* certain possibilities stand out. Such situations 'provide concrete and precise motivations'[47] for particular imaginaries. They are needed to ground them. An image can appear 'only on the ground of the world and in connection with that ground'.[48] This allows him to say 'every concrete and real situation of consciousness in the world is pregnant with the imaginary in so far as it is always presented as a surpassing of the real'.[49] This metaphor of pregnancy is picked up later by Merleau-Ponty and marks a point where their phenomenological descriptions are remarkably close. How it is to be understood marks a key point of contention between them.

The analysis which Sartre offers in the concluding section of *The Imaginary* informs the ontological framework of *Being and Nothingness*. Here the negation which is at the heart of the imaging consciousness is the means by which the *being-for-itself* manifests its freedom. Such imagining consciousness is what distinguishes being-for-itself from *being-in-itself*, whose existence remains within the domain of the actual and whose changes are determined by mechanistic causality. This freedom is instanced in projects towards which the for-itself directs its activities. These activities are revealed by imagining consciousness as possibilities grounded in the present situation but *absent* from it and *undetermined* by it. They require a negation of that situation, 'a cleavage between the ... past and the present'.[50] To exercise freedom 'it is necessary that conscious being constitute itself in relation to its past as separated from this past by a nothingness'.[51] It is in this way that 'nothingness haunts being'.[52] 'The for-itself arises as the nihilation of the in-itself.'[53] For Sartre, then, in the act of perception, consciousness posits a real, which is distinct from the perceiver and which makes itself evident as presence, positivity. However, within the act of imagining, which is an exercise in spontaneity, and undetermined by the perceived real, though grounded in it, possibilities are opened out. These require a negation of the positivity that is offered to perception, and a positing of irreal images, towards which we direct our projects. These are possibilities for consciousness to transform reality. In this way the imaginary is the basis of our freedom.

Imagining consciousness is also the *source* of the value and significance which we, pre-reflectively, experience the world as carrying. Phenomenologically, 'values are sown on my path as thousands of little real demands, like the signs which order us to keep off the ground'.[54] The alarm clock demands we get up, like an instruction issued from outside. But, Sartre argues, this appearance is misleading. Values are not part of the real, 'they ... derive from an original projection of myself, which stands as my choice of myself in the world'.[55] The original choice of myself in the world does not occur at a moment. The whole life is the choice. It manifests itself in our patterns of empirical projects over our lives; but is the 'transcendent meaning'[56] of such projects. They are informed by the imaginary, by a sense of an ideal self, which frames the way in which these empirical choices present to us. (For further discussion see Chapter 6.) So the pregnancy of the world, its field of possibilities which appear to confront us, the values which seem to justify our responses, have their origin in the exercise of our freedom in the positing of an imaginary ideal.

Sartre's distinction between imagining and perceiving seems to have its anchorage in two sources. One is phenomenological. He draws our attention to differences in the experience of perceiving Pierre and in imagining him. Where imagining is restricted to the context of what we might call 'conjuring up', there clearly are phenomenological differences. But the category of the imaginary is wider than the category of mental imaging for Sartre. His recognition of continuities between imagining an absent friend, seeing a performer in a role, recognising a portrait and seeing a doodle as a cloud, is one of the strengths of his account. Within this wider category the insistence that imagining plays no role in perceiving seems to have more than a phenomenological motivation. Moreover, his distinction between perceiving the arabesque continuing under the chair (a combination of sensory perception and knowledge that it goes under the chair) and imagining it as continuing under the chair, seems a forced one, as do his other accounts of what we are terming the absent present in perception. Our experiences here seem immediate, and not to involve the application of knowledge. Furthermore there do not seem to be sufficient *phenomenological* grounds for assuming the acts of a positing, imaging consciousness that he requires in looking at portraits and pictures. In the case of value and significance, he admits his account is in tension with the phenomenology. We experience such features as perceived, and we are unaware of their need for originary acts of imagining. But for Sartre the phenomenology is deceptive here and needs correcting by acts of reflection.

Further motivation for Sartre's division is found within a framework of reflective metaphysics, anchored in a distinction between the for-itself and in-itself. This ontology is offered as a way of breaking the deception of everyday experience, in which the perceived world seems to condition our agency. He wants to make space for a freedom for us to make our lives. As he sees it, it is a condition of this freedom that we can surpass the givenness of the real towards a future of our own imagining. So his ontology, and the distinction of the acts of imagining and perceiving, is offered as something like a transcendental condition of possibility for our phenomenal world having the characteristics it has, but our nonetheless operating freely within it.[57]

Perception and bodily synthesis in the *Phenomenology of Perception*

Merleau-Ponty, in his account of the phenomenology of perception, rejects the ontological framework informing Sartre's account. Instead he offers us a phenomenology in which the imaginary is interwoven into the texture of perception itself. If what we pay attention to is the *character of perceptual experience itself*, we find the imaginary within it. In this he follows the lead which Kant has provided. Nonetheless he also rejects a Kantian metaphysics of transcendental idealism, and for the same reason. We need to pay attention to the phenomenology, the world as perceived, without metaphysical speculation as to its source. This is a world in which the absent present, to which Sartre draws our attention, and which is characterised by him as an *irreality*, cannot be distinguished from the positivity of the real (a positivity which Sartre needs to assume, but cannot phenomenologically justify).

In the preface to the *Phenomenology* Merleau-Ponty writes:

> What distinguishes intentionality from the Kantian relation to a possible object is that the unity of the world, prior to being posited by knowledge through an explicit act of identification, is *lived* as *already accomplished* or as *already there* [my emphasis]. In the *Critique of Judgement* Kant himself demonstrated that there is a unity of the imagination and of the understanding ... In the experience of beauty, for example, I undergo the experience of a harmony between the sensible and the concept ... which is itself without any concept. Here the subject is no longer the universal thinker of a system of rigorously connected objects, no longer the subject ... that imposes the law of the understanding upon the manifold: rather he discovers himself and appreciates himself as a nature spontaneously [responding] ... But if the subject has a nature, then the hidden art of the imagination must condition the categorical activity; it is no longer merely aesthetic judgments that rest upon this hidden art, but also knowledge ...[58]

Merleau-Ponty therefore endorses the Kantian insight that knowledge and not just aesthetic judgment requires the art of the imagination. For Kant this was a capacity to *generate* unities in the experienced world. But Merleau-Ponty registers important dissentions on this point. He dissociates himself from the view of the subject that itself *imposes* the laws of understanding onto the manifold, in favour of a subject that finds itself able to respond to harmonies encountered in nature. He writes:

> Beginning from our experience of the world reflective analysis works back towards the subject as if towards a condition of possibility distinct from our experience, and presents universal synthesis as that without which there would be no world. To this extent reflective analysis ceases to adhere to our experience and substitutes a reconstruction for a description. From this we can understand how Husserl could criticise Kant for a 'psychologism of the faculties of soul'.[59]

He wishes to reject the postulation of a transcendent subject as the source of the syntheses of the world in favour of a view in which a synthesised world is encountered as already there, lived in our everyday encounters with it. He does away with the transcendent constituting subject, bestowing, via the exercise of spontaneity, form onto a mass of intuitions which have been passively received. Such, he argues, takes us away from the character of the perception itself. To grasp that character we must return to pre-reflective experience:

What have we then at the onset? Not a given manifold with a synthetic apperception which ranges over it and completely penetrates it, but a certain perceptual field against the background of the world ... not a mosaic of qualities, but a total configuration.[60]

In perception, we are drawing attention to characteristics of the world as we perceive it, without commitments to transcendent (or empirical) stories about what might be required for perceptual experience to have that shape. '"Form" is not privileged in our perception because ... it makes a world possible (in the Kantian sense), but rather because form *is the very appearance of the world not its condition of its possibility*' (my emphasis).[61]

For Merleau-Ponty, the world taking shape for us is not the work of a transcendent subject, but an aspect of our bodily immersion in the world we perceive. He articulates the organisational shape of perceptual experience utilising the vocabulary of gestalt psychology. The gestalt is what we grasp 'when we say we have found the rabbit in the foliage of a visual puzzle',[62] or more generally when we move beyond mere 'visual data' to 'the sense, the structure, and the spontaneous arrangements of parts'.[63] 'To perceive is not to experience a multitude of impressions ... it is to see an immanent sense bursting forth from a constellation of givens.'[64] This is what is primary in perception. The form takes shape under our eyes or under our touch.[65] The possibility of experiencing the gestalt of the world, for him, is a consequence of a bodily existence which is part of that world and which, pre-reflectively and pre-conceptually, can focus on objects and practically negotiate the space in which it finds itself. The nature of the subject here is a bodily nature, immersed in the spatiality of a world to which it is responding. We take up, grasp, the shape in the world we encounter and which emerges in relation to our body. I perceive an object as a door handle by means of a body that reaches out to grasp it:

> I perceive with my body. To have a body is to possess ... a schema of all perceptual arrangements and developments ... a thing is not [simply] *given* in perception it is ... taken up by us ... and lived by us ... linked to a world ... of which this thing is just one of several possible concretions.[66]
>
> When I move about in my house, I know immediately ... that walking towards the bathroom involves passing close to the bedroom, or that to look out the window involves having the fireplace on the left. I hold 'in my hands' or 'in my legs' its principal distances and directions.[67]

We have not, in this text, lost the synthesising activity which, for Kant, distinguished the productive imagination. But the synthesising activity is not the imposition of conceptual form onto intuited matter. It is rather the *taking up* or *grasping of shape* in the world we encounter, and which emerges in relation to our body. The productive imagination here is bodily, and it does not so much impose form as take up form, as a consequence of its sensitivity to the world in which it is placed. This is, initially, a pre-reflective and pre-conceptual activity of the body. It does not rule out conceptual syntheses, but for Merleau-Ponty these are secondary and rest on a prior ability of the body to find shape and meaning in what it encounters, 'my body ... the common texture of all objects'.[68] Such bodily abilities are often ones which are learnt, and become sedimented into bodily habits; the shape of our world being not individual but social. We learn how to perceive by a process of bodily training which becomes sedimented into bodily habits which serve to constitute the shape our world takes for us. Here Merleau-Ponty has modified the Kantian synthesis, the art of the imagination in perception, so that it is both bodily and social.

The thing we perceive remains transcendent to any of our perceptual experiences. But it is not a pure positivity offered to us. It has infinite possibilities of manifesting, which our bodily positionality, in relation to it, may anticipate and explore 'unperceived things ... not unbounded entities whose laws of construction we possess a priori ... [but] open, inexhaustible systems'.[69] Merleau-Ponty is not returning us to a naive realism, here, in which the world has an organisational structure independent of us, so that 'perception reveals objects as the lamp illuminates them at night'.[70] Rather the form takes shape under our eyes or under our touch. He refers to the work of the painter Cézanne who attempts to depict the process whereby matter takes form, 'breaking the skin of things, to show how the things become things'.[71] The process of perception is a process *in time*, in which I must keep hold of the past and an eye to the future to be able to grasp a determinate object and locate it in space:

> I open my eyes in the direction of my table; and my consciousness is immediately flooded with colours and confused reflections ... Suddenly, I focus on the table, which is not yet there ... my body centres upon an object ... The act of seeing is indivisibly prospective (since the object is at the end of my focusing movement), and retrospective (since it will be presented as anterior to its appearance) ... The spatial synthesis and the synthesis of the object are based upon this deployment of time ... a present, a past and a future together.[72]

Perception is never a pure positivity of the temporal present. It yields a form in which the spatial and temporal elsewhere are also given. We hear the notes as part of a melody, we see the carpet continuing under the cupboard and that the table has an underside. He rejects the account offered by Sartre, in which such features are injected into perception by our knowledge of what has passed or should follow, or our knowledge that the cupboard is resting on the carpet. Instead these are features yielded pre-cognitively by the gestalt of the perception itself.

Merleau-Ponty (here in common with Sartre) also rejects an account of such features which invokes mental images. Instead he explains them in terms of 'a *practical* [my emphasis] synthesis: I can touch the lamp, and not only the side turned towards me but also the other side; I have only to extend my hand'.[73] The sides not turned to me are, nonetheless, given in the perception, integrated into the bodily awareness which enables our negotiation of our world. He therefore integrates together within perceptual experience what for Sartre are distinct intentional acts. The pretension and retension which mark the temporal aspects of our experience and the spatial continuity which extends beyond what is immediately presented (for Sartre a combination of perception and knowledge), *and* the future possibilities which the situation we perceive suggests, yielding its meaning and significance (for Sartre the result of imagining consciousness) are, for Merleau-Ponty, all aspects of the rich content of perception. The possibility of such perceptual gestalts rests on constitutive interrelations, the echoing of the shape of our world in the shape of our bodies, and vice versa. We can perceive the world, he says, through 'co-naturality'[74] with it. I see blue because 'I am *sensitive* to colours'.[75] This is a picture of body and world as co-natural, so that we can discover sense without endowing it (even though the sense so discovered is a sense *for us*).

For Sartre meaning was introduced into the world by an imaging consciousness, envisaging its own possibilities, by an act of *negating* the world as perceived. For Merleau-Ponty we experience the world as *offering possibilities* to our bodies. We can make sense of our activities within it by pointing to worldly characteristics in which they are implicit. Merleau-Ponty argues freedom only makes sense within a field of possibilities. Within this field of possibilities 'a collection of things emerge from a background ... by presenting themselves to our body as "to be touched", "to be taken", "to be climbed"'.[76] Against this background our freedom emerges as a normatively intelligible response, rather than an exercise in transcendence. As a consequence my relation to my past is neither one of its determining the present, nor one in which it provides a ground to be negated. Though not a fate, the past has a weight which bears on my present decisions, and gives 'the atmosphere of my present'.[77] The significance of the world is perceived, encountered, available to others, and *assessable and re-assessable* in the light of the significance which others find there. And such significance provides the intelligibility of my projects. And, this, he suggests, is not accountable for within the characterisation that Sartre offers.

These differences between Sartre and Merleau-Ponty exist despite close similarities in many of their phenomenological descriptions. As previously noted, the image of a situation as pregnant with possibilities, found in both *The Imaginary* and *Being and Nothingness*, is one which Merleau-Ponty uses repeatedly throughout his work. In Sartre's account of the workings of the imaginary in works of art, the role of the artist is to create a physical entity which could serve as an analogon for imagining consciousness. Although he also claims that, individually, we can use almost anything as the basis for an image, the work of the artist requires a certain publicness. It must *suggest the form* which imaging consciousness can take. The implication seems to be that the individual reading of the artwork must be, in some sense, demonstratively anchored in what has been presented to us. 'The painter ... constitutes a material analogon such that anyone can grasp that image if only they gaze at the analogon'[78] (here he is discussing a portrait). What this formulation suggests is that irrealities can be *manifest*, appropriate to, certain material analogons. As Merleau-Ponty remarks: 'nothingness, Sartre himself is obliged to fulfil it somewhat with the *analogon*, with the living imaginary as it is in the actor'.[79] 'From the moment that there is an *analogon*, and this *analogon* is apprehended as "evoking" the real being of the absent object, imagining consciousness is not empty.'[80] The degree of spontaneity that Sartre stresses is, then, highest in purely mental images, and more strongly motivated when the possibilities are manifest in the analagon.[81] Such a model can be applied more widely. As Beauvoir points out,[82] Sartre stresses that our actions are grounded in *situations*. It is only in relation to concrete situations that certain possibilities emerge. These might also be interpreted as *irrealities* which are nonetheless *manifest*, grounded, not only in the sense that there is something to be negated to reach them, but also in the sense that there is something which suggests them, something which makes some and not others appropriate, normatively required. This indeed is the way that Beauvoir reads Sartre here.

But despite these similarities in the phenomenological descriptions, Sartre offers a metaphysical underpinning for this phenomenology which Merleau-Ponty rejects for failing to accommodate our perceptual experiences and our experiences of agency. For Sartre, manifest possibilities are a consequence of original projects, themselves acts of imagining, shaping our way of experiencing the world. They are manifest only within the context of these projects. The alarm clock seems to summon us, but only because we have imagined possibilities for it, the source of which was ourselves. For Merleau-Ponty all projects are anchored in the shape the world takes in our encounters with it.

The visible and invisible

As we have commented above, in the *Phenomenology of Perception* Merleau-Ponty does not articulate his disagreements with Sartre in terms of the imagination. However, in later texts,[83] he introduces the terms *visible and invisible*, as terms that echo and replace Sartre's sets of distinctions, between the present and the absent, being and nothing, the perceived and the imagined. And in some of these texts the 'invisible' and the 'imaginary' are used interchangeably. Throughout this later work there is an ongoing challenge to the account of our perceptual encounters which Sartre offered. Sartre's account 'assumes then a bipartite analysis: perception as observation, a close-woven fabric, without any gaps ... the imaginary as locus of the self negation'.[84] Sartre, he complains, offers us a perceived world without depth. This he rejects: 'There is no thing fully observable, no inspection of the thing that would be without gaps and that would be total ... conversely, the imaginary is not an absolute unobservable. This distinction ... is not that between the full and the void.'[85] In place of Sartre's picture he offers an account of perception in which the visible, what we might initially characterise as the perceptually present, is woven through with the invisible, the absent present, 'a visible is not a chunk of absolutely hard, indivisible being, offered all naked to ... vision ... but ever gaping open'.[86] He wishes to replace Sartre's account of the imaginary with 'an operative imaginary ... which is indispensable for the definition of Being itself'.[87] This imaginary is not the freely postulated irreality which Sartre suggests but the latent depth in the perceived world. Pregnancy is again the recurrent metaphor. The visible is pregnant with the invisible. The invisible is not the non-visible. It is made manifest through the visible, giving it 'immense latent content of the past, the future and the elsewhere, which it announces and which it conceals'.[88] In Sartre's account we *posit* the imaginary and fix its content, but Merleau-Ponty suggests, in contrast, that 'the invisible is a hollow in the visible, a fold in *passivity, not pure production*'[89] (my emphasis). What he is offering us, therefore, is an account of 'the visible as in-visible' (in the visible),[90] in place of a binary opposition between the perceptual and the imaginary; being and nothingness. 'The proper essence [*le propre*] of the visible is to have a layer [*doublure*] of invisibility ... which it makes present as a certain absence.'[91]

The framework of the visible and the invisible which Merleau-Ponty offers us here, and which we carry forward as anchoring the account of the imaginary put forward in this present work, proves to be a rich resource for articulating multiple features of our perceptual experience. In the *Phenomenology of Perception* he pointed out that to recognise an object as red requires an awareness of other actual and possible reds; to take an impression as that of a continuous thing requires holding on to its past and potential future as well as to the sides which are not immediately visible. But it is not to *conjure up* these other reds or other sides. For Merleau-Ponty, the imaginary (the invisible) is explicitly separated from the domain of representation. There is no question of memories of past experiences or anticipations of future ones being lined up in the inner realm of consciousness alongside present sensory data. Rather, for him, the other possible reds are *alive* in the red which we see. (There is a parallel here with Strawson's interpretation of the reproductive imagination in Kant.)[92]

> This red is what it is only by connecting up ... with other reds about it, with which it forms a constellation ... a certain node in the woof of the simultaneous and the successive ... A punctuation in the field of red things, which includes the tiles of roof tops, the flags of gatekeepers ... also a punctuation in the field of red garments, which includes the dresses of women, robes of professors.[93]

These connections are not a result of an intellectual process of generalising, or the workings of an empirical psychological process of association. They are part of the texture of perceptual experience: 'the visible landscape under my eyes is not exterior to ... other moments of time and past, but has them really behind itself in simultaneity'.[94] Such simultaneity of other moments of time within the audible present is also the feature which allows us to hear a melody in a piece of music. And the interweaving of the visible and invisible is what we experience when we see the carpet as extending under the cupboard and experience the completion of the pattern. The gestalt of the world is like that of a gesture. It is a movement across time in which a visible or positive presence carries with it an expressive depth. Equally, for Merleau-Ponty, to experience a spatio-temporally continuous thing is to recognise a certain *style*, holding together experiences in a way that requires both the visible and invisible to be in play: 'a certain manner of modulating time and space'.[95] So the detection of a gestalt (what Kant would call an image or a schema), including the gestalt of a *thing*, is only possible once the visible is experienced as carrying the invisible within it.

The framework can also be used to articulate the unity of the senses. Already in the *Phenomenology* he had pointed out that when we perceive, each of our senses suggests what is available to others:

> we see the rigidity and fragility of the glass, and when it breaks with a crystal clear sound, this sound is borne by the visible glass. One sees the elasticity of steel, the ductility of molten steel, the hardness of the blade in a plane, the softness of its shavings. The form of a fold in a fabric of linen or cotton shows us the softness or the dryness of the fibre. In the movement of the branch from which a bird has just left, we read its flexibility and its elasticity ... we see the weight of a block of cast iron that sinks in the sand.[96]

When I perceive an object, via one sense, a whole range of other possible sensory encounters are implicated, including those involving other senses. And he extends this range of possibilities to include a grasp of possible perceptual encounters which would be had by other perceivers. Our perceptual experience of the world has implicit within it the possibility of what we see being perceived by others, whose experiences of it may be different from ours. The possibility of such *differing* experiences latent within our own perceptions is part of what makes those perceptions to be of things, of a world. We experience our world as both available to all of our senses and as open to a potentially infinite range of possible modes of perception from different positions within it, perceptions which can never exhaust it. 'Every landscape of my life ... is ... pregnant with many other visions besides my own.'[97]

The work of art

In *The Visible and the Invisible* Merleau-Ponty enigmatically describes 'Being. as containing everything that will ever be said, and yet leaving us to create it'.[98] (Again there are echoes of the model Kant offers us in his account of the beautiful.) The invisible is something which is *offered* to our senses, but not as a positivity and not determinately. We are creatively involved in bringing it to expression, in gesture, in language, and in works of art. It is in painting, particularly, that Merleau-Ponty thought that the features of vision and visibility were made most evident to us. Sartre's account whereby 'the picture ... [is a] device to be borrowed from the real world to signify prosaic things which are absent'[99] is rejected. For him, the invisible, or imaginary, being *a dimension* of the visible, undermines the Sartrean picture. 'The animals painted on the walls of Lascaux are not there in the same way as the fissures and limestone forma- tions. But they are not *elsewhere*.'[100] They inhabit those rocky surfaces in a way that has been made available to us by the work of the artists.

Painting, for him, is the artist '*lending his body to the world*',[101] so that *it* can be expressively accomplished through him. Merleau-Ponty is not here concerning himself with a purely figurative art, for some viewed as trying to reproduce on canvas something bearing a relation of similarity to the observed scene. Art for him, figurative or not, is not imitative, the artist does not 'appropriate what he sees; he merely approaches it … he opens on to the world',[102] and by lending his body makes evident a physiognomy of existence. What art is bringing to expression is the salience and significance of the world we encounter; of colour and of space, drawing our attention to the possibilities of a line. Although he returns time and again to Cézanne, and his workings and reworking of the way a perceived scene comes into focus for us as a world of things, he also engages with colour in the work of Matisse and the line in Klee: 'as Klee said the line no longer imitates the visible; it "renders visible," it is the blueprint of the genesis of things. Perhaps no one before Klee had let a line muse.'[103] Art does not describe or depict an already determinate reality, but as with other expressive gestures, brings a world into focus, opening a 'hollow' or 'fold' in existence. Here Merleau-Ponty's thinking echoes that of Heidegger,[104] and although he does not talk of art as disclosive or unconcealing, art, along with other expressive gestures, is capable of a truth in a way that is similar to the Heideggerian picture, accomplishing the world alongside other expressive gestures. Such gestures can be truthful, but truth here is not conceived as a coincidence with a separate reality. The gestures instead unfold a shape which that reality can carry. And it is a truth which remains ambiguous. There are not, then, two stages, the world appearing and the painter somehow translating this into public expression. The appearance only becomes determinate as the paint- ing takes shape. Discussing Matisse's brush strokes, captured in slow motion on film, he draws our attention to the way a particular line 'was called for … in order that the painting might finally be that which it was in the process of becoming'.[105] This painting was not determined by the visible of the world, but nonetheless offers us its 'allusive logic'.[106] It brings into being a signification that offers one of the infinite possibilities of landscape, light or colour. It is not expressive of an inner subjectivity, but of the world thinking itself through the painter. It is for this reason that others can engage with the work, that a painting can be revelatory, making evident an imaginary which could not have been realised through our own hands. The painting 'opens … a texture of being' which, for the painter, 'emanates from the things themselves'.[107] A painting must, in some sense, *recognisably* offer us the imaginary of a visible world; and also our interpretations of the painting, open as they may be, must be anchored intelligibly in the patterns of colour and shape which we are offered. It cannot float free of what is visually offered to us. Pictures, then, offer to 'vision its inward tapestries, the imaginary texture of the real'.[108]

This account of art as bringing the imaginary of the perceived world to shape under our hands is one which Merleau-Ponty offers for other expressive mediums. Bodily gestures and language also express the world in this way, making manifest its possibilities. What becomes central to his account in the later works is not simply our bodily manipulations as giving shape to the world (the bodily syntheses of the *Phenomenology*), but the fact that we *can bring the world to expression*, which we need our bodies to do (see Chapters 4 and 7). While works of art may offer us new imaginaries, at the heart of Merleau-Ponty's work is the recognition that imaginary texture informs and animates *all* our perceptual experiences. The character of our perceptual experience is a gestalt, a style, or form, which is a relation between the sensible and a perceiving body, a body which is itself both sensing and sensible. The shape the world takes for us, therefore, is not that which it would take for an all-seeing eye positioned at no particular place within it. It is nonetheless not subjective. For our world has the character of a shared world and the character we assign it is answerable to others within it:

> the in-visible is not the contradictory of the visible, the visible itself has an invisible inner framework ... and the in-visible is the secret counterpart of the visible, it appears only within it ... it is *in the line* of the visible ... it is inscribed within it (in filigree).[109]

There is a continuity in these writings with the discussion in *The Phenomenology of Perception*, but the stress which was laid there on the personal habit body yielding a synthesised world is replaced by one in which the notion of synthesis is itself removed. 'If one starts from the visible and the vision, the sensible and the sensing, one acquires a wholly new idea of "subjectivity." There are no longer "syntheses." There is contact with being through its modulations, or its reliefs.'[110] Merleau-Ponty later held that in *The Phenomenology of Perception* he had maintained a distinction between subject and world; even while recognising that subjectivity was embodied and engaged in the world it was perceiving. In discussing the relation between body and world, in his later work, he no longer talks of the body as performing a practical synthesis. Rather he speaks of the body being 'the carnal formula' of the world; the gestalt of each constitutively (invisibly) contained in the other. We will return to this in Chapter 7.

Conclusion

Close reading of the works of both Merleau-Ponty and Sartre allows us to recognise what we have termed the absent present in our perceptual experience of the world, woven into the gestalts of everyday experience. For Sartre the texture of everyday experience was misleading. It disguises from us the distinction between the perceived and the imagined, and thereby the extent to which the possibilities we seem to find in the world are of our own making. In contrast, for Merleau-Ponty, the invisible/imaginary texture of the perceived world is something which emerges from our corporeal immersion within it, a manifestation of the multiple possibilities of the real.

Notes

1 See: Whitford, M., 1982, *Merleau-Ponty's Critique of Sartre's Philosophy*, French Forum Publishers, Lexington KY; and Stewart, J., ed., 1998, *The Debate Between Sartre and Merleau-Ponty*, Northwestern University Press, Evanston IL.
2 Sartre, J.-P., 1962, *Imagination*, trans. F. Williams, University of Michigan Press, Ann Arbor.
3 Sartre, J.-P., 2004, *The Imaginary: A Phenomenological Psychology of the Imagination*, trans J. Webber, Routledge, London and New York. Previously published in English as *The Psychology of Imagination*, 1948, Citadel Press, New York. Quotations and page references in this book are from the 2004 translation.
4 Sartre, J.-P., 1969, *Being and Nothingness*, trans. H. Barnes, Routledge, London.
5 Sartre, J.-P., 1964, *Saint Genet: Actor and Martyr*, trans. B. Frechtman, Mentor, New York; 1981–93, *The Family Idiot*, trans. Carol Cosman, 5 vols, University of Chicago Press.
6 Merleau-Ponty, M., 2012, *Phenomenology of Perception*, trans. Donald A. Landes, Routledge, London and New York.
7 Merleau-Ponty, M., 1968, *The Visible and the Invisible*, ed. C. Lefort, trans. A. Lingis, Northwestern University Press, Evanston IL.
8 Merleau-Ponty, M., 1964, *The Primacy of Perception*, ed. J. M. Edie, Northwestern University Press, Evanston IL, p. 164.
9 *Imagination*, and *The Imaginary*.
10 Husserl, E., 1970, *Logical Investigations*, vol. 2 bk 6, trans. J. Findlay, Humanities Press, New York; 1962, *Ideas; General Introduction to Pure Phenomenology*, trans. W. Gibson, Collier, New York.
11 *The Imaginary* 7.
12 Ibid., 7.
13 Ibid., 9.
14 Ibid., 11.
15 Ibid., 14.
16 Ibid., 19.
17 Ibid., 14.
18 Ibid., 19.
19 Ibid., 19.
20 Ibid., 30.
21 Ibid., 23.
22 Ibid., 26.
23 Ibid., 27.
24 Ibid., 93.
25 Ibid., 10.
26 Ibid., 188.
27 Ibid., 189.
28 Ibid., 190.
29 Ibid., 120.
30 Ibid., 120.
31 Ibid., 120.
32 Ibid., 121.
33 Noë, A., 2006, *Action in Perception*, MIT Press, Cambridge MA, pp. 8–9.

34 Hume, D., 1888, *Treatise of Human Nature*, trans. L. A. Selby Bigge, Oxford University Press, part III, section 6; Kant, I., 1929, *Critique of Pure Reason*, trans. N. Kemp Smith, Macmillan, London, A 120.
35 *The Imaginary* 181.
36 Ibid., 181.
37 Ibid., 122.
38 Ibid., 181.
39 Husserl, E., 1991, *On the Phenomenology of the Consciousness of Internal Time*, trans. J. Brough, Kluwer, Dordrecht, Netherlands.
40 *The Imaginary* 181.
41 Ibid., 75.
42 Ibid., 182.
43 Ibid., 182.
44 See Goldthorpe, R., 1997, 'Sartre and the Self: Discontinuity or Continuity?' *American Catholic Philosophical Quarterly* LXX, no. 4, p. 531.
45 *The Imaginary* 183.
46 Ibid., 186.
47 Ibid., 185.
48 Ibid., 185.
49 Ibid., 186.
50 Sartre, J.-P., 1969, *Being and Nothingness*, trans. H. Barnes, Routledge, London, p. 27.
51 Ibid., 28.
52 Ibid., 11.
53 Ibid., 565.
54 Ibid., 38.
55 Ibid., 39.
56 Ibid., 564.
57 Gardner, S., 2011, 'The Transcendental Dimension of Sartre's Philosophy', in J. Webber, ed., *Reading Sartre on Phenomenology and Existentialism*, Routledge, New York and London.
58 *The Phenomenology of Perception* lxxxi.
59 Ibid., lxxiii.
60 Ibid., 251.
61 Ibid., 62.
62 Ibid., 58.
63 Ibid., 58.
64 Ibid., 23.
65 *The Primacy of Perception* 181
66 *The Phenomenology of Perception* 341
67 Ibid., 131.
68 Ibid., 244.
69 *The Primacy of Perception* 5.
70 *The Phenomenology of Perception* 251.
71 Merleau-Ponty, M., 'Eye and Mind', in Galen A. Johnson, ed., 1993, *The Merleau-Ponty Aesthetics Reader*, Northwestern University Press, Evanston IL, p. 141.
72 *The Phenomenology of Perception* 248–249.
73 *The Primacy of Perception* 14.
74 *The Phenomenology of Perception* 225.
75 Ibid., 223.
76 Ibid., 465.
77 Ibid., 467.
78 *The Imaginary* 189.

79 Merleau-Ponty, M., 2010, *Institution and Passivity*, trans. L. Lawlor and H. Massey, with a foreword by C. Lefort, Northwestern University Press, Evanston IL, p. 238.
80 *Institution and Passivity* 148.
81 Goldthorpe, R., 1984, *Sartre: Literature and Theory*, Cambridge University Press, p. 143.
82 Beauvoir, S. De, 'Merleau-Ponty and Pseudo-Sartreanism', reprinted in J. Stewart, ed., 1998, *The Debate between Sartre and Merleau-Ponty*, Northwestern University Press, Evanston IL.
83 Merleau-Ponty, M., 1968, *The Visible and the Invisible*, ed. C. Lefort, trans. A. Lingis, Northwestern University Press, Evanston IL.
84 *The Visible and the Invisible* 266.
85 Ibid., 77.
86 Ibid., 132.
87 Ibid., 85.
88 Ibid., 114.
89 Ibid., 235.
90 Ibid., 242.
91 *The Merleau-Ponty Aesthetics Reader* 147.
92 Compare Strawson, P., 1974, 'Imagination and Perception', in P. Strawson, *Freedom and Resentment*, Methuen, London.
93 *The Visible and the Invisible* 132.
94 Ibid., 267.
95 Ibid., 208.
96 Ibid., 238.
97 Ibid., 123.
98 Ibid., 170.
99 *The Merleau-Ponty Aesthetics Reader* 126.
100 *The Primacy of Perception* 164.
101 *The Merleau-Ponty Aesthetics Reader* 123.
102 Ibid., 124.
103 Ibid., 143.
104 Heidegger, M., 1971, 'The Origin of the Work of Art', in *Poetry, Language, Thought*, trans. A. Hofstadter, Harper, New York.
105 *The Merleau-Ponty Aesthetics Reader* 83.
106 Merleau-Ponty, M., 1973 [1951], *The Prose of the World*, trans. J. O'Neill, Northwestern University Press, Evanston IL, p. 65.
107 *The Merleau-Ponty Aesthetics Reader* 127.
108 *The Primacy of Perception* 164–165.
109 *The Visible and the Invisible* 215.
110 Ibid., 269.

4   An 'affective logic'

we must no longer ask why we have affections in addition to 'representative sensations' since the representative sensation also … is affection, being a presence to the world through the body and to the body through the world.[1]

In this book we are exploring the claim that the perceived real has an imaginary texture. The imaginary on this account is not the realm of pure fancy and illusion. When it is manifest in perception, it is the animating form of perceived experience, weaving together the present and the elsewhere in our everyday encounters with the world. We have thus far unpicked several elements in this account. The imaginary texture involves a *gestalt*, a schema or organising form, which we find in the world as experienced by us. This gestalt we have suggested, following Kant and Merleau-Ponty, is neither imposed nor simply discovered, but emerges from a *creative interplay* between corporeal subjects and the world within which they are placed, and to which they are sensible. The gestalt is an interwoven mesh of a manifold of the *present and the elsewhere*, the visible and what is in the visible,[2] giving immediate perception an experienced depth. There are two further elements which require extended treatment. One, which will be the focus of this chapter, is *the affective* character, the salience and significance, which is carried in the imaginary texture of the perceived world. The second is the social nature of our imaginary worlds, which will be considered in the following chapter.

The notion of affect has two aspects. One is the capacity of our bodies *to be affected*, to bear the marks of our interactions with the world and other bodies. Another is our capacities *to respond*, expressively or purposively. Both receptivity and spontaneity are in play. Sartre and Merleau-Ponty, as discussed in the previous chapter, articulated the way in which the world, as experienced, offered possibilities for response. They differed, of course, as to the source of these manifest possibilities, and that issue will be returned to here. Nonetheless for both writers these possibilities were anchored in the imaginaries informing our experiences, *the imaginary carrying the affective salience*. In this respect their work intersects with that of other thinkers who recognise the interdependencies of image and affect. Below we will make these links: with thinkers who derive their accounts from psychoanalytic sources; those informed by the writings of Spinoza; and with the romantic poets, particularly Coleridge.

This chapter also clarifies what is involved in the claim that images carry affect, by unpacking that claim in relation to two other concepts. It is suggested that the imaginaries found within perceptual experience are *expressive*, in the sense of expressive offered in the work of Merleau-Ponty; that is, that they bring the world to expression, and interdependently that they are *reason-constituting*, in the sense of that term articulated by John McDowell. What both these articulations capture is that the imaginaries of our perceived world are co-constituted with our responses to it.

The psychoanalytic imaginary

The concept of the imaginary which derives from psychoanalytic sources has influenced much twentieth-century writing.[3] Castoriadis remarks: 'Psychoanalysis obliges us to see that the human being is not [an animal possessing reason] ... but essentially an imagining being ... in the unconscious, representation, affect, desire are mixed together ... it is impossible to separate them'.[4] The interdependence between image and affect is central to psychoanalytic writing. For Freud *phantasy* provided us with a way of representing ourselves, our biological processes and our relations to the world and others, that was governed, not by judgment, but by the demands of the passions. In one example a man had a recurrent dream in which he imagined his father had hungry rats on his bottom, which ate their way into his body. Despite his insistence that he and his father were the best of friends, attention to the images within the dream revealed a terror of the father and a desire of the son to return punishments which had been received.[5] In the Freudian framework images embody our emotional relations to the world and others. By means of images the emotional contours of the subject's world are revealed. (The way in which the shape the world takes for us is *an affective shape* is illustrated particularly clearly in Freud's discussion of the formation of our image of our body; see Chapter 7.) For Freud, imaginary or phantasmatic relations, recognised as the domain of passion or emotion, were regarded as problematic. Such relations, being informed by emotions rather than considerations of truth and falsity, meant, for him, that they were not subject to 'the reality principle', by means of which they needed to be curtailed. However, he also recognised that such modes of relating to the world pervasively co-existed with knowledge derived from such a reality principle, providing an affective substratum to it, so that, for him, in the words of one writer, 'even aspects of behaviour which ... appear at first glance to be governed solely by the demands of reality, emerge as ... derivatives of unconscious phantasy ... the subject's life as a whole ... seen as shaped and ordered by what might be called ... a *phantasmatic*'.[6]

Lacan developed Freud's ideas by positing the Imaginary as a stage (moment) in the development of the ego, a dimension of consciousness which remains in play throughout life: 'the Imaginary as the order of identification with images'.[7]

Lacan stresses our relationship to the image seen in the mirror (later, for him, the screen),[8] a relation which forms our affective sense of self.[9] The mirror stage is the stage of development in which a baby first sees itself in a mirror and becomes fixated with that image. Gradually and jubilantly the child comes to view the image in the mirror as an image of itself. For Lacan the baby's relation to the mirror, and identification with the image it finds there, is not cognitive but affective.[10] It is joyful or jubilant, sometimes aggressive and angry, in relation to the image which the mirror reflects back. Grasping the image in the mirror, and consequently its own body as a whole, is achieved not through the application of concepts, but through the fascination and seduction which the image provides. The image provides an ideal in relation to which the ego becomes formed, by acts of affective identification. The domain of the Imaginary, as the domain of *experiencing* ourselves, others, and the world at large *in terms of images which carry affective charge*, is pervasive throughout our lives. This concept of the Imaginary has been carried forward by multiple writers independently of whether they accept or modify the founding picture of the baby and the mirror. Lacan also argued that the Imaginary was problematic. For him the Imaginary offers us a *misrecognition* of ourselves: as the apparently unified, coherent self of humanist discourse. He argued therefore that the Imaginary dimension of experience needs to made subject to the Symbolic order, the structure of language and signs, which releases desire from the grip of the Imaginary and into the inter-subjective social (see Chapter 5) world.[11]

For other writers making use of the Lacanian notion of the Imaginary the strict distinction between the Imaginary and the Symbolic dimensions of experience is not maintained. Lacan's assumption that the domain of the Imaginary is *necessarily* a domain of illusion and misrepresentation is challenged by a recognition that all experience has an imaginary dimension, and indeed it is by means of such a dimension that a world takes shape for us at all, a world which may, nonetheless, be captured in a public symbolic order.[12] What is retained from Lacan is the account of the image as fascinating, seductive, repulsive or enraging. The images which structure our experience of the world are affectively charged. Nonetheless, all knowledge, it is suggested, bears the marks of the imaginary. The work of Luce Irigaray has been particularly influential here. She makes what may seem like a rather startling claim; namely that the public cognitive structure of western rationality is marked by imaginaries of the masculine and the feminine; so that principles of identity, non-contradiction, binarism, assuming the possibility of individuating, and distinguishing one thing clearly from another, reflect the imaginary 'one of form, of the individual, of the (male) sex organ'. In contrast the imaginary of 'the contact of at least two (lips) [which] keeps woman in touch with herself'[13] suggests an ambiguity of individuation, a fluidity and mobility, a rejection of stable forms. Here in contemporary thought we have a version of the Kantian thesis that the imagination is required for knowledge of the world, informed by the recognition (which Kant only accepted for aesthetics) that images carry with them affect. Irigaray paid particular attention to unpacking the imaginaries attaching to philosophical and psychoanalytic thought, and the way in which these were marked by sexual difference. Michelle Le Doeuff, among others, has unpacked the distinctive imaginaries underpinning key philosophical texts.[14] Science writers, including feminist philosophers of science, have looked at the images invoked in the models and metaphors informing scientific theories.[15] We will not have space to pursue these explorations here.

Sartre: the affective–cognitive synthesis

The interweaving of the cognitive and the affective, which we find within the psychoanalytic imaginary, was given extended treatment by Sartre. In the section 'Affectivity' in Sartre's text *The Imaginary*, he characterises the 'affective–cognitive synthesis' which is none other than 'the deep structure of image consciousness'.[16] In these discussions he rejects an account of feeling/affect as a 'purely subjective and ineffable shiver' linked externally (causally) and contingently with representations. In its place he offers a 'living synthesis'. First, he reiterates the intentionality of affective consciousness. Feelings have intentional objects. Hate is hate of someone. But to hate Paul is not just for Paul to be the object of an intellectual judgment, it is to be conscious of Paul as hateful, and this is to make a certain sense of Paul, to experience him as appearing to me with a certain 'affective structure'.[17] If I love 'the long fine white hands' of someone, 'this love ... could be considered as one of the ways that they have appeared to my consciousness'. But this is not a cognitive sense but an affective one: 'the affective form entirely permeating the object'.[18] He quotes a passage of D. H. Lawrence: 'It was always the one man who spoke. He was very young, with quick large, bright dark eyes that glanced sideways at her. His long black hair, full of life, hung unrestrained on his shoulders.' Sartre comments: 'Lawrence excels at suggesting, while he seems only to be describing the form and colour of objects, those subdued affective structures that constitute their deepest reality.'[19]

These affective structures are, for Sartre, the work of imaging consciousness. Desire is provided with an imaginary object which tells us what the desire is a desire for: 'desire and disgust exist at first in a diffuse state ... in being organised ... into an imaging form, the desire is made precise and concentrated'.[20] I awake restless. It is not clear whether the physiological discomfort is hunger or sexual desire. The matter is settled by the direction which my imagining consciousness takes. To experience the desirability of the hands is to surpass (sometimes unaware) their *physiological form* and constitute them into an image of desirability, giving the hands to me in their *affective form*. It is only by means of these affective forms (images) that we can become aware of our desires, whose intentional objects are the posited images of imaging consciousness. 'The image is a kind of ideal for the feeling.'[21] For Sartre the image is 'a certain way that an object has of being absent within its very presence'.[22] Confronted with the hands about which we have certain pieces of intellectual knowledge, this knowledge is synthesised with the affective structure, the image, which is the absence within the presence. (Despite their ontological differences the account of the phenomenology here is very close to Merleau-Ponty's characterisation of the invisible in the visible.) My love for Annie consists, in part, by my making her 'irreal face'[23] appear when she is absent, and, crucially, by the form it takes for me when it appears. However, even when Annie is present, her attribute of being lovable is an imagined one. These affective qualities for Sartre enter phenomenologically into the experience of the perceived object, and cannot be detached by the unreflecting consciousness. Faced with such qualities I react: 'this book for example ... is entirely suffused by ... affectivity ... faced with this book I do not remain inactive. I pick it up or put it down, I do not like its binding, I make judgments of fact and value.'[24] And these responses register the affective qualities it holds for me. For Sartre, then, as for the other writers discussed below, image and affect are internally related: 'if the image of a dead one appears to me suddenly ... the ache in my heart is part of the image'.[25]

Affective content is given in terms of images and, conversely, the synthesis required in the act of imagining itself is, for Sartre, an affective synthesis. When discussing my response to a portrait the painting becomes recognisable as a portrait by means of the affective structure (expressiveness) in terms of which I experience it, which is, in turn, manifest by the affective responses which I make to it. Watching Franconay, the affective meaning is the route to the synthetic unification of the body, into the person of Chevalier. When I see Franconay's impersonation, what needs to be invoked in me is the *affective* response which I had to Chevalier, so that the figure which invoked such a response can be imagined through her:

> The affective sense of the face of Chevalier will appear on the face of Franconay. It is this that realises the synthetic union of the different signs ... gives them life and a certain depth ... giving to the isolated elements of the imitation an indefinable sense ... and ... unity ... the signs united by an affective sense, which is to say *the expressive nature*.[26]

It is in manifesting the affective sense of Chevalier that the personification is achieved. The *affective cognitive synthesis* is thus 'the deep structure of the image consciousness'.[27]

Motifs and mobiles

The affective cognitive synthesis which Sartre articulates as our relationship with the world is one whose ontological status remains ambiguous for him. For Hume, and his twentieth-century followers such as John Mackie,[28] we are simply mistaken about the shape of the world. We fail to realise that the affective significance, which we seem to encounter, is simply a *projection* of our own inner emotional states onto the world. What we actually encounter, they argue, is neutral. It has no significance until we bestow one. This picture is that espoused in what has become a standard account of reasons for acting. We have a reason to act only if we have a desire for a goal and a belief that some course of action will promote that goal. The possibilities, which on the phenomenological accounts haunt our perceptions, are reduced to present inner states linked by relations of efficient causation to future actions. In this standard picture, although our beliefs might be justified by our encounters with the world, our desires are inner states which may have causes, but are not the kind of thing for which we can seek justifications. Some desires may be motivated, have reasons, because they are desires for things which promote the satisfaction of prior goals; but ultimately there must be some desires which are simply given, at which the justificatory chain ends.[29]

Sartre warns us against such accounts, which 'refer us ultimately to inexplicable original givens' and against 'considering desires as little psychic entities dwelling in consciousness'.[30] He rejects an account of agency which refers us to 'inexplicable original givens ... determined desires (or "drives")'.[31] He asks: 'if I desire a house or a glass of water or a woman's body ... how can my desire be anything but the consciousness of these objects as desirable?'[32] Nonetheless Sartre's own account is ultimately one in which we constitute the affective qualities of the world. In discussing motivations for actions he draws a distinction between what he terms *motifs* and *mobiles*. The motif is an aspect of the objective situation. What we might point to in justifying our decisions or actions. But these aspects are aspects of the situation as 'revealed in the light of a certain end as being able to serve as the means for attaining this end'.[33] The features are objective but instrumental. In contrast to the motif is the *mobile*, 'the ensemble of the desires, emotions and passions which urge me to accomplish a certain act'.[34] Nonetheless these two features are not separate aspects, joining together to rationally or causally (or both) produce the action, as in the picture of the previous paragraph. They are internally related. The motifs of a situation only become revealed to us because we have an implicit awareness of our projects and goals, our mobiles; they are only revealed as motifs through these mobiles. But these mobiles are not psychic givens, but themselves ways of experiencing our situation. I experience my kitchen as lacking milk.[35] I experience a cake as appetising. However, this is not a picture in which value is perceptually given. For these affective qualities are themselves constituted by imagining consciousness. To experience milk as absent is only possible within the light of my overarching projects. These projects are not the result of deliberation or reasoning, nor are they traceable back to brute desires or drives. They are my imagining *choices of myself in the world*, choices manifest in my pattern of action over time.

For Sartre it is the imagination which gives us the affective texture of the world, a texture which we cannot pre-reflectively disentangle from the intellectual knowledge which we have of it. But he also says: 'when they [images] disappear ... perception remains intact, things are not touched, and yet the world is singularly impoverished'.[36] Perception remains intact because for Sartre such affective qualities are constituted as irreal properties, imagined through surpassing the positivity of perception. 'To become conscious of Paul as hateful, annoying, sympathetic ... is *to construct him* along a new dimension'[37] (my emphasis). 'The very feeling of disgust, which emerges in constituting in the object the quality "disgusting" ... becomes conscious of itself only in the form of an irreal property, this very feeling is produced by the intentional animation of certain physiological phenomena.'[38] The affective qualities of objects are imagined qualities, and Sartre's account of the image is an intentional surpassing of the factive world, in the postulation of goals, for him ultimately unified in terms of a fundamental project. Nonetheless he also claims that it is such properties which give our experienced world its depth. The tension here in Sartre's account was highlighted in the previous chapter, and it is noted by Judith Butler: 'whether affectivity is an "apprehension" of the real or an indicator of solipsism, is a question that haunts Sartre's discussion of the imaginary, emotions, and desire'.[39] Affective quality is given with the shape the object takes for us, but ultimately that shape is one which has been constituted by imaging consciousness.

In contrast to Sartre, Heidegger insists that 'affectedness implies a disclosive submission to the world, out of which we can encounter something that matters to us'.[40] The picture in which we choose projects and the world is seen as a means to satisfy them is here replaced with one in which those projects reflect our openness to the world.

> We do not, so to speak, throw a 'signification' over some naked thing which is present-at-hand, we do not stick a value on it; but when something within-the-world is encountered as such, the thing in question already has an involvement which is disclosed in our understanding of the world.[41]

And, for Merleau-Ponty, as we have previously noted: 'I am capable ... of finding a sense in certain aspects of being, without myself having given them this sense through any constituting operation'.[42] The world we perceive is *the world to which we appeal in making sense of our own responses*, and those of others, in acts of public justificatory explanations. These seem to have an empty circularity on subjectivist accounts, whether these are anchored in inner emotions or original (and ultimately unmotivated) choices of ourselves in the world. 'Why did you get up early?' I might be asked. 'Look outside', I might reply. But on accounts in which we are the source of such value such an answer is empty; unless there are prior goals we share and such a gesture is a shorthand way of pointing out a means to their promotion. 'Why are you smiling?' we might be asked. 'Look at her', we might say, pointing to a smiling child, 'Doesn't that deserve a smile in response?'

In our discussion of Kant's theory of Beauty we stressed what the writer Galen Johnson terms the *contagion* of aesthetic judgments.

> The claim that something is beautiful is not a cognitive judgement, but at the same time it speaks in a voice that is plural and not merely personal. Therefore, one needs to speak about the features ... that evoke pleasure

and delight – the shape of the tree and its sensuality ... the texture of the bark, the symmetry and asymmetry of its crossing branches, or the colours and patterns of its leaves.[43]

Aesthetic judgment, for Kant, as we discussed in Chapter 2, is rooted in feeling, but makes universal claims: 'Whoever declares something beautiful holds that everyone ought to give his approval to the object at hand and that he too should declare it beautiful.'[44] Johnson points out that the subjectivist account misses that 'our feelings of the beautiful opens us up to a world beyond ourselves and this world is shared with those around us ... whom we expect to share our experience'.[45] The expectation here is logical not causal. And we might add this openness, and the contagion, or implicit publicness, applies to affective concepts in general and not simply to beauty. The 'subjective universality'[46] which Kant detects in aesthetic forms is, as we have noted, a consequence of such forms being created by the play of the imagination, yet making claims on the feelings of others. Merleau-Ponty shares Kant's account of what Johnson calls the contagion of imaginary shapes, and the picture of imaginary form being both a passive 'taking hold of the self from outside'[47] and an act of creation.

Merleau-Ponty and the expressive character of the world

Merleau-Ponty, along with Sartre, views the imaginary as providing us with the affective depth of the experienced world. 'The thing's sense inhabits it as the soul inhabits the body; it is not behind appearances ... The sense of the ashtray ... animates the ashtray, and is quite evidently embodied in it.'[48] And 'Love is in the bouquet that Felix de Vandenesse prepares for Madame de Mortsauf. Its significance is the trace of an existence for another existence.'[49] The account which Sartre offers of affective content as imaginary shape is for Merleau-Ponty articulated in terms of expression. And he spells out the notion of expression in terms of the internal relation between the shapes of the world and the shapes our bodies take in response to it. The body and world each experienced as 'the possible of the other'.[50] This is what we mean by the world having an 'affective logic'. This world is something which is offered to our senses, but not as a positivity and not determinately. We are creatively involved in bringing it to expression, in gesture, in language, and in works of art.

We experience the imaginary of the world, because we are able to express it; *finding the world expressive and being able to express it being, for Merleau-Ponty, equivalent claims*. We are able to *accomplish* features of our world by gestures, including linguistic gestures of our own; such gestures offering a physiognomy of things. These, however, are not acts of a constituting subject, but of an expressive one. What is offered is a world which comes into focus alongside us, by means of creative expressive acts, whose legitimacy rests on their being able to be recognised and taken up by others. Our expressions, linguistic or otherwise, are not operating as signs, to draw attention to a world whose characteristics could be grasped independently of the gestures. Rather our gestures draw our attention to a shared world which is such that it *can be expressed* in this way, accomplished, as he says, through us: 'words, vowels, and phonemes … so many ways of singing the world'.[51]

The account which Merleau-Ponty offers of expression with its central interdependency between recognition and response can be seen in the discussion of bodily gestures and works of art, and both of these are continuous with the account he gives of the expressive character of the perceived (and imagined) world. What is involved in the process of perceiving gesture is grasp of a certain kind of gestalt,[52] recognition of a certain kind of patterning of the body as that of fear, or joy or grief. The gestalt which is distinctive of particular expressions has woven into it a pattern of movements over time, the broader context and background, and crucially the responses of others. The expressive content of a gesture is internally related to the response which it invites/requires. What response is invited is part of the invisible which we perceive in the visible behaviour. So to grasp expressive gestures *as* expressive is to grasp them as invitations for a response. Without such recognition, the expressive content has not been perceived.[53] (For a detailed discussion of bodily expressions see Chapter 7.) In *The Phenomenology of Perception*, after discussing bodily expressions, Merleau-Ponty says 'this revelation of an immanent or nascent meaning in the living body extends, as we shall see, to the entire sensible world, and our gaze … will discover the miracle of expression in all other "objects"'.[54] As with bodily expressions, to experience the world as expressive is to experience it in terms of a gestalt which weaves together, in his terms, both visible and invisible characteristics, including possibilities for responses of ourselves and others towards it. The capacity for expression, that is for bodily gestures which make manifest, to ourselves and others, aspects of our shared world, is one of our fundamental carnal possibilities. 'Quality, light, colour, depth, which are there before us, are there only because they awaken an echo in our bodies and because the body welcomes them.'[55] 'Things … arouse in me a carnal formula of their presence.'[56] This carnal formula is the manifestation of the affective shape of the world.

In his account of the expressive content of works of art Merleau-Ponty rejects the individualism and subjectivism which leads to an account of *style* in painting (put forward, for example, by Malraux) as the projection of the personal meanings and values of the painter.[57] It is not something 'shut up in the depths of the … individual'.[58] Expressive content is not fixed by its relation to a prior feeling of the artist, seeking a perceptual form which can evoke parallel or complementary feelings in the audience. Expressive content is rather an intersubjective quality of the work, a gestalt, a shape, an image, which reaches out to the viewer and *invites* a response. We are not dealing with *causal* associative links here, certain patterns invoking causally certain kinds of responses, for most or some people or some people in a given cultural setting. In a way that parallels bodily expressions, expressive quality is a character seen in the materiality of the work of art, but irreducible to it,[59] and the shape which is at issue is only recognised when its link to possible responses is grasped (though we may need certain kinds of training and initiation to detect what shape is manifest). As with bodily expressions, the expressive content of works of art invites/requires/gives reasons for responses from those who encounter it. These may simply be bodily responses such as finger tapping or dancing to music. Or they may take more extended forms, such as the places that pictures are hung, whether they are just looked at or also woven into our lives in other ways. 'You could say', says Wittgenstein, that insofar as people understand a work of art, they 'resonate' in harmony with it, respond to it.[60] And this conception of harmonising with the imaginary shape of both art and world is central to the picture which Merleau-Ponty offers. 'The accomplished work', says Merleau-Ponty, 'is ... not the work which exists in itself, like a thing, but the work which reaches the viewer and invites him to take up the gesture which created it.'[61] Grasping the expressive quality of an image, is, therefore, to be distinguished from a mere description of it, in which we are not implicated. It is to immediately recognise the call to our own bodies, to our own way of looking and feeling. (Although there is an openness and indeterminacy in these calls which Merleau-Ponty is at pains to stress.) The work of art continues the expressive operations of the body in breaking the silence of the world: 'the quasi eternity of art is of a piece with the quasi eternity of incarnate existence ... the use of our bodies and our senses, in so far as they involve us in the world'.[62]

The imaginary shape the world takes for us is therefore constitutively tied up with ways of responding to and acting in relation to it, and this is what we mean by claiming that it has affective texture. In the remark which heads this chapter Merleau-Ponty draws attention to the fact that once we experience the world as having a certain shape we already have a world which is expressive, which carries affective content. 'We must no longer ask why we have affections in addition to "representative sensations" since the representative sensation also ... is affection, being a presence to the world through the body and to the body through the world.'[63] And he follows such an observation with another. 'Reason too is in this horizon.' Reason here is anchored in the possibility of body and world finding the harmonious relation which he has been at pains to characterise, that is, what is involved in the world having an affective *logic*. The world, on this account, does not offer the perceiver 'a set of recipes' but 'a radiant image, a particular rhythm'.[64] Our relation to it is one of a productive passivity which yields shape to the world and thereby shape to our desires in relation to it. Galen Johnson compares and contrasts Merleau-Ponty's descriptions of the affective shape of experience with Kant's form of beauty in the *Critique of Judgement*:

> though the word 'shape' may appear quite close to Kant's stress upon 'form' the absence of colour and sensuousness from Kant's conception differentiates them. [It pulls Merleau-Ponty] away from the word 'form' towards the domain of the more sensuous term 'shape' [... for Merleau-Ponty] ... desire is awakened by the smells and tastes and touches of things

... by sight and sound ... desire has a shape – the shape of a face, or a place, or a time.[65]

The constitutive interrelation between the imagined shape of the world and the shape of our response to it, which Merleau-Ponty captures in his account of expression, has contemporary parallels in the work of John McDowell, who points out that the character we experience the perceived world to have suggests and demands the desiring and sometimes fearful responses we make to it (cf. the discussion in Chapter 1). There is *an intelligible link* between the perceived world and our responses. The content of our perceptions therefore stands in a different kind of explanatory relation to our responses, from that simply of causal connections supported by empirical laws. Our responses are explained by showing that they are, in some sense, as they should be. McDowell terms these intelligible links *reason giving links*. Other writers reject the suggestion that all intelligible links are rational ones. Jaspers,[66] for example, draws a distinction between showing that a connection was in accordance with a logical norm and making it psychologically intelligible. McDowell, in not making this distinction, extends the scope of the rational. It is not the case for him, that, wherever we have examples of intelligibility, we have examples of the application of logical norms.[67] In the example of fear, which he discusses, we find intelligible, in this special way, a fearful response, by attention to the way the world appeared to the subject who is afraid. We point out the aspects of the situation which give it a threatening appearance. Walking down the garden I reach over to smell the roses, an action both making evident their sweetness, and being rendered intelligible by it. These examples seem a long way from displaying the rationality of belief by giving a sequence of reasoning. Yet there is continuity between the cases. In each case the response is shown as in some sense appropriate or merited by the situation. Given that the world appeared in a certain way, a fearful response was at least one of the appropriate ways of responding to it. And indeed we have no grasp of its fearfulness unless we grasp the necessity for such a response. What is central to McDowell's account also is the *internal relation* between the perceived character of the world and the responses we make to it. This has clear parallels with phenomenological descriptions which highlight the affective texture of the world in terms of the possibilities which it opens up for our body. For these writers our affective responses are modes of apprehending the world, and the characteristics of the world, which we are apprehending, are ones which we need such responses to grasp.

Affectively laden thought patterns

In the writings so far discussed in this chapter what has been explored is the interplay between the cognitive and the affective in the imaginary shape which the world takes for us, echoed in the shapes which our bodies take in response to it. The legitimacy of those shapings is then ascertained by the recognition they invoke in others. For some contemporary writers[68] the exploration of the role of the imagination in this affective/cognitive synthesis is anchored in the work of Spinoza. What these writers derive from Spinoza is a concept of our imaginaries as 'affectively laden thought patterns'[69] which constitute our modes of being in the world. For Spinoza the imagination was the way in which bodily perturbations, resulting from our bodily encounters with the world and other bodies, manifested themselves to consciousness:

> An imagining [*imaginatio*] is an idea whereby the mind regards a thing as present ... which indicates the disposition of the human body rather than [perhaps this should be as well as] the nature of the external thing ... Therefore an emotion ... is an imagining in so far as it indicates the disposition of the body.[70]

The imagination provides us with an image of the world which captures the impact that world has on us. It is just this thought that we have been unpacking in the psychoanalytic and phenomenological writings discussed above. Spinoza suggests that for most of us, most of the time, images are the way in which we motivate our actions and mediate our practical engagements with the world and other people.

For Spinoza, although the imagination failed to yield the kind of certain knowledge which was offered by philosophical reflection, it was one of the key ways in which we try to persevere in our being, 'we try, as it were, to experience the world in ways that are empowering rather than debilitating'.[71] Indeed, although 'true knowledge of good and evil', derived from rational understanding, can provide motivations, these motivations, for Spinoza, were weaker than those provided by the emotions. For him we are required to cultivate the imagination to provide empowering images to enable the perseverance of our own being and thereby our harmonious relations with others.[72] Imaginative thinking, then, is contrasted with the kind of thinking which philosophers go in for. Philosophical thought, using only principles of rationality, deals in clear and distinct ideas. Its goal is indubitable truth. It deals with the abstract and the universal. The imagination, involved in the perception of individual things and events, gives us images of the world which are inadequate when subject to the scrutiny of philosophical reflection, but indispensable in everyday dealings with the world. Such an account informs the distinction he draws between philosophy and theology.[73] Theological thinking necessarily uses stories and images; its goal is to motivate people to good behaviour by means of the images it presents.

> They did not seek to convince people of the truth of their revelations through argument and logic. Their powers of persuasion lay with their capacity to form awe-inspiring images and visions – winged seraphims, chariots of fire and the blare of heavenly trumpets[74]

from which they constructed compelling narratives concerning God as creator, king, lawgiver, punisher and redeemer. The prophets' visions, recorded in scripture, 'appeal to and engage men's fantasy and imagination'[75] in order to instruct even 'the most sluggish mind'.[76]

Spinoza recognises that most people are not philosophers, and, those that are, do not engage with the world only in philosophical mode. In their everyday lives (and social communities, see Chapter 5) they are negotiating the world in terms of images which motivate and justify everyday interactions, just because they capture the affective character of the world. Spinoza notes that imaginary form has a particular resilience, and engagement with it becomes essential if we are to persuade and instruct. 'No affect' he claims 'can be restrained by the true knowledge of good and evil insofar as it is true, but only insofar as it is considered as an affect'.[77] What he means by this is that we cannot change people's way of looking at the world simply by offering them philosophical reflections. We need to offer them *alternative images* which make emotional and not just cognitive sense. This insight is pivotal to the discussion of ways in which our imaginaries may be subject to change, and we will return to it in the following chapter.

Not the mirror or the lamp

Coleridge, in his poem *Dejection*, laments his inability to respond to the beauties of nature:

> All this long eve, so balmy and serene,
> Have I been gazing on the western sky,
> And its peculiar tint of yellow green:
> And still I gaze and with how blank an eye!
> And those thin clouds above, in flakes and bars,
> That give away their motion to the stars;
> Those stars, that glide behind them or between,
> Now sparkling, now bedimmed, but always seen:
> Yon crescent Moon, as fixed as if it grew
> In its own cloudless, starless lake of blue;
> I see them all so excellently fair,
> I see, not feel, how beautiful they are![78]

Here we might note a similarity to Sartre's claim that there are times when 'perception remains intact, things are not touched, and yet the world is singularly impoverished'.[79] The themes which preoccupied Coleridge and Wordsworth were directly linked to the themes which have been preoccupying us in this chapter: the link between imagination and feeling, the interdependence between (what they considered) the inner and the outer, the role of creativity and discovery in the poetic evocations of the natural world. Thus Wordsworth early on in *Tintern Abbey*:

> All the mighty world
> Of eye and ear, – both what they half create,
> And what perceive.[80]

For these poets the view of poetry as simply imitative of reality had been replaced by one in which the feelings of the poet transformed the world which they set out to describe. J. S. Mill claims that things are 'arranged in the colours and seen through the medium of the imagination, set in action by the feelings'.[81] Coleridge claims poetry impregnates sights and sounds 'with an interest ... by means of the passions'[82] instead of the mirror or the lamp. Mill's characterisation of this process has projectionist and associative echoes. The world is perceived by poets and by a process of causal associations elicits certain feelings within them. These they project back onto the world, colouring it; describing it in such a way as to provoke such feelings universally. And such a picture sometimes seems endorsed by Wordsworth, who often speaks of the imagination as working by association, 'conferring additional properties on an object, or abstracting from it some of those it actually possesses'.[83]

Despite this account, for Coleridge (and sometimes for Wordsworth when in discussion with him) more than a projection of inner feelings is involved in the poetic endeavour. Coleridge makes a distinction between Fancy, working mechanically via associations, and Imagination, which, influenced by Kant, he viewed as creative and productive:

> The IMAGINATION then, I consider either as primary, or secondary. The primary IMAGINATION I hold to be the living Power and prime Agent of all human Perception, and as a repetition in the finite mind of the eternal act of creation in the infinite I AM. The secondary Imagination I consider as an echo of the former, co-existing with the conscious will, yet still as identical with the primary in the kind of its agency, and differing only in degree, and in the mode of operation. It dissolves, diffuses, dissipates, in order to recreate. FANCY, on the contrary, has no other counters to play with, but fixities and definites. Fancy must receive all its materials ready made from the law of association.[84,85]

The secondary imagination was exercised by the artist, who, in an account which echoes that offered by Kant in the third *Critique*, both creates and discovers forms in nature, which, when offered to others, invoke recognition. For Coleridge there is a harmony not just between the forms our imagination derives from our encounters in the world, and the understanding, as Kant suggests, but also between these imaginative forms and our feelings. Coleridge speaks of the 'shaping spirit of Imagination' which 'Nature gave me at my birth'.[86] This capacity of imagination allowed him 'not to think of what I needs must feel'. The power of feeling, rather than cognition, was what enabled him to find forms in nature, which made just those feelings the appropriate ones to hold: 'to make the external internal, the internal external, to make nature thought and thought nature'.[87] The poet then offers these forms to others, who, if they grasp them, will grasp the emotional content they convey. There are parallels here with the account of expression offered by Merleau-Ponty, discussed above.

Coleridge claims the imagination reanimates 'the dead world of the materialists'[88] to enable us to feel 'at home' in it. As Mary Warnock remarks, for Coleridge 'in understanding one's feelings one can understand the riddle of the world'.[89] They provide the world with the depth to which Merleau-Ponty also drew our attention, a depth whereby possibilities for being, our own and that of other creatures, are revealed. The picture that Coleridge is offering us here is not that sometimes suggested by Wordsworth, in which we are searching for the laws of human nature to find which images provoke which feeling, universally, in human beings. The relation between the images and the feelings, for Coleridge, seems, instead, to be the internal one we have been at pains to describe in the rest of this chapter. The images carry the salience the world has for us, but it is a salience which we have to creatively uncover by the search for appropriate images.

What then has happened to Coleridge which he laments in the poem *Dejection*? Is he indeed able to perceive the world in a way which should occasion joy, but nonetheless finds that his feelings fail him? If so how does that fit with the picture characterised above? In the characterisation which Merleau-Ponty offers of our body intertwined with the world, there does not seem room for the situation Coleridge describes here. For it is via our bodily responses that the shape of our world is detected and made manifest. Yet Coleridge is aware that joy is what he *should* feel, and is unable to feel it. There are tensions in the way in which he describes this. He claims that Nature lives only in our lives and that

> from the soul itself must issue forth
> A light, a glory, a fair luminous cloud
> Enveloping the Earth.

Yet it is also clear that such a glory is what the earth *merits* and that a breakdown in the capacity to shine such a light is an impoverishment in the world and not just ourselves.

The situation which Coleridge describes has perplexed writers who see our feelings as manifesting the way in which the world shows up for us. For that makes seeing in the same way, but failing to feel in the same way, paradoxical. Yet this is not quite what Coleridge is offering us. What he offers us in the poem as a whole is a characterisation of the way the world is now experienced by him, which captures his feelings of desolation and lassitude. He has not given us a neutral characterisation of the world, the affective charge simply lifted. Even when he offers us the features which should occasion joy they are not 'placed' as they were previously, and emotional character is very much a result of such positioning. Consequently he has not painted the world in either a neutral or a joyful way. He has pointed to features which he is aware, cognitively, have been the occasion for previous joyful figuring, but with the recognition that features of the world, thus grasped, offer possibilities for a depth, which alludes him, and without which he cannot respond. The failure he is lamenting is not just a failure of feeling. It is also a failure of seeing. It has parallels in our relations with others when we fail to read the expressiveness of their features and consequently are unable to respond appropriately.

Conclusion

In this chapter a constitutive relation between the imagination and the domain of affect has been explored across a range of philosophical texts. It is through the images in terms of which we perceive the world that the world makes 'affective sense' to us. We experience it as a world of possibilities for us, both for intentional projects and expressive responses.

For many of the writers discussed here the imaginary shape of the world is something both encountered and created, prompting or requiring our responses. The world itself is enticing. From our point of view, as experiencing subjects, we have no access to a supposedly neutral world onto which we are then supposed to cast a veil of significance (as Heidegger reminds us). The imaginary world, as described here, is our most direct and immediate mode of perception. In the way in which we can see a face as joyful, without being aware of its spatial coordinates, we also experience the freshness of the morning without having access to some alternative characterisation of it which lacks affective resonance. The interdependence between image and affect does not exclude our imaginaries from the domain of reflective scrutiny. But such scrutiny does not require us to step out from our customary realms of seeing into a domain of neutral facts, augmented with a reflective reason. We cannot simply peel off the affective dimension of our modes of seeing. The reflection to which our imaginary modes of experiencing must be subject is a process in which our images are held up to public scrutiny. Any assessment of the appropriateness or inappropriateness of imaginary formations has then to involve the confrontation of different ways of inhabiting our world and living affectively and effectively within it. It is to this social aspect of the imaginary that we turn in the following chapter.

Notes

1 Merleau-Ponty, M., 1968, *The Visible and the Invisible*, ed. C. Lefort, trans. A. Lingis, Northwestern University Press, Evanston IL, p. 239.

2 Merleau-Ponty in using the terms visible and invisible privileges sight over the other senses. This has been pointed out by Luce Irigaray (*An Ethics of Sexual Difference*, trans. C. Burke and G. Gill, Cornell University Press, Ithaca NY, 1993) and Elizabeth Grosz (*Volatile Bodies*, Indiana University Press, Bloomington, 1994). But the point that he is using this terminology to make, namely the haunting of perception by an imaginary, extends to all the senses. Proust's example of the *madeleine* would be a good illustration.

3 Lacan, Jacques, 2006 [1966], *Ecrits*, trans. Bruce Fink, Norton, New York; Castoriadis, Cornelius, 1998 [1987], *The Imaginary Institution of Society*, trans. Kathleen Blamey, MIT Press, Cambridge MA; Irigaray, Luce, 1985, *Speculum of the Other Woman*, trans. G. Gill, Cornell University Press, Ithaca NY; 1985, *This Sex Which Is Not One*, trans. C. Porter and C. Burke, Cornell University Press, Ithaca NY. For an illuminating discussion of the imaginary see Whitford, M., 1991, *Luce Irigaray*, Routledge, London and New York, ch. 3.

4 Castoriadis, Cornelius, 1997, *World In Fragments: Writings on Politics, Society, Psychoanalysis, and the Imagination*, ed./trans. David Ames Curtis, Stanford University Press, Stanford CA, pp. 351–353.

5 Freud, S., 1974, 'Notes on a Case of Obsessional Neuroses', in *The Standard Edition of the Collected Psychological Works of Sigmund Freud*, trans. J. Strachey, Hogarth Press, London, vol. X, pp. 153ff.

6 Whitford, M., 1991, *Luce Irigaray: Philosophy in the Feminine*, Routledge, London and New York, p. 64.

7 Grosz, E., 1990, *Jacques Lacan*, Routledge, London and New York, p. 43.

8 Lacan, J., 1977, *Ecrits*, Tavistock, London.

9 Ibid., 1–7.

10 Lacan, 'The Mirror Stage as Formative of the "I"' in *Ecrits*.

11 In such a way the mistaken narcissism of ego psychology is replaced with a recognition of the way in which the self is not individual but constituted by its position in such social relations. (We will not pursue that aspect of his thought here.)

12 Castoriadis, Cornelius, 1998 [1987], *The Imaginary Institution of Society*, trans. Kathleen Blamey, MIT Press, Cambridge MA; Irigaray, Luce, 1985, *Speculum of the Other Woman*, trans. G. Gill, Cornell University Press, Ithaca NY; 1985, *This Sex Which Is Not One*, trans. C. Porter and C. Burke, Cornell University Press, Ithaca NY.

13 *Speculum of the Other Woman* 79.

14 Le Doeuff, M., 2002 [1989], *The Philosophical Imaginary*, trans. Colin Gordon, Continuum, London and New York.

15 See Haraway, Donna, 1989, *Primate Visions*, Routledge, London; Keller, E. Fox, 1985, *Reflections on Gender and Science*, Yale University Press, New Haven CT; Latour, B., 1993, *We Have Never Been Modern*, trans. C. Porter, Harvester, Brighton.

16 *The Imaginary* 73.

17 Ibid., 69.

18 Ibid., 69.

19 Ibid., 69–70.

20 Ibid., 139.

21 Ibid., 72.

22 Ibid., 72–73.

23 Ibid., 141.

24 Ibid., 141.

25 Butler, J., 1999, *Subjects of Desire*, Columbia University Press, New York, p. 113.

26 *The Imaginary* 28–29.

27 *The Imaginary* 7; I am indebted here to the discussion in Denoon Cumming, R., 1992, *Phenomenology and Deconstruction, Volume Two, Method and Imagination*, University of Chicago Press, Chicago and London.

28 Mackie, J., 1990, *Ethics: Inventing Right and Wrong*, Penguin, London.

29 Smith, M., 1994, *The Moral Problem*, Blackwell, Oxford.

30 *Being and Nothingness* 557.

31 Ibid., 560–561.

32 Ibid., 557.

33 Ibid., 446.

34 Ibid., 446.
35 See the discussion in Morris, K., 2008, *Sartre*, Blackwell, Oxford, pp. 148–150.
36 *The Imaginary* 69.
37 Ibid., 69.
38 Ibid., 137.
39 *Subjects of Desire* 112.
40 *Being and Time* 177, H 138.
41 Ibid., 150.
42 *Phenomenology of Perception* 225.
43 Johnson G., *The Retrieval of the Beautiful*, Northwestern University Press, Evanston IL, p. 211.
44 *The Retrieval of the Beautiful* 211; Kant, I., 2007 [1790], *Critique of Judgement*, trans. J. C. Meredith, Oxford University Press.
45 *The Retrieval of the Beautiful* 210.
46 Ibid., 212.
47 Ibid., 214.
48 *Phenomenology of Perception* 333.
49 *Phenomenology of Perception* 335–336.
50 *The Visible and the Invisible* 228.
51 *Phenomenology of Perception* 193.
52 Both writers were reading and responding to gestalt psychology. See paper by Katherine Morris in Komarine Romdenh-Romluc, ed., *Wittgenstein and Merleau-Ponty*, Routledge, forthcoming.
53 Lennon, K., 'Wittgenstein and Merleau-Ponty on Expression', in Komarine Romdenh-Romluc, ed., *Wittgenstein and Merleau-Ponty*, Routledge, forthcoming.
54 *Phenomenology of Perception* 203–204.
55 Merleau-Ponty, M., 1993, 'Eye and Mind', in Galen A. Johnson, ed., *The Merleau-Ponty Aesthetics Reader*, Northwestern University Press, Evanston IL, p. 125.
56 Ibid., 126.
57 'Indirect Language and the Voices of Silence', *The Merleau-Ponty Aesthetics Reader* passim.
58 Wittgenstein, L., 1970, *Lectures and Conversations on Aesthetics, Psychology, and Religious Belief*, Blackwell, Oxford, p. 90.
59 Stephen Davies, for example, defends a version of what he calls 'appearance emotionalism', attributed to himself and Peter Kivy. For these writers the emotional characteristics of a piece of music are part of the 'appearance' of the piece. To recognise them the detection of a certain kind of pattern or shape in the music itself is necessary. This is a shape or pattern which it may take some kind of training or initiation to discover, and is something which people can be particularly apt or inept at detecting. Davies, S., 2003, *Themes in the Philosophy of Music*, Oxford University Press.
60 Wittgenstein, L., 1980, *Culture and Value*, ed. G. H. Von Wright, Blackwell, Oxford, p. 58e.
61 'Indirect Language and the Voices of Silence' 88.
62 Ibid., 107.
63 *The Visible and the Invisible* 239.
64 Merleau-Ponty, M., 2004, *The World of Perception*, trans. O. Davis, Routledge, London and New York, p. 99.
65 *The Retrieval of the Beautiful* 156.
66 Jaspers, K., 1963, *General Psychopathology*, Manchester University Press, vol. 1, p. 255.
67 McDowell, John, 1998, *Mind, Value and Reality*, Harvard University Press, Cambridge MA, p. 337.
68 Gatens, Moira and Lloyd, Genevieve, 1999, *Collective Imaginings: Spinoza, Past and Present*, Routledge, London and New York; Gatens, M., 1996, *Imaginary*

Bodies: Ethics, Power and Corporeality, Routledge, London and New York; James, S., 2012, *Spinoza on Philosophy, Religion and Politics*, Oxford University Press.

69 *Collective Imaginings* 5.

70 Spinoza, B., 1992, *Ethics*, trans. S. Shirley, Hackett, Indianapolis and Cambridge, IV, proposition 9. See discussion in Gatens and Lloyd, *Collective Imaginings*, p. 52.

71 James, *Spinoza on Philosophy, Religion and Politics*.

72 Spinoza, *Ethics* 18.

73 *Spinoza on Philosophy, Religion and Politics*.

74 Spinoza, B., 1951, *Theologico-Political Treatise*, trans. R. H. M. Elwes, Dover, New York, p. 164.

75 Ibid., 80.

76 Ibid., 153.

77 See: Lloyd, G., 1998, 'Spinoza and the Education of the Imagination', in A. Rorty, ed., *Philosophers and Education*, Routledge, London, p. 162; and Spinoza, *Ethics* 13.

78 Coleridge, *Ode to Dejection*, available at: http://classiclit.about.com/library/bl-etexts/scoleridge/bl-stcole-dejection.htm. My discussion in this section is indebted to Warnock, M., 1976, *Imagination*, Faber and Faber, London.

79 *The Imaginary* 69.

80 Abrams, M. H., 1953, *The Mirror and the Lamp*, Oxford University Press, New York, 62.

81 Mill, J. S., 1833, 'What Is Poetry?' in *Early Essays*, available at: https://archive.org/details/earlyessays00lyttgoog

82 *The Mirror and the Lamp* 54.

83 *The Mirror and the Lamp* 181.

84 Coleridge, S. T., 1817, *Biographia Literaria*, ch. xiii, available at: www.online-literature.com/coleridge/biographia-literaria/13/

85 Fancy on this account has clear parallels with the workings of the reproductive imagination described by Hume. See the discussion in Chapter 2.

86 *Ode to Dejection* stanza VI.

87 *The Mirror and the Lamp* 53.

88 *The Mirror and the Lamp* 65.

89 Warnock, *Imagination* 102.

5 Imaginary institution(s)

The imaginary texture of the experienced world, which this work is exploring, has an affective character. The imaginary content expresses a world which makes a call to our bodies, initiates a response. This was the focus of the previous chapter. In this chapter we turn to the social dimension of that imaginary. The theorist who has done most to provide an account of what he terms *The Imaginary Institution of Society*[1] is Cornelius Castoriadis, and much of this chapter will be taken up with a discussion of his work. The affective, bodily and social aspects of the imagination were under-theorised by Kant. In the writings of Castoriadis we find them theorised together. His is an approach to the imaginary informed by Kant, incorporating insights from psychoanalysis and put into conversation, in its social application, with the writings of Marx. In the first part of the chapter Castoriadis is read alongside Merleau-Ponty, to explore the role the social plays in instituting our imaginaries. In the second part he is read alongside Marx, to examine imaginaries *of* the social. In the third part he is read alongside contemporary theorists, Gatens and Lloyd, to discuss critical reflection on, and transformation of, social imaginaries. We will, however, start with some examples, from which we can consider what kinds of questions people have employed the notion of the social imaginary to address.

At the beginning of her book *Imperial Leather*, Anne McClintock[2] discusses a map made by Rider Haggard to guide imperial explorers in Southern Africa. What she draws our attention to is the way the image Haggard presents mirrors a woman's body. In much nineteenth-century discourse, the land to be explored, often characterised as virgin territory, is imagined as a female body, to be ravished and explored, but also as, potentially, a threatening engulfment. This map, then, carries an imaginary of what it purports to be representing, which suggests, and legitimises, certain kinds of responses to that land. McClintock's work highlights the intersecting imaginaries of sexed difference, raced difference, class difference, domesticity, and empire, in nineteenth-century writings about imperialism. She does not use the term social imaginaries, which has since become ubiquitous, but she draws attention to what others have captured by it, in her explorations of the meanings attached to 'home' and 'empire', and the images (in the wide sense in which we have been using this term, to

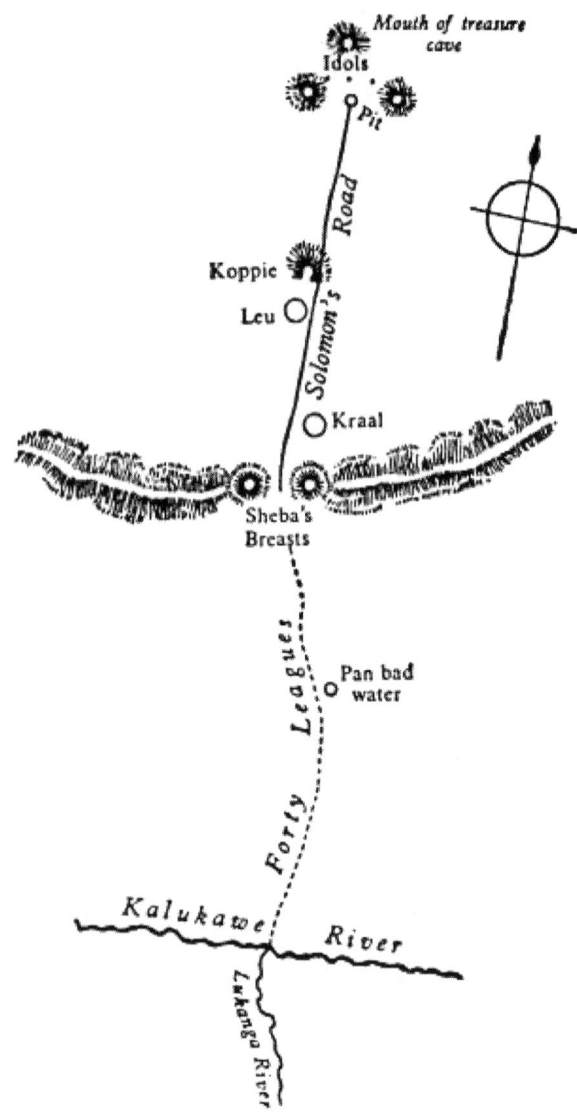

Figure 5.1 Rider Haggard's map
Source: McClintock, Anne, 1995, *Imperial Leather: Race, Gender, and Sexuality in the Colonial Contest*, Routledge, London and New York, p. 2.

incorporate more than visual images) whereby these significances were conveyed. These are images in terms of which we experience and make sense of our social world.

The goal, for those for whom the concept of the social imaginary has become central, is to provide an account of the social as consisting of more than objective, thing-like institutions. Interwoven with these, in any society, making them possible and being made possible by them, are both shared and differing imaginaries. These are imaginaries of the world, ourselves, other people, and of the social groupings in which we live; both local and national. Such imaginaries both make possible social life and are themselves social entities carried in stories, myths, practices, visual representations, and institutional structures. And this more recent use of the concept of the imaginary continues much older lines of thought which regard 'imagination and memory, mingled with affect [as] the materials from which ... community identities are built'.[3]

In Benedict Anderson's[4] famous analysis *nations* are imagined communities. He draws a contrast, not between the imagined and the real (for here the imagined is constitutive of the real), but between the imagined and the face to face. In thinking of ourselves as part of a national community, he suggests, we think of ourselves as linked to those we never encounter. Such awareness, he argues, was facilitated by the rise of print mediums which allow representations of, and shared understandings with, those we do not meet. Anderson's book, however, also illustrates the importance of the imaginary to the constitution of the nation in the somewhat wider sense of the imaginary with which this book has been concerned (and not just with the imagined as the not-present). In the sense of the imaginary which has become distilled from the previous chapters, the imaginary is the shape or form in terms of which we experience the world and ourselves; a gestalt which carries significance, affect and normative force. Our activities and responses are both motivated and legitimised by the shape which the world, including the social world and its imagined history, carries for us. So for Anderson, we are linked to imagined others by shared ways of imagining the nation of which we are all a part. He himself was responding to a series of writings which saw nations as invented and therefore as *fictional* or illusory entities.[5] To counter this he points out 'the attachment people feel for the inventions of their imaginations ... people are ready to die for these inventions ... nations inspire love, and often profoundly self sacrificing love'.[6] They also, of course, can inspire hatred of those imagined as foreign or other to them. In claiming nations are imagined, and thereby in some sense invented, communities, Anderson was not dismissing them as fantasies, the social groupings they inform unreal. But neither is it the case that the way they are imagined is immune from critical reflection. Given the emotional pull such imaginings generate it is important to consider how they are to be assessed, how we are to reflect on their legitimacy.[7]

For those theorists for whom the concept of the social imaginary has become central it can be playing different roles, and part of what this chapter will do is unpack and evaluate the claims made on its behalf. One job of the social imaginary is to provide an account of how we come to experience the world, ourselves, etc., as having a certain imaginary shape, and how that imaginary shape is one which we share with others. The concept of the social imaginary shifts attention away from the imagination as a faculty of an individual subject, and onto imaginaries as features of socio-historical contexts which can be

encountered and shared; anonymous daily creations in which everyone partici-
pates. Imaginaries conceived as social and inter-subjective are both *instituted* and
instituting; broadly, both passively found or encountered as conditions for
experiencing the world, and actively and innovatively transformed as they are
re-experienced. The imaginary as both instituted and instituting will be the
focus of the first part of this chapter.

The other use to which talk of social imaginaries has been put regards them
as, at least partially, *constitutive of social groupings*, for example cultural,
ethnic or national groupings. In Charles Taylor's terms the social imaginary is:

> the ways people imagine their social existence, how they fit together with
> others, how things go on between them and their fellows, the expectations
> that are normally met, and the deeper normative notions and images that
> underlie these expectations ... common understandings that make possible
> common practices and a widely shared sense of legitimacy.[8]

Society, on this account, does not simply consist of inter-subjective material
encounters and thing-like structures but also of patterns of meaning and significations which structure experience and condition such encounters and
structures. It is the social imaginary in this sense that will be the concern of the
second part of the chapter. It is, as we shall see, a contested question as to how
much communality of imaginary signification can be assumed within social
groups, and the question of *differing imaginaries* turns out to be a central one.

As the examples of the imagined lands of colonial conquests and that of
nations as imagined communities make clear, the issue of reflective scrutiny,
evaluation and change within social imaginary significations is a central one.
This will be addressed in Part III of this chapter.

Part I: the instituted and instituting imaginary

We start with the social imaginary's role in providing an account of how we
come to experience the world, ourselves, etc., as having a certain imaginary
shape; and how this imaginary shape is one which is sometimes shared and
sometimes not.

Castoriadis: the individual and social workings of radical imagination

In the work of Cornelius Castoriadis we are offered a concept of the imaginary
which weaves together the Kantian productive imagination, yielding images or
forms to our experience: the romantic creative imagination, and the domain of
the affective, derived, for him, from psychoanalysis. He gives us an account of
the radical imagination at work within the individual and within the social, and
an account of the relation between the two. For Castoriadis, prior to questions
of the truth or rationality of our representations of the world, comes the question of how it is possible for a world to exist for a subject in the first place. His

answer to this question makes the radical imagination a condition of possibility of experience. It is via such imagination, the productive imagination in Kant's sense, that we are able to both create and grasp form in the flux of sensation which is presented to us: 'radical imagination (as source of the perceptual quale and of logical forms) is what makes possible for any being-for-itself (including humans) to *create for* itself an own world (*eine Eigenwelt*) "within" which it also posits itself.' He adds, with another Kantian echo: 'It is clear that no being for itself could "organise" something out of the world, if this world were not intrinsically organis*able* – which means that it cannot be simply "chaotic". But this is another dimension of the question.'[9] The imagination here is conceived of as an originary capacity to create figures or images and bring them into relation to each other. In common with Kant he views this capacity as some-thing prior to the distinction between the real and the fictitious. It is necessary if we are to have a world at all. He illustrates this with reference to Eddington's two tables, both of which require the imagination.

> *This* table – the one I touch, I see, I lean on etc. – contains an indefinite plurality of 'elements' created by the singular imagination *and* the social imaginary. The other 'table' – in fact no table at all – is a scientific con-struct, *such as* science makes it *today*. (And this does not make it any less imaginary in the sense of the word I am intending.)[10]

He castigates Kant for failing to appreciate the openness and creativity of such a capacity. Focusing on the Kant of the first *Critique*, he accepts the necessity of the categories to capture what he calls the *ensemblistic-identitarian* dimension of thinking, yielding a logical order to our world, but nonetheless criticises Kant for failing to see how much the creative dimension of the ima-gination is exercised even in 'the cognitive (scientific or philosophical) domain'.[11] Where Kant does recognise creativity, he suggests, as in the third *Critique*, he links it too closely to the Ideas of Reason. For Castoriadis the creativity of the imagination floats free of any such constraints. He insists on what he calls the *defunctionalisation* of the imagination. It is not tied to the Kantian Ideas of Reason, but neither is it determined in other ways. It is not fixed by biological needs, fundamental psychic drives or (in the social realm) by material and economic necessity.

The Kantian framework, which Castoriadis revives, is put together, by him, with insights from psychoanalysis. Within the figures and forms which the imagination delivers, 'representation, affect and desire'[12] are mixed together in ways that resist disentanglement (see discussion in Chapter 4). The imagination is the means by which the world is endowed with meaning, and in this process of endowment, what he would term the codifying aspects of meaning, go hand in hand with a poetics, an affective signification which delivers the world with an emotional colouring. Continuing the quote we utilised in the previous chapter: 'Psychoanalysis obliges us to see that the human being is not an ... [animal possessing 'reason'], but essentially an imagining being, one endowed with radical, unmotivated,[13] de-functionalised imagination'.[14] In psychoanalysis, however, the imagination was the realm of phantasy, an illusory realm from which we need to be freed. (Imagination as *Phantasie*, rather than, as for Castoriadis, *Einbildungskraft*.) For Freud the world of phantasy needed correction by engagement with the real. For Castoriadis, in contrast, the imaginary made the real possible, preceding the division into the real and the fictive.

As we have noted, for Lacan, for us to emerge as socialised individuals the imaginary has to be put to one side, as we enter and become positioned within the public symbolic realm of language and public symbols. For him this realm has an ontological status distinct from the imaginary. We have no option, if we are to become socialised individuals, other than to position ourselves in relation to it. For Lacan, the process of becoming a subject requires a double alienation from the plenitude of immersion in the Real, which marks our existence prior to our emergence as subjects. First we become enthralled by external and illusory images. Then we are released from this by subjectification to an external symbolic order.[15] For Castoriadis the imaginary is not constituted out of a relation to an external, and illusory, image. It is instead the product of the originary and creative capacity for making and grasping image or form in what is presented to us. Although such imaginary formations are multiple and historically variable, they are not necessarily distorting and illusory. Moreover, although, for Lacan, they are distinct moments, the imaginary and symbolic functions are intertwined for Castoriadis, as for other theorists we discussed in the previous chapter. The codifying and affective dimensions of thought are woven together in the way in which we experience our bodies and worlds.

The picture which Castoriadis paints of the psyche is one which gives a certain kind of priority to the singular, interior, first person perspective. The psyche is constituted via *its own* imaginary, set against the social, also constituted via the imaginary (of which more below). An initial monadic meaning is given by the psyche to its own world, initially closed in on itself, which is disrupted by the process of socialisation, when 'the psyche is forced to (never fully) abandon its pristine solipsistic meaning for the shared meanings provided by society'.[16] But even when this process of socialisation takes place, what is introjected is always reinterpreted 'on the basis of the existing own scheme'.[17] This prior psyche interiority is already bodily: 'there is no frontier between this living, animated body and the originary psychic monad'.[18] The originary imagination for Castoriadis is a bodily one. While drawing on psychoanalysis in the picture which he offers of the psyche, he rejects any suggestion that a determining role be given in its constitution to fundamental drives. The radical imagination is not simply put to use to provide objects for independently given drives, in a way that would be suggested by a hydraulic reading of Freud's account.[19] The point of the imagination is not simply to provide images which will satisfy fundamental drives universally present in each psyche. It is rather that the nature of such psychic drives is not fixed independently of the images which express them. These images can be multiple and variable, and constitute the affective texture of the psyche's interior world.

The structure of the imaginary *within singular subjects* is repeated at the level of the social. Our social/cultural/historical position influences the imaginaries in terms of which we experience the world. These imaginaries are shared and we are initiated into them by our upbringing. In this sense social imaginary significations are, from the point of view of the individual, something which we encounter. Social imaginaries also have the characteristics of the radical imaginary. They give form to the world, including the social world. They are encountered by the subject and internalised, such that we never encounter individuals in a pure, unsocialised state, we only encounter 'socialised individuals'.[20] The imaginaries which we share, like individual imaginaries, endow the world with meaning and significance which is affectively laden. These social imaginaries, and the institutions they both enable and constitute, are creations, but not of identifiable individuals, rather of an 'anonymous collective'.[21] They are undergoing continual modification, even when we are unaware of this. There are multiple social imaginaries, even within a given socio-historical configuration. Imaginaries can change and new imaginaries emerge. The creativity which he made a central feature of individual imagination is repeated at the level of the social. (So he suggests capitalism was the emergence of a 'new social imaginary signification, the unlimited expansion of "rational" mastery'.[22] Slavery marked 'the emergence of a new imaginary significance, a new way for society to live'.[23] And this in turn was challenged by an opposing imaginary in which human beings were conceived of as equal.) Social imaginaries, though undetermined, are not unconstrained. They are constrained by the 'natural stratum ... and natural habitat ... an ensemblistic–identitary dimension – two stones and two stones make four stones'.[24] They are constrained by the psychic demand for meaning, which includes affective meaning, and by the requirement to have some kind of internal coherence. They are 'Not freely chosen, nor imposed upon a given society, neither a neutral instrument nor a transparent medium'.[25]

The social for Castoriadis is both *instituted* and *instituting*:

> The social is, on the one hand, given structures, 'materialized' institutions and works, whether these be material or not and, on the other hand *that which structures, institutes and materializes* ... the union and the tension of instituting society and of instituted society, of history made and of history in the making.[26] (my emphasis)

'There will always be distance between society as instituting and what is, at each moment instituted.'[27] Here society is given the instituting role which, in the individual, is given to the productive, in Castoriadis' terms, radical imagination. But society is also the temporary stabilisations of structures which such instituting makes possible. In his account of the workings of the imaginary Castoriadis offers a picture of the relation between the psyche and the social in which neither is reduced to the other. There is rather a relation of interdependency which he terms 'leaning on'.[28] The psyche maintains a certain

independence of the social, while necessarily being modified by the social imaginaries to which it is exposed. Nonetheless these social imaginaries are reinterpreted in its own terms. An individual is always socially formed, but also
bears the distinctiveness of its own psychic formation. The social imaginary
derives some of its creativity from the individual psyches of those that make it
up, but also has a creative potential of its own which cannot be reduced to this.
The anonymous social works in a way that parallels but is not simply constituted out of individual radical imaginaries. Nonetheless it *leans on* intrinsic
possibilities of the human psyche. It exploits and becomes intelligible in the
light of these possibilities, without the psychic features determining the form
the social must take.[29]

Merleau-Ponty on institution

In the writing of Castoriadis the distinction between the individual imagination
and the social imaginary is retained. But they are interdependent. The social
imaginary is internalised and modifies the individual psyche, and the social
imaginary is realised in, but remains independent of, individual psyches. Both
display the features of the radical imagination. They are both instituting and
instituted, formed and forming, displaying both stability and creativity. In
Merleau-Ponty's later work on institution, *Institution and Passivity*,[30] the picture of an individual subject, constituting its world via the faculty of imagination, is rejected. In the *Phenomenology of Perception* the imagination had
become embodied and it was an embodied subject which gave form or shape
mutually to itself and the world. But in the later work this picture has been
replaced by one of a process, instituted and instituting, passive and active,
which yields the meaning, the significance (what we have been terming imaginary form) which makes up the world for us. He writes: 'Understand the imaginary sphere ... as the true *Stiftung* [institution] of Being of which observation
and the articulated body are special variants'.[31] Lefort comments: 'he has used
Stiftung to designate the fecundity deriving from a moment in time ... the
workings of culture which opens a tradition'.[32] The distinction between constitution and institution is key here. The world as constituted is dependent on
and makes no sense independent of the constituting subject(s). In contrast, sense
as instituted is encountered. It is encountered in the socio-historical field: '[the]
inter-subjective or symbolic field, [the field of] cultural objects, ... is our milieu,
our hinge'.[33] It is an imaginary organisation of existence that is socio-cultural
as well as bodily.

Castoriadis reflects on the socio-historical anchorage, though not determination, of Merleau-Ponty's instituted and instituting imaginary, via a discussion
of the visible and invisible elements of 'red' (cf. discussion in Chapter 3).
Merleau-Ponty writes:

> a certain red is ... a fossil drawn up from imaginary worlds ... a punctuation
> in the field of red things, which includes the tiles of roof tops, the flags of

gatekeepers, and of the Revolution, certain terrains near Aix and Madagascar ... also the dresses of women, robes of professors ... or that of gypsies dressed like hussars who reigned twenty five years ago over an inn on the Champs-Elysées.[34]

Castoriadis points out that such a red requires a historically specific institution:

> It is likely that my grandchildren ... will understand nothing about those gypsies on the Champs-Elysées ... and none of the examples cited would make Aristotle see anything at all. [Moreover,] the red of the Revolution introduces another and new differentiation ... a new modulation to those that the colour red had made until that point ... And then we can no longer speak of 'a fossil drawn up from the depths of imaginary worlds'; as these imaginary worlds continue to *make themselves*, the red is not *finished*.[35]

But the thought Castoriadis expresses here is one with which Merleau-Ponty was in agreement. Meaning or form is encountered by us as something which has been deposited, as a residue of prior engagements; but it is experienced also as something to be *continued* in a way that is open, rather than determined. We find ourselves in a field of culturally mediated objects which we can surpass, but only on the basis of what has been given. Lefort comments: 'if institution is openness to, openness is always produced – on the basis of'.[36] We can engage in transformative activity, but only on the condition of our position in an already meaningful world. And the world as instituted suggests the initiation of the new; the invitation to a future. Such an opening for Merleau-Ponty is always a collective one, for the 'field' is always 'a double horizon' 'for others and not for me alone'.[37]

The structure of institution, both instituted and instituting, is found in all areas of life: 'birth [is] the institution of a future. There will be later decisionary institutions ... but they will be understood on the basis of birth'.[38] It is not simply that birth is the causal origin of what happens to us later. It is rather that what comes later is understood in the context of that birth. Subjects, no longer conceived of as constituting origins, are themselves, from birth, both instituted and instituting:

> [there is an] instituted and instituting subject, but inseparable, and not a constituting subject ... [this instituted/instituting subject is] exposed to ... an event ... which is productive after it ... which opens a future. The subject [is] that to which such an order of events can advent, [open], field of fields.[39]

Social and cultural groups are also instituting and instituted. Neither form a determined foundation for meaning: 'sense is deposited ... not as an object left behind ... a residue ... [but] as something to continue ... without it being the case that this sequel is determined. The instituted will change but this very change is called for by its Stiftung'.[40] Complexes of human/non-human life are involved. We find 'a certain variation in the field of existence already instituted, which is always behind us and whose weight, like that of an object in flight, only intervenes in the actions by which we transform it'.[41] This instituted variation has sources which are material/biological and socio-historical, but which are determined by none of these sources. The imaginary worlds, both material and social, which we encounter 'sediment in me a meaning as the invitation to a sequel, the necessity of a future'.[42] What Merleau-Ponty emphasises is the openness of such sequels. Even though each is grounded, he insists on the dimension of difference in the way in which different subjects/times may form a sequel, further institutions which are 'echoes and exchanges'[43] of each other and that which they follow. And on the basis of which new instituting events will take place.

For Merleau-Ponty, then, institution

> is the wherewithal on which I count at each moment ... which is assumed by everything that is visible for a human being, is what is at issue each moment and which has no name and no identity in our theories of consciousness.[44]

The imaginary is here conceived of as a process with non-determining sources which are both material and cultural, and in relation to which individual subjects and social groups are moments, always engaged in creative transition. Castoriadis, though working with the notions of the imaginary as both instituted and instituting, has not finally broken with the model of the constituting individual imagination. As we have noted, he sees the creativity of the social imaginary as *leaning on* the creativity of the psyche. For Merleau-Ponty such creativity is a result of a process which is both instituted and instituting and the sources or grounds of which are multiple. Creativity is integral to the process of institution itself as it plays across the individual, the social and the other elements informing it. We, as subjects, encounter an imaginary significance which requires and suggests a sequel to which it must bear an intelligible relation, but does not fix. The imagination as an individual faculty bestowing order has gone. For both writers we require the social imaginary, within which we find ourselves, for perception; to provide us, in Castoriadis' term, with a 'home'. But also for both: 'we cannot live without a home, but neither can we remain hermetically sealed within our home'.[45]

Part II: the imaginary institution of society

The concept of the social imaginary was central to Castoriadis' conception not only of *the origin* of imaginary significations, but also of *what made up* society, or social groups. 'Society is ... a quasi-totality held together by institutions (language, norms, family forms, tools and production modes etc.) and by the significations these institutions embody' (totems, taboos, gods, God, *polis*, commodities, wealth, fatherland, etc.).[46]

The magma

For Castoriadis shared social imaginaries are a necessary component of a social grouping:

> the total world given to a particular society is *grasped* in a way that is determined practically, affectively and mentally ... an articulated meaning is imposed on it ... distinctions are made concerning what does or does not possess value ... and what should and should not be done.[47]

Such grasping is made manifest in activity: 'It is in the doing of each collectivity ... that embodied meaning is made manifest'.[48] The social imaginary significations of any society form an immensely complex web of meanings, which nonetheless, for Castoriadis, display some unity and internal cohesion. This network of meanings he termed a *magma* of 'social imaginary significations that are carried by and embodied in the institution of a given society and that, so to speak, animate it'.[49] Shared imaginaries make possible social institutions, and these institutions are constitutively linked to the imaginary significations which we have of them. These institutions are 'self sanctioning'.[50] Their imaginary form gives shape to the social world in a way that makes appropriate certain ways of behaving in relation to it, and legitimates certain forms of social organisation.

For Castoriadis, social imaginaries also yield a sense of what constitutes the society itself and what constitutes our own identity as members of the society. Our participation in social groupings is then mediated by the imaginaries which we have of such groups and our own position in relation to them (as in Benedict Anderson's account of the nation). There is a stronger claim, which he sometimes seems to imply here: that social groupings require a *shared imaginary* about just that grouping (culture, nation, etc.; Englishness requiring a shared way of imagining what it is to be English), a sense of a 'we' transparent between individual and collective which constitutes both individual and group identity. 'Every society up to now has attempted to give an answer to a few fundamental questions: Who are we as a collectivity? ... Society must define its identity. Without these definitions, there can be no human world, no society, no culture.'[51] But this stronger claim seems problematic. We will return to it below.

Castoriadis and Marx

Castoriadis developed his ideas in conversation with a Marxism to which he always maintained an allegiance. But he criticises Marx for failing to understand the imaginary and not therefore grasping the nature of institutions. This criticism incorporates several strands. For Castoriadis the role of the imaginary and its constitutive necessity for institutions challenges: a Marxist distinction between infrastructure and superstructure; a broadly functional view both of the organisation of social relations and of the superstructures which supposedly facilitate them; and a distinction between ideological and scientific accounts of social relations.

In contrast to Marxist views, for him, the ways in which we make sense of our world, our imaginaries, cannot simply be conceived of as part of a super-structural *level* deriving from a more fundamentally determining level of material forces, and the productive relations by which they are developed. Rather they are themselves *part of* the social relations in terms of which society organises itself: 'the relations of production articulated on the social scale ... signify *ipso facto* a network, one both real and symbolical, which is self sanctioning – hence [in Castoriadis' terms] an institution'.[52] If it is, in his terms, an institution, it incorporates and requires the workings of the imaginary. This imaginary has the characteristic of openness and creativity (in the terminology of the previous discussion, is both instituted and instituting) and is not simply functional. So, even at the level of the organisation of productive relations, an imaginary is at work, organising and legitimising sets of social interactions in ways that are not simply required or suggested by the material forces and levels of technology. Such an imaginary as constitutive cannot then be assigned to a supposed super-structural level. Instead he suggests the material and the imaginary are 'a matter of moments in a structure – which is never rigid and never identical from one society to another'.[53] Furthermore, Castoriadis' insistence on the *defunction-isation* of the imagination, in the social as in the individual sphere, has the consequence that the imaginary forms in terms of which we make sense of our worlds are not simply those which are *functional* to retaining a social order – a structuring of social relations which maximises the development of the material and technical resources available to us, or facilitates change to an order which would so maximise them.

> We find, in every case, at the heart of this imaginary and in all of its expressions something that cannot be reduced to the functional, an original investment by society of the world and itself with meaning – meanings which are not dictated by real factors, since it is instead this meaning that attributes to these real factors a particular importance and a particular place in the universe constituted by a given society – a meaning that can be recognised in both the content and style of its life.[54]

Consequently, Marxist theories of ideology cannot be accepted. Marx himself did not see the level of sense making and meaning as purely epiphenomenal; the links between the productive relations and the superstructure were dialectical. The images in terms of which people made sense of their social world affected the docility, or otherwise, with which they accepted or sought to change it. So for Marx, images of the heavenly family distracted members of earthly families from conflict, oppression and exploitation. (Currently the fantasy world of celebrity and royalty might serve a similar function.) However, images remained functional. They promoted the interests of the group within society which was dominant. In this theory of ideology the imaginary becomes something like a collective *fantasy*, a *distorted* set of images which served to conceal from the participants of society (including those whose interests it served) the *real* laws of working. It also distracted them from suffering and conflict by means of the pleasures and promises such fantasies incorporated.[55] The job of revolutionaries was to *expose the falsity and distortion* of such fantasies and *open people's eyes to the real structures and to the real fact* that, via collective agency, they could be changed. Given the functionality of the fantasies to certain forms of social organisation, however, changes to such imaginings could not be achieved without some destabilisation at the level of what was regarded as real material structures. So the bringing about of revolutionary change required an ongoing dialectical process between the level of what we are calling the imaginary and what Marx regarded as the real relations grounding it.

This picture was unacceptable to Castoriadis, not only for the functionality of the imaginary which it incorporates, but also because it rests on a fundamental distinction between the real and the imaginary; between what Marx terms ideology and science, which Castoriadis rejected. For Marx it was possible to replace imaginary understandings with scientific accounts of the world, including crucially the social world, on the basis of which revolutionary change could be brought about, leading to a society in which imaginary (for him ideological and distorted) views would no longer be functional. But for Castoriadis:

> when it is asserted that the imaginary plays a role with respect to the institution only because there are 'real' problems that people are not able to solve, this is to forget, on the one hand, that people manage to solve real problems, precisely, to the extent that they do solve them, only because they are capable of the imaginary; and on the other hand, that these real problems can be problems, can be constituted as these specific problems, presenting themselves to a particular epoch or a particular society as a task to be completed, only in relation to an imaginary central to the given epoch or society.[56]

The imaginary is therefore in play in both the scientific and the ideological depictions of society, and cannot therefore be dispensed with. The so-called real conditions of society cannot be articulated independently of imaginary configurations: 'If by communism ... is meant a society that would be purely transparent to itself ... which would never be weighted down with symbolism ... we must clearly state that this is an incoherent reverie, an unreal and unrealisable state.'[57] The task of revolutionary change and that of creating an alternative social order is not, then, that of dispensing with imaginaries, but of *providing alternative ones*. We return to this below.

Difference

For Castoriadis:

> every society defines and develops an image of the natural world ... in which a place has to be made not only for the natural objects ... but also for the collectivity itself. This image, this more or less structured vision of the whole of available human experience makes use ... of what is given ... but arranges ... [it] according to ... significations [which] belong ... to the imaginary. This is just as self evident in the beliefs of archaic societies as in the religious conceptions of historical societies; and even the extreme 'rationalism' of modern societies does not ... escape this perspective.[58]

He, along with some more recent theorists,[59] sees shared imaginary salience, including shared imaginaries of the social group itself, as part of what constitutes membership of the group and leads to its coherence. Because he sees shared imaginary significations as what holds society together, where they fragment, as he saw in many contemporary societies, he saw a crisis of 'identification'[60] occurring. There is some tension in his writings between his insistence on the openness and creativity of the workings of the imaginary at both the individual and the social level and his insistence on the sameness and closure of meaning in many societies and, moreover, his lament for loss of shared meanings in contemporary culture.

For many commentators, his account is problematic for the extent to which it assumes a homogeneity in the imaginaries of given societies and glosses over the divisions within them. Irigaray[61] and other feminist theorists have pointed out the difference between male and female imaginaries. These are not simply differences in the imaginaries of actual men and women, but rather differences which reflect or implicate different and unequal social positions. John Thompson[62] suggests that an overemphasis on homogeneity ignores divisions of class, sexual difference, sexuality and ethnicity, for example. Castoriadis does not discuss either the imaginaries that each of these social categories carry or their role in maintaining social inequality. What is clear, however, is that at whatever level we posit social groupings there are divisions, which the imaginary *unity* of the nation or indeed the religious or cultural or sexed group glosses over.

Many contemporary writers have drawn our attention to the *different* imaginaries which can surround what may appear, materially, to be the same practices. Anne McClintock[63] reflects on Fanon's earlier discussion of the veiled woman in the context of colonial conquest. 'In "Algeria Unveiled" Fanon ventriloquises – only to refute – the long Western dream of colonial conquest as an erotics of ravishment ... the Algerian woman ... unveiled and laid bare for the colonials' grip.'[64] In this context the apparel of women became a key issue in the nationalist struggle: 'for male nationalists women served as the visible markers of national homogeneity', and, for them, this required the wearing of the veil; whereas, for colonialists, unveiling was imagined as a sign of rescuing women from the control of Algerian men. (We can recognise parallels in today's debates.) Some militant Algerian women unveiled themselves, an act mistakenly taken by colonialists as a sign of cultural conversion, and later appropriated by nationalists to enable infiltration of colonialist domains with bombs. Since Fanon's discussion there have been many debates over the significance of the wearing of the veil or the headscarf, within both post-colonial societies and European ones.[65] The tensions in Turkey (whose public discourses carry both secular and religious imaginaries), over the wearing of the headscarf, were made clear when Merve Kavaki, a headscarf-wearing woman from a pro-Islamic party, was unable to take the oath on the opening day of parliament. But the ambiguity of its symbolism (its imaginary supposedly opposed to modernisation) was complicated by her being a 'divorced, United States trained computer engineer ... dressed fashionably in modern suits'.[66] In a discussion of the wearing of the burka in present-day France, Paul Gilbert identifies[67] different saliences which the practice may have for its participants: a pleasing unobtrusiveness within a community of those with whom we pass most of our time; an assertion of difference in the context of a wider community experienced as hostile; an expression of religious beliefs – and so on. None of these are necessarily conscious or chosen meanings, but they emerge from the pre-reflective encounters with a practice to which differing social imaginaries may be attached. Antony Cohen points out that a community may share a symbol but not necessarily share its meaning:

> Age, life, father, purity, gender, death, doctor, are all symbols shared by those whose use the same language, or participate in the same symbolic behaviour through which these categories are expressed and marked. But their meanings are not shared in the same way.[68]

For Cohen these different meanings are because 'each is mediated by the idiosyncratic experience of the individual',[69] something which, of course, Castoriadis also stressed in his discussion of the intersection of the individual and social radical imaginary; and which sits in some tension with the view that there is a homogeneity in the imaginaries of a society. Even within societies which he considers closed, the workings of the individual and the social imaginaries will lead to differences. For Thompson such differences reflect the conflicts and distinct material and economic positions of different participants within a shared social grouping; while it is also the case that there are dominant imaginaries, which people adopt, whether or not they make sense of their experience or support their interests. For Merleau-Ponty, in common with many poststructuralist writers,[70] such variations are the way in which an instituted and instituting imaginary works: 'institution ... is open, because it is a divergence in relation to a norm of sense, *difference*. It is this sense, by divergence, deformation, which is proper to institution.'[71] From which we may conclude that while Castoriadis was right to draw our attention to the role of social imaginaries as yielding our sense of the social order and framing our possibilities within it, he was mistaken in seeing, or recommending, homogeneity within such imaginaries.

Part III: reflective scrutiny and imaginary transformations

Some of the examples of social imaginary significations which we have met in this chapter have served to draw attention to the way in which imaginaries can be damaging, put to use to justify power hierarchies. The colonial imaginaries of virgin lands or savage peoples justified imperialist adventures. Nationalist imaginaries can both produce and pathologise the 'foreigner' and justify hostility, prejudice and war. Sexed imaginaries, informing a division into male and female, also maintain and motivate unequal social positioning for men and women. (The way in which imaginaries not only attach significance to pre-established social groupings, but also form such groupings, will be discussed further in the following chapter.) This makes urgent the question of how imaginary significations can be brought to reflective scrutiny and transformed. This is the concern of this part of the chapter.

Habermas and Castoriadis

Jürgen Habermas has criticised Castoriadis' account of imaginary institution on several interrelated grounds, pertaining to issues of assessment, validity and change. Castoriadis, he says, offers us:

> the originless creation of absolutely new and unique patterns. This ... comes uncomfortably close to a Being operating without reason ... one cannot see how this ... could be transposed into the revolutionary project proper to the practice of consciously acting, autonomous, self-realising individuals particularly if 'socialized individuals are merely "instituted" by the "social imaginary."'[72]

He uncouples, Habermas suggests, 'the productivity of language from the consequences of an intermundane practice', so that 'any interaction between world disclosing language and learning processes in the world is excluded'.[73] The consequence is 'to entrust the rational content of socialism ... to a demiurge creative of meaning, which brushes aside the difference between meaning and validity'.[74] He leaves no room 'for an inter-subjective praxis for which socialized individuals are *accountable*'.[75] Habermas insists 'social praxis is linguistically constituted, but language, too, has to *prove itself* through this praxis, in terms of what is encountered within the horizon disclosed by it'.[76]

However, the refusal by Castoriadis to endorse a dualism between the real (captured by science) and the imaginary (found in distorted ideologies) does not mean that he gave all imaginary significations the same status. He retains much of the emancipatory impulse behind theories of ideology, but addresses them by his consideration of autonomy. As McNay points out,

'Castoriadis recasts the idea of autonomy within the instituted–instituting dynamic of the social imaginary'.[77] At the personal level autonomy is conceived of as an individual entertaining a questioning rather than submissive attitude to received knowledge: a 'reflecting and deliberating subjectivity'.[78] Such reflection is then repeated at the social level. He distinguishes '*heteronomous* societies where closure of meaning prevails' and where questions of legitimacy are answered from within such a closed set of meanings; and *open* societies where activities of autonomous reflection lead to open sets of possibilities.[79] Most societies, for him, establish *closure* of their imaginary significations, not allowing their essential features to be called into question. But in some, reflection can take place, including reflection on the social order itself; though, following Marx, he saw this as requiring an 'upheaval ... in the entire socio-historical field'.[80] Reflection at the social level involves the recognition that collectively we make the social laws and could make them differently. But, this is not, as often thought, a reining-in of imaginary understanding by the workings of an objective reason. Rather, autonomy itself requires the workings of the radical imagination, enabling us to detach ourselves from immersion in the certainty of our given social imaginaries and raise the prospect of their being replaced with others. Moreover, it is the imagination which then provides us with new models for thinking, whether in the field of mathematics or science or in social and political understanding. But, he makes clear, such imaginings are not unconstrained:

> what we are able to imagine and, on that basis, to theorise about ... is not 'falsifiable' in Popper's sense; but stating that is a far cry from abolishing the distinction between truth and falsehood. An infinity of stupid statements can be made ... and these inanities can be shown to be inanities.[81]

Reflection is therefore 'the effort to break closure ... whether such closure comes from our personal history or from the socio historical institution'.[82]

Some imaginaries are deeply problematic because they disguise from participants in society the possibility of agency which could bring about social transformation. In accepting this, he shares elements of Marx's theory of alienation ... He also follows Marx in recognising that such imaginaries (called by him mythologies), even if unfounded, structure institutions and have real consequences. One such example, which he discusses, is the imaginaries of the nation, which we have considered above. Our identification of ourselves as part of a nation is not just a spatial-temporal positioning of ourselves within a region governed by objective political and judicial structures. Such a position has a significance; an imaginary salience which gives content to such an identification. So to lay claim to being British or Irish or American carries such (diverse) content. Such content often makes use of assumptions about a common history, a certain set of values and cultural practices, maybe an allegiance to certain ideals, and sometimes a set of religious practices. Castoriadis agrees with Marxist critiques of nationalism in their recognition that much of this imaginary content is ungrounded, in his terms mythical: 'this history ... is not really common ... and what is known of it and what serves as the basis for this collectivising identification in people's consciousness is largely mythical'.[83] But to point this out is in no way the end of the matter. This mystification 'has effects so massively and terribly real, that it proves itself to be much stronger than any "real" forces (including even the instinct of self preservation)'.[84] Such imaginaries cannot, therefore, be ignored as merely distorting, with a promise that they will disappear with world revolution. Such mythologies, distorting and damaging fictions, need to be engaged with *at the level of the imaginary and without trying to dispense with it.* (We should be reminded here of Spinoza's remark, quoted in the previous chapter: 'no affect can be restrained by the true knowledge of good and evil insofar as it is true, but only insofar as it is considered as an affect'.[85] We return to Spinoza below.) For Castoriadis:

> the most important social and historical transformation of the contemporary era ... is neither the Russian Revolution nor the bureaucratic revolution in China but the changing situation of woman and her role in society. This change ... has been carried out collectively, anonymously, daily, by women themselves ... in the home, at work, in bed, in the street, in relation to children, to their husbands, they have gradually transformed the situation.[86]

These changes have interwoven material and imaginary elements.

How are we to relate this to his discussion of autonomy and reflection? For Merleau-Ponty the instituting nature of the imaginary lent it a necessary instability, a creative openness which for Castoriadis was also integral to the workings of the radical imaginary at both the individual and the social level. But for Castoriadis such openness needs to be married to a possibility for reflective autonomy in unpicking the dominant social imaginaries, which allows for the possibility of a conscious praxis in social transformation. What some of his critics point out is that while requiring such reflective autonomy he is less clear how it is to be brought about. For many writers, however, starting from Marx, the tension which generates such praxis comes from the *differences* which are found within the social order, so that dominant imaginaries are experienced variably from different positions within it.[87] Merleau-Ponty has been subject to criticism for paying insufficient attention to social differences, sexed difference, raced differences or class difference. Nonetheless his framework is one which suggests them. It is the anchorage of bodies in material and social worlds which forms the basis of instituted and instituting imaginaries, and different forms of embodiment and social positionality yield expressive imaginaries of different kinds, part of the infinite possibilities of interpretation, he reminds us, to which the world is susceptible. For more recent theorists, it is just this dimension of difference which must be woven into the public conversation if assessment and transformation of social imaginaries is to be possible.

Gatens and Lloyd: collective imaginings

Moira Gatens and Genevieve Lloyd explore these issues, utilising a concept of the imaginary which they anchor in Spinoza,[88] but which nonetheless has many overlaps with that employed by Castoriadis. As we noted in Chapter 4, for Spinoza the mind is a form of direct bodily awareness, the imaginary an awareness of the environment and context as they impinge on our bodies. Because each mind is the idea of a different body, with a different life history, there will be divergency between different imaginary orders. These differences, however, will not be entirely individualistic. For our modes of being in the world, though variable, are inherently social: 'the affections of individual bodies, Spinoza says, lay down widely divergent associational paths, from traces of a horse seen in the sand, the soldier passes to thought of horsemen and war, the farmer to ploughs and fields'.[89] But although these patterns are individual and idiosyncratic – multiple in contrast to the supposed unitary order of reason – the variations are not a product of the affections of individual bodies in isolation from others. 'Farming and military activity give rise to different associational paths which reflect different practices.'[90] Different imaginaries are therefore tied up with different ways of responding to and acting in relation to our environment.

Spinoza notes, as does Castoriadis, that the imagination has a logic of its own, and has a resilience which can result in its persistence even when challenged by claims of truth or falsity. We cannot, therefore, modify damaging representations of, for example, women, simply by claiming they are false (women too can reason or carry heavy weights), for the way women are imagined, the response of men (and women) to female bodies, will not necessarily be changed. Gatens gives a good illustration of this point in her discussion of the attitudes of judges and jurors in rape trials. Judges and jurors are subject to training which instructs them that neither a woman's sexual history nor her trustworthiness can be gauged from her appearance. If asked to express their beliefs on this matter, many would express them in just this way. Nonetheless their responses to witnesses as trustworthy or provocative can remain in an imaginary realm governed by both social imaginaries and individual histories.[91] Gatens and Lloyd also discuss the social imaginary in which white Australians, thinking of their history, imagine Australia as a 'tabula rasa' prior to British colonisation, an image conditioning their relation to their land, their past and their future, and crucially their relation to indigenous peoples. 'The founding fiction ... was the "discovery" of a vast and ... empty land ... devoid of law and society and so without a history.'[92] Pointing out that there were people in Australia when British settlers arrived can have a bearing on the image of tabula rasa. But it is not sufficient. To dislodge this image those people and their social arrangements and relationships to the land have to be imagined in ways that give them rights over its use and disposition.

Gatens and Lloyd point out that, in a way comparable to Castoriadis' discussion of autonomy, Spinoza thought it was possible to reflect rationally on the workings of the imagination. The patterns of associations which were generated by specific images could be made a subject of scrutiny: 'he sees these organised patterns of affect and image as changeable through challenging the appropriateness of the images at their core'. In this way we can 'learn to replace misleading and debilitating illusions with better fictions'.[93] The legal fiction of *terra nullius* was overturned in 1992. Paul Keating, then prime minister, in response to activism from indigenous groups, emphasised that non-indigenous Australians needed to change their ways of thinking: 'it was we who did the dispossessing. We took the traditional lands and smashed the traditional way of life ... we committed the murders. We took the children from their mothers'.[94] Keating was not simply amassing facts. He was trying to bring about a change in the way the past is imagined, and consequently felt about. He was putting a different image or form on that past, which carried with it a different mode of feeling, and thereby acting in response to it. It was a *re-imagining*, provoked by the activism of indigenous peoples, of a dominant image which made no sense of the lives of themselves and their ancestors. Our imaginary worlds are perspectival. They are worlds from the perspective of embodied subjectivities whose corporeal forms, personal histories and social and cultural anchorage are implicated in the imaginary which their worlds possess. They are not, however, private. Others who can grasp the context should be able to grasp the imaginary form as a possible one. This process, however, is not that of checking an independently accessible reality to see if the representation of it is accurate. It is more like seeing if the world and subject *can carry* the signification suggested. Assessment as appropriate or inappropriate has to involve the confrontation of *different* ways of inhabiting our world and living affectively and effectively within it. The transformation of social imaginaries cannot be arbitrary or capricious. It must be capable of making sense to participants, in what Castoriadis would characterise as both codifying and affective ways.

Artistic interventions

For Castoriadis improved understanding of the world comes, then, from critical consideration of the images in terms of which we experience it. Autonomy requires us to both reflect on and expand our powers of imagining. For the writers discussed above, such reflection requires an engagement with social difference. However, we are frequently *unaware* of the images in terms of which we experience the world, and they are often unarticulated. In his philosophical writings Wittgenstein constantly draws our attention to the way in which philosophical problems often result from our being in the grip of a certain picture.[95] One way of addressing them is to make the picture with which we are working (the mind as inner, perhaps) explicit. Then it can be subjected to reflective scrutiny. This is not just the job of philosophers. It often takes the creative insights of artists to enable such awareness and to suggest alternative patterns of imagining.

Genevieve Lloyd draws our attention to a writer doing just this. Virginia Woolf,[96] in her talk to the Women's Service League in the early 1940s, identifies a pervasive image structuring our experience of the world, and, in her distinctive manner, the difficulties involved in shifting it.

> I discovered that if I was going to review books I should need to do battle with a certain phantom. I called her after the heroine of a famous poem, The Angel in the House. It was she who bothered me and wasted my time and so tormented me that at last I killed her ... – you may not know what I mean by the Angel in the House, I will describe her as shortly as I can. She was intensely sympathetic. She was immensely charming. She was utterly unselfish. She excelled in the difficult arts of family life. She sacrificed herself daily. If there was a chicken she took the leg; if there was a draught she sat in it ... above all – I need not say it – she was pure. When I came to write ... the shadow of her wings fell on my page ... she made as if to guide my pen ... whenever I felt the shadow of her wing or the radiance of her halo upon my page, I took the inkpot and flung it at her.[97]

It was part of Woolf's particular talent that she could articulate this image, which for many structures and inhibits their life without their being explicitly aware of it. Its articulation enables evaluation and rejection. She realised that such an image, of what is involved in being a woman, had to be destroyed if she was to become the kind of writer she aspired to be.

It was an image which also needed to be replaced, but its replacement was a difficult business. It required many people to envisage possibilities for their lives in new ways; ways that she thought were only just emerging: 'I mean, what is a woman ... that is one of the reasons I have come here – out of respect for you, who are in the process of showing by your experiments what a woman is'.[98] What it is to be a woman is not something that could be simply discovered. It is something that has to be imagined in a way that opens up and creates possibilities for agency in the world. But such imagining is not a fantasy; for a fantasy floats free of the world, whereas images of women must be able to take hold. They must make both cognitive and affective sense. It was just such images which emerged in the revolution Castoriadis described above; the advent (in Merleau-Ponty's term) of new imaginaries, emerging from the encounters of bodies and world, and previously instituted imaginaries.

Where Lloyd evokes Virginia Woolf, Gatens discusses the writing of George Eliot,[99] herself familiar with the works of Spinoza, but, unlike him, unequivocal in viewing the imagination as playing a central role in the development of knowledge. Gatens points out that Eliot thought it her duty to instruct and not merely entertain her readers, and contrasts 'powerful imagination' with 'the fictions of fancy'. Powerful imagination can 'create new combinations from a store of patient and meticulous ... observation ... imbued with affective force ... artistic representation a matter of re-visioning'.[100] 'Eliot conceived of her ... fiction ... as an ... agent ... in the revision of belief and in the promotion of more adequate understandings of the world within which we act and are acted upon.'[101] In pursuing this end she both makes explicit the imaginaries within which people are acting (Dorothea's invocation of St Teresa of Avila; Lydgate's imaginary of what makes a truly womanly woman), and traces out the damaging consequences these have in their lives. She also opens possibilities for other imaginaries and other modes of living which might have less damaging consequences.

The position which Gatens and Lloyd here allocate to writers in making explicit, evaluating and re-envisaging our imaginaries, Merleau-Ponty extends to politicians. He says:

> Neither art nor politics should consist of simply pleasing or flattering its audience. What they expect of the artist or the politician is that he draws them towards values ... which they will only later recognise [as their] own values. The public he aims at is not given; it is precisely the one his oeuvre will elicit.

And, of course, for him, it draws them by its evocation of an imaginary.[102] If we supplement Castoriadis' own insistence on reflective criticism with the writings of Gatens and Lloyd, then Habermas' criticisms seem misplaced. In insisting on the role of the imaginary within the social world we are not delivering ourselves to 'the originless creation of absolutely new and unique patterns ... a Being operating without reason'. Reason and the imaginary are not in opposition for Castoriadis. We do not remove ourselves from myths and fictions by stepping out from the imaginary into a world of objective facts ascertained by Reason. That itself is a myth which will not stand up to scrutiny. The imaginary for him, as for Kant and Merleau-Ponty, is that without which there would be no 'real' for us. This does not free us from the necessity of reflective scrutiny, but makes that task the more complex one of both articulating and re-envisioning the imaginaries which structure our social interactions.

Notes

1 Castoriadis, Cornelius, 1998 [1987], *The Imaginary Institution of Society*, trans. Kathleen Blamey, MIT Press, Cambridge MA; 1997, *The Castoriadis Reader*, ed./ trans. David Ames Curtis, Blackwell, Oxford; 1997, *World In Fragments: Writings on Politics, Society, Psychoanalysis, and the Imagination*, ed./trans. David Ames Curtis, Stanford University Press, Stanford CA; 1991, *Philosophy, Politics, Autonomy: Essays in Political Philosophy*, ed. David Ames Curtis, Oxford University Press, New York and Oxford; 1984, *Crossroads in the Labyrinth*, trans. M. H. Ryle and K. Soper, MIT Press, Cambridge MA; 1997, *Thesis Eleven*, special issue 'Cornelius Castoriadis', no. 49, May, Sage Publications, London.
2 McClintock, Anne, 1995, *Imperial Leather: Race, Gender, and Sexuality in the Colonial Contest*, Routledge, London and New York, p. 2.
3 Gatens, Moira, 2012, 'Compelling Fictions: Spinoza and George Eliot on Imagination and Belief', *European Journal of Philosophy* 20, no. 1, February, pp. 74–90.

4 Anderson, Benedict, 1983, *Imagined Communities*, Verso, London and New York.

5 For example Ernest Gellner, 1983, *Nations and Nationalism*, Oxford, Blackwell.

6 Ibid., 141.

7 Gilbert, Paul, 1998, *The Philosophy of Nationalism*, Westview Press, Oxford and Boulder CO.

8 Taylor, Charles, 2004, 'What is a "Social Imaginary"?' in *Modern Social Imaginaries*, Duke University Press, Durham NC, p. 23.

9 Castoriadis, Cornelius, 1994, 'Radical Imagination and the Social Instituting Imaginary', in Gillian Robinson and John F. Rundell, eds, *Rethinking Imagination*, Routledge, London and New York, p. 143.

10 Ibid., 140.

11 Ibid., 144.

12 Castoriadis, *World in Fragments* 353.

13 That is not anchored in prior desires.

14 Ibid., 351.

15 Lacan, Jacques, 2006 [1966], *Ecrits*, trans. Bruce Fink, Norton, New York.

16 Robinson and Rundell, *Rethinking Imagination* 146.

17 Ibid., 147.

18 Ibid., 147.

19 See discussion of desire in Chapter 4.

20 *Rethinking Imagination* 148.

21 Ibid., 149.

22 *World in Fragments* 15.

23 *The Imaginary Institution of Society* 154.

24 Ibid., 150.

25 Ibid., 125.

26 Ibid., 184.

27 Ibid., 189.

28 See discussion of this in McNay, Lois, 2000, *Gender and Agency*, Polity, Cambridge, ch. 4.

29 This relation of 'leaning on' has interesting implications for how we think about the inter-implication of explanatory relations at different levels of description. It is beyond the scope of this chapter to discuss them here.

30 Merleau-Ponty, Maurice, 2010, *Institution and Passivity*, trans. L. Lawlor and H. Massey, with a foreword by Claude Lefort, Northwestern University Press, Evanston IL.

31 Merleau-Ponty, Maurice, 1968, *The Visible and the Invisible*, trans. Alphonse Lingis, Northwestern University Press, Evanston IL.

32 Lefort, foreword to *Institution and Passivity* xv.

33 *Institution and Passivity* 6.

34 *The Visible and the Invisible* 32.

35 *The World in Fragments* 291–292.

36 Lefort, foreword to *Institution and Passivity* xi.

37 *Institution and Passivity* 11–12. See discussion in Diprose, Rosalyn, 2010, 'Review of Maurice Merleau-Ponty, Institution and Passivity: Course Notes From the Collège de France (1954–1955)', *Notre Dame Philosophical Reviews* 11.

38 *Institution and Passivity* 8.

39 Ibid., 6.

40 Ibid., 9.

41 Ibid., 49–50.

42 Ibid., 49–50.

43 Ibid., 15.

44 Ibid., 12.

45 *Rethinking Imagination*.

46 *Rethinking Imagination* 149.
47 *Imaginary Institution of Society* 145–146.
48 Ibid., 147.
49 *World in Fragments* 7.
50 *Imaginary Institution of Society* 124.
51 Ibid., 147.
52 Ibid., 124.
53 Ibid., 125.
54 Ibid., 128.
55 Marx, Karl, 1981 [1845], 'Theses on Feuerbach', in Lucio Colletti, ed., *Early Writings of Marx*, Penguin, London, pp. 421–423.
56 *Imaginary Institution of Society* 133.
57 *The Castoriadis Reader* 186.
58 Ibid., 149.
59 Taylor, 'What is a "Social Imaginary"?'.
60 *Thesis Eleven* 85.
61 Irigaray, Luce, 1993, *An Ethics of Sexual Difference*, trans. C. Burke and G. Gill, Cornell University Press, Ithaca NY.
62 Thompson, John, 1982, 'Ideology and the Social Imaginary', *Theory and Society* 11, no. 5, pp. 659–681.
63 McClintock, *Imperial Leather* 364–365.
64 Fanon, Franz, 1969, 'Algeria Unveiled', in *The New Left Reader*, ed. Carl Oglesby, Grove Press, New York. Available at: http://home.comcast.net/~platypus1848/fanonfrantz_algeriaunveiled1959.pdf.
65 For an indication of the complexities, subtleties and variety of the imaginaries which they can carry, see Pamuk, Orpam, 2004, *Snow*, trans. M. Freely, Faber and Faber, London.
66 Gaonkar, D. P., 2002, 'Towards New Imaginaries: An Introduction', *Public Culture* 14, no. 1, p. 17.
67 Gilbert, P., 2010, *Cultural Identity and Political Ethics*, Edinburgh University Press, Edinburgh, ch. 5.
68 Cohen, Antony, 1985, *The Symbolic Construction of Community*, Routledge, London, p. 14.
69 Ibid.
70 Derrida, Jacques, 1978, *Writing and Difference*, trans. Alan Bass, University of Chicago Press; Butler, Judith, *Gender Trouble*, Routledge, New York and London.
71 *Institution and Passivity* 11.
72 Habermas, Jürgen, 1987, *The Philosophical Discourse of Modernity*, trans. Frederick Lawrence, Polity, Cambridge, p. 318.
73 Ibid., 319.
74 Ibid., 321.
75 Ibid., 330.
76 Ibid., 335.
77 McNay, *Gender and Agency* 152.
78 *Rethinking Imagination* 153.
79 Ibid., 151.
80 *World in Fragments* 268.
81 Ibid., 270.
82 Ibid., 271.
83 *Imaginary Institution of Society* 148.
84 Ibid., 148.
85 See: Lloyd, G., 1998, 'Spinoza and the Education of the Imagination', in A. Rorty, ed., *Philosophers and Education*, Routledge, London, p. 162; and Spinoza, B., 1992, *Ethics*, trans. S. Shirley, Hackett, Indianapolis and Cambridge, p. 13.

86 Castoriadis, *Philosophy, Politics, Autonomy* 204–205.
87 This has been discussed particularly within standpoint epistemology, initially Marxist and then feminist. See L. Alcoff and E. Potter, eds, 1993, *Feminist Epistemologies*, Routledge, London and New York; and K. Lennon and M. Whitford, eds, 1994, *Knowing the Difference*, Routledge, London and New York.
88 Castoriadis, *Philosophy, Politics, Autonomy* 204–205.
89 Lloyd, Genevieve, 1996, *Spinoza and the Ethics*, Routledge, London and New York, p. 25.
90 Ibid., 76–77.
91 Gatens, M., 1996, *Imaginary Bodies: Ethics, Power and Corporeality*, Routledge, London and New York, pp. 136–141.
92 Gatens, Moira and Lloyd, Genevieve, 1999, *Collective Imaginings: Spinoza, Past and Present*, Routledge, London and New York, pp. 142–146.
93 Ibid., 26.
94 Ibid., 143.
95 Wittgenstein, Ludwig, 1968, *Philosophical Investigations*, trans. E. Anscombe, Blackwell, Oxford.
96 Lloyd, G., 1998, 'Spinoza and the Education of the Imagination', in A. Rorty, ed., *Philosophers on Education*, Routledge, London and New York.
97 Woolf, Virginia, 1961, 'Professions for Women', in *Death of a Moth and Other Essays*, Penguin, London, pp. 202–203.
98 Ibid., 204.
99 Gatens, 'Compelling Fictions'.
100 Ibid., 83.
101 Ibid., 86.
102 Merleau-Ponty, Maurice, 1993, 'Indirect Language and the Voices of Silence', in *The Merleau-Ponty Aesthetics Reader*, ed. Galen Johnson, Northwestern University Press, Evanston IL, pp. 110–111.

6   Imaginary selves

Thus far in this work, with the help of the key theorists, Kant, Sartre, Merleau-Ponty and Castoriadis, we have set up the apparatus of the imaginary as capturing the character of our everyday perceptions. Our world, including our social world, has a gestalt, interweaving the present and absent, echoing the past and the elsewhere, and holding out possibilities for the future. In the broad sense of the term, it is grasped as an *image*, with an affective salience, suggesting or requiring responses from us. Imaginaries are both encountered and modified in our ongoing, socially anchored interactions with the world and others. They are, in the terminology of the previous chapter, both instituted and instituting.

In this chapter and the next (in which we pay particular attention to the body), this framework will be utilised to explore the role the imaginary plays in the mutual constitution of ourselves and others. In this chapter we will explore the role of the imaginary in the formation of both individual and social selves. The latter will return us to some of the issues raised in the previous chapter. The case of social identities is one particularly important example of the way in which social imaginaries can be damaging or progressive. By looking at the role of the imaginary in the formation of such identities, and in challenging them, we are continuing the discussion of reflection and transformation, outlined in Part III of the previous chapter. Our sources in this chapter will primarily be the phenomenologists: Sartre, Merleau-Ponty, Beauvoir and Fanon; and a contemporary theorist giving a poststructuralist turn to Sartrean insights, Judith Butler.

Sartre's *personnages*

Sartre claimed his late biographical work on Flaubert, *The Family Idiot*,[1] as a sequel to his work *The Imaginary*.[2] In this work, as in his biographical work on Genet, *Saint Genet*,[3] he gives centre stage to the imaginary in the formation of the self. As we have seen in previous chapters, Sartre draws a sharp distinction between the real, primarily the spatial-temporal provider of unlimited sensory data to perception, and the imaginary, the irreal content posited by acts of imagining consciousness. But in the discussion of the self it is the *interplay* between these two which is central to the constitution of the self. For it is the imaginary of the self which governs the patterns of choices and projects, the performances which make up our 'real' lives; and it is the imaginaries in terms of which we experience others which mediate our relations to them. Moreover, our own imaginary selves are not here contrasted to 'real' selves, which might be available to introspection. Subjectively all that we encounter is our being-towards-the-world (self as *ipse*), an active, spontaneous self immersed in our projects. A unified conception of ourselves as an object (ego) can only be reached by an act of reflection in which we view ourselves as others might view us (we will return to this below), and detect a coherence or unity in our projects, a certain style, which itself can only be captured by invoking a character or personage;[4] something like an imagined role or ideal. Similarly the selves we attribute to others, which we also unify by such imaginary personages, cannot be trumped by their own authoritative access to an inner 'real' self which is unavailable to us. It can only confront their own imaginary of themselves, which may or may not conform to that in terms of which we interpret them.

Such an account unifies the range of examples which Sartre discusses from *The Imaginary* onwards. In *The Imaginary* the examples given are ones which are explicitly those of performance. Franconay,[5] the actor playing Hamlet;[6] and, in his play, the actor Kean[7] even when he leaves the stage, is still acting. In *Being and Nothingness* he gives us, most relevantly for our purposes, the example of the waiter.[8] Later we have Genet and Flaubert,[9] biographies in which the imaginary is given centre stage. Franconay has been discussed in previous chapters, so we will start with the waiter:

> Let us consider this waiter in a café. His movement is quick and forward, a little too precise, a little too rapid. He comes towards the patrons with a step a little too quick. He bends forward a little to eagerly ... finally there he returns, trying to imitate in his walk the inflexible stiffness of some kind of automaton while carrying his tray with the recklessness of a tightrope walker. All his behaviour seems to us a game. He is playing, he is amusing himself. But what is he playing ... he is playing at being a waiter in a café.[10]

He is playing because, 'from within' he is not a waiter 'as an inkwell is an inkwell'. But 'from within' he does not have some other 'real' self. For a being-for-itself does not have objective characteristics. Consequently I (as *ipse*) cannot be the waiter:

> I can only play at being him, that is imagine to myself that I am he ... as the actor is Hamlet ... aiming at myself as an imaginary café waiter through those gestures taken as an 'analogue'. Yet there is no doubt that I am, in a sense, a café waiter.[11]

From within, Sartre claims I am 'that divine absence of which Valery speaks'.[12] He extends the analysis to an account of myself as sad. Being sad is a making of myself sad. It is not a mode of being which is simply discovered: 'if I make myself sad, I must continue to make myself sad from beginning to end'.[13] And in this making I am informed by an imaginary of sadness. For Sartre it is only from the outside, myself as others would see me, or myself as an object of reflection in which I see myself as others see me, that I am a waiter (or, in a reversal of classical accounts, sad). We are, however, in bad faith if we treat the characteristics thus evident as constituting our *being* in the way an inkwell is constituted as an inkwell. For then we would miss the fact that our being a waiter is, in a key sense, a performance, and one we could choose to perform differently or not at all. In this performance we are aiming at an imaginary waiter, which provides an ideal which can never be fully realised. Similarly 'being sad ... is a value which I cannot realise; it stands as a regulative meaning of my sadness, not as its constitutive modality'.[14] The performance, governed by the imaginary, is not in opposition to the real here, but rather all it amounts to.

The framework which Sartre offers in *Being and Nothingness* is put to work in his biographical accounts of Genet and latterly Flaubert. In Sartre's recon-struction of Genet's early life he portrays him as a solitary and imaginative child, engaged in imaginary performances in which he is his own audience, with two favourite games of pilfering and saintliness. The pilfering occurs within the project of gaining desirable objects, by means of which he can play the more privileged child he desires (and thereby imagines) himself to be.[15] A crisis occurs, however, when he is confronted with a judgment from outside, from the adults around him, and learns what he is 'objectively'.[16] 'You are a thief' he is told. He is confronted with himself as a thief, and thereby a moral monster in the eyes of others. Here we have the conflict, which Sartre immortalised in *Being and Nothingness*, via the discussion of the look. We are caught listening at a door (absorbed in our own projects which make this necessary) and are seen by others and categorised as 'listeners at doors'.[17] Our own sense of our-selves enters into conflict with the verdict delivered by others and we struggle to make our own view prevail. In his work on Genet, Sartre comments that when things go well, we can prioritise our being for ourselves, from our being for others. Genet could then hang on to his imaginary of himself as saintly and a child who deserves desirable objects. But when things go badly the view of others gains priority and we accept the view of others and regard it as our nature or destiny. Genet would then accept the view that he is a thief.[18] Initially for Genet things went badly. Nonetheless, for Sartre, there always remains a tension, an *unrealisability*[19] between the subjective sense of self, with its sense of being the source of its projects, and the objective judgments from without. Genet resolves this tension by 'making himself a thief',[20] regaining subjectivity by adopting the imaginary of the other and performing in terms of it (the structure we encountered in the waiter). Later Genet himself described his thefts as 'poetic acts', creative ways of inhabiting the imaginary role of 'thief'. Instead of stealing because he was a thief (destiny), he now steals in order to be a thief.[21] 'He made himself become the Other,[22] which he already was for others',[23] a pattern which Sartre traces throughout his account of Genet's life. This is one way in which Genet regains subjectivity in the face of the clash of imaginaries which Sartre reports him as experiencing as a child. Later the priority of his own imaginary view is ensured by his *making himself a writer*, a creator of imaginary worlds, in which he attempts to control the responses of his audience by his writing, and thereby take control of their imaginary, in response to the way in which an imaginary from outside had been imposed onto him. What is important to note is that the conflict of imaginaries which Genet encounters, and which we will see below is central to the account Sartre offers of oppressive relations, is not answered by an appeal to a *deep inner self* which at least some of the imaginary selves cannot make sense of. For Sartre there was no real self with which Genet could confront his accusers, no 'deep' saintliness he could pose against the monster they presented.

The pattern which Sartre uncovers in his account of Genet's life is manifest again in his biography of Flaubert. The stages of Flaubert's life are marked by the imaginary *personnages* which are offered to him to inhabit. Initially these come from within the family, 'you would make an excellent actor'; and later from social imaginaries, including those found in literature, which are encountered at school. Sartre says that in this biography he was asking himself the question 'What was the imaginary social world of a dreamy bourgeoisie in 1848',[24] one who moves from actor to poet, and finally to the novelist and creator of *Madame Bovary*? The last of these shifts Sartre locates following a traumatic collapse in 1844, and it is the moment when he sees Flaubert as making an imaginary of his own, a *conversion*[25] from one imaginary to another, that allows him to surpass those he had previously adopted, and constitute his own personalisation. As was the case for Genet, by making himself a creator of imaginary worlds, an artist, a writer, he takes back control of the imaginaries gleaned from those surrounding him and offers imaginaries of his own creation. In creating Madame Bovary he is also creating himself. 'Madame Bovary, c'est moi', he famously claimed.

For Sartre the imaginary selves which govern our performative constitution of ourselves have some kind of unity or coherence. They can be organised in terms of some fundamental project or overarching ideal which is manifest in our choices over time. The original choice of myself in the world does not occur at a moment. Our whole life is the choice. It manifests itself in our patterns of empirical projects over our lives; but is the 'transcendent meaning'[26] of such projects. It is the imaginary, the ideal self, which frames the way in which these empirical choices present to us, and the light of this imaginary makes certain situations in the world light up for us in terms of possibilities. So the pregnancy of the world, its field of possibilities which appear to confront us, the values which seem to justify our responses, have their origin in the exercise of our freedom in the *positing* of an overarching imaginary ideal self. In contemporary thought the unity and coherence which Sartre requires for our imaginary selves has been replaced by a recognition of the multiple and sometimes conflicting imaginaries of ourselves which can take hold at different times of our lives and even simultaneously. Sartre did, however, allow that there could be radical shifts in this ideal (the conversions referred to above). His account gives a central role to a spontaneity which involves both choice and reflectivity. Although the imaginary selves, which frame the way the possibilities of the world show up for us, are commonly pre-reflective, they can be brought to reflective scrutiny. And they are subject to conversions in which we reflectively take an imaginary for ourselves.[27] Here there are links between his work and concerns which have been found in other writers we have discussed: Kant, Castoriadis, Habermas, Spinoza, McDowell, for whom a capacity for reflective evaluation is required for the autonomy they wish to make room for. The nature of this process, however, remains a point of contention between Sartre and Merleau-Ponty.

Sartre's account insists that our imaginary ideal self is *chosen*. In combination with his account of the imaginary as the surpassing and negation of the real, this can make our choice of self seem both unconstrained and unmotivated. Merleau-Ponty criticises him on just this account, and here we are back to the key disagreement between them which we highlighted in Chapter 3. As we saw there, for Merleau-Ponty, our freedom emerges as an *intelligible response* to a situation whose meaning and significance is encountered, rather than an exercise in transcendence. The imaginary of the self is a *dimension* within my experience of myself in the world. It is not an unconstrained and irreal ideal which I posit. But neither is it offered as a facticity to be observed. It is the invisible in the visible of body and world. He discusses our identities as middle class or working class:

> I am not conscious of being a worker or a bourgeois because I in fact sell my work or because I in fact show solidarity to the capitalist machine, and I certainly do not become a worker or a bourgeois the day that I commit to seeing history through the lens of class warfare. Rather 'I exist as a worker' or 'I exist as a bourgeois' first and this mode of communication with the world and society motivates both my revolutionary projects and my explicit judgments.[28]
>
> It is not because the day labourer has *decided* to become a revolutionary and consequently to confer a value upon his actual condition, but rather because he perceived concretely the synchronicity between his life and the lives of workers ... the commands issued by the so called agitators are immediately understood as if through some pre-established harmony and find complicity everywhere, because they crystallise *what is latent in the life* to all producers.[29]
>
> (my emphasis)

Our identifications must reflect our ways of experiencing the world, such that the identification *makes sense of* my mode of dealing with the world and society. My relation to my past is neither one of its determining the present, nor one of pure negation. The gestalt of myself, which involves my past and a possible future, is interwoven with a gestalt of the world which I cannot intelligibly ignore.[30]

However, despite Sartre's view that our imaginary selves are posited, he is nonetheless insistent that the past constitutes a facticity which must be accommodated. To pretend that we had a past different from the one we have had is one form of self-deception and bad faith. It would be incoherent for the waiter to imagine himself as Napoleon,[31] for this would require denying the facticity of past events. It is not only the facticity of the past which must be accommodated in this way, but features of the present situation. In his play *Les Sequestres d'Altona*, the protagonist Franz is enacting an imaginary world which requires the denial of not only past but also present events. It is illusory and ultimately self-destructive. He can maintain it only by keeping himself in a locked room and by the connivance of his visitors.[32] Freedom, then, is the choice of ends in terms of the past and present situation. Here Sartre and Merleau-Ponty seem very close. However, conversely,

> the past is what it is only in terms of the end chosen ... my past is pressing urgent and imperious, but its meanings and the orders it gives me I choose by the very project of my end ... Who shall decide whether that mystic crisis of my fifteenth year 'was' a pure accident of puberty or ... the first sign of a conversion? I myself, according to whether I shall decide – at twenty years of age, or thirty years – to be converted.[33]

The need to accommodate the facticity of the past, therefore, constrains imaginings but still leaves us freedom with regard to the shape we bestow on our past and future lives. It leaves the possibility of radical conversions in which the past is cast off, like the skin of a snake, and left behind.[34]

However, in his later autobiographical and literary writings, Sartre shows himself very aware of the constraints and motivations surrounding that 'choice'. As Rhiannon Goldthorpe makes clear,[35] Sartre, in these writings, is concerned with comprehending, understanding in the hermeneutic sense, the lives and thereby imaginary selves which he is outlining. In *Les Mots* he shows 'the opacity of childhood and through mediation of the family, of formative historical and socio-political pressures ... the child seeks selfhood by adopting the roles imposed on him by his adult milieu'.[36] In the portrayal of Genet, and particularly Flaubert, the personages in terms of which they conduct their lives are not only partially (causally) explained by their circumstances, but *made sense of* in terms of them. The choices made are *comprehensible* not only in terms of individual history but also in terms of the socio-historical circumstances and the pervasive social imaginaries.[37] He places Flaubert psychologically within the history of his family, where the relationship with an insufficiently loving mother and an authoritarian father play a key role in explaining the personages he finds available. To these conditions are added the socio-historical conditions he grows up in and the social imaginaries which are offered to him.[38] For this later Sartre this leaves room only for a certain *improvisation* in the claiming of subjectivity in the face of the objectifying gaze of others. Even in the case of their 'conversions', as Sartre reconstructs things, at moments of crises; the adoption of the identity of 'writer' is a way *of resolving conflicts* in their lives and circumstances. It is a possibility inherent in such circumstances, in a way which seems close to the picture offered by Merleau-Ponty. Moreover (to return to an earlier example), if my sadness is a performance of sadness, it is nonetheless one which I take to make sense in the context of my life, a context which requires/justifies sadness from me. It is this which makes it susceptible to reflective evaluation, both by myself and others. Here we seem to have moved from Sartre's imaginary self as an irreal ideal, and closer to Merleau-Ponty, for whom the imaginary of the self is a dimension of the experienced body/world. And conversely the workings of spontaneity stressed by Sartre find an echo in the openness and creativity Merleau-Ponty stresses in the way in which self and world are brought to expression.

For both writers our sense of self involves an imaginary and is interdependent with our imaginaries of others and our situation. Yet, despite the commonalities, there remain key differences between them. However anchored the imaginary becomes, for Sartre, even in his later writings, it remains an ideal which is posited by an act of imagining consciousness, pre-reflectively or as a consequence of reflection. A transcendent consciousness remains in a constituting relation to it. For Merleau-Ponty, the notion of constitution has been replaced by the instituted/instituting structure. This structure, as we discussed in Chapter 5, is conceived of as a process with non-determining sources which are both material and cultural, and in relation to which individual subjects and social groups are moments, always engaged in creative transition. The self, along with other aspects of the world, becomes a 'hollow' or 'fold' in being, which emerges from the complexity by means of which an imaginary finds expression. It does not rest on a transcendent and constituting consciousness.

Oppressive social imaginaries

In the previous chapter we drew attention to the way in which the imaginary both had its anchorage in an instituted and instituting social, and provided a way of experiencing the social world, including others. There are imaginaries at play not only in our individual relations with others but also in terms of the *social positioning* of ourselves and others, what are often called our social identities. Here we will look at Sartre's account and compare it to that offered by Beauvoir and Fanon, and more recently by Judith Butler.

What is important about Sartre's account is that he not only discusses the imaginaries *attaching* to social groups, but also articulates the way in which the imaginary is involved in the *formation* of such groups. In *Anti-Semite and Jew*[39] Sartre gives an account of the way in which the category 'Jew' is created from the imaginary of dominant groups in society. The Jew is imagined as *Other*, and attributed the characteristics which the dominant group wishes to dissociate from themselves. There is a double objectification involved in this. The normal gaze from another, attempting to fix our objective characteristics, is for Sartre reciprocal. We return the gaze to individual others in our turn. But in the case of the Jews (and later black people) there is an additional level. A whole group is imagined in ways which ensure a social positionality, from which they have *no power* to cast an objectifying eye back on the dominant group:

> the root of Jewish disquietude is the necessity imposed on the Jew of subjecting himself to endless self examination and finally of assuming a phantom personality, at once strange and familiar, that haunts him and which is nothing but himself – himself as others see him. You may say that this is the lot of all, that each of us has a character familiar to those close to us which we ourselves do not see. No doubt: this is the expression of our fundamental relation to the Other, but the Jew has a personality like the rest of us, and on top of that he is Jewish. It amounts to a doubling of the fundamental relationship with the Other.[40]

This structure of oppressive imaginaries which Sartre outlined is put to use and added to by both Beauvoir and Fanon in their characterisation of the lived experiences of respectively women, old people and black people. Although she does not use the term imaginaries, in *The Second Sex*[41] Beauvoir explores the 'myths' which are attached to women:

> it is always difficult to describe a myth; it does not lend itself to being grasped or defined; it haunts consciousness … the object fluctuates so much and is so contradictory that its unity is not at first discerned; Delilah and Judith, Aspasia and Lucretia, Pandora and Athena, woman is both Eve and the Virgin Mary. She is idol, a servant, source of life, power of darkness, she is the elementary silence of truth, she is artifice, gossip and lies; she is medicine woman and witch; she is man's prey; she is his downfall, she is everything he is not and wants to have, his negation and his raison d'etre.[42]

In this account woman is imagined as the Other to man, who is the One: 'He is the Subject; he is the Absolute. She is the Other.'[43] As with Sartre's description of the Jew, this is an othering additional to the reciprocal conflict, inherent for both writers, in the look of an individual other. Here there is no reciprocity, for power differences ensure that the imaginaries attached to women have been formed by men. One of the key elements of Beauvoir's characterisation of this process is her recognition of the way in which these social imaginaries of women are adopted by women themselves (cf. Genet, 'you are a thief'), yielding their own sense of identity, and structuring their sense of themselves and experiences of their body. Being a woman is experienced as a destiny, the content of which has its source outside of us. Such myths then frame the range of possibilities in terms of which women can conceive of their projects, can imagine their lives.

In her later work, *Old Age*,[44] Beauvoir also saw the way in which old age was imagined by others and this imaginary espoused by the self. This creates crises of identification for those who shift their sense of themselves as worker, mother, artist, etc. (all of which have imaginary content), to a sense of someone whose life is one of loss and decline, a burden to society. The structure of the One and the Other, found in her account of Woman, and Sartre's account of the Jew, is here applied to age, with the young occupying the position of the One and old people that of the Other:

> Old Age is particularly difficult to assume because we have always regarded it as something alien, a foreign species: … People have said to me 'so long as you feel young you are young' [but] this shows a complete misunderstanding of the complex truth of old age … within me is the Other – that is to say the person I am for the outsider, who is old; and that Other is myself.[45]

The Sartrean structure of an imaginary self grasped through the gaze of the other, and adopted by the self, is also used to devastating effect in the work of Franz Fanon, particularly in *Black Skins White Masks*. In the chapter 'The Lived Experience of the Black', he describes how, on his arrival in France, he discovers his blackness:

> 'Dirty nigger!' … I discovered myself as an object among other objects … the other fixes me, just like a dye is used to fix a chemical solution. It is not a question of the Black being black anymore, but rather of his being black opposite the White … we came to have to confront the white gaze … I was all at once responsible for my body, responsible for my race, for my ancestors … I ran an objective gaze over myself, discovering my blackness, my ethnic characteristics and then I was deafened by cannibalism, intellectual deficiency, fetishism, racial defects, slaveships, and above all, above all else, 'Sho good Banana.'[46]
>
> I can see in the white gaze that it is not a new man who is coming in, but a new type of man, a new kind – why a negro … Shame. Shame and self contempt.[47]

Anne McClintock describes a prevalent imaginary which attached to the working class in the nineteenth century, portrayed as 'childlike, irrational, regressive … the Irish, Jews, feminists, gays and lesbians, prostitutes, criminals, alcoholics, and the insane – who were collectively figured as racial deviants, atavistic throwbacks to a primitive moment in human prehistory', associated with 'biological images of disease and contagion' and consequently viewed as social outcasts refusing integration into society.[48] There are echoes here of contemporary imaginaries of 'benefit scroungers', placed in opposition to 'hard working families', and in contemporary uses of the term, imaginaries of 'chavs', to refer to working-class youths: chavs, as Owen Jones writes in a recent book, unremittingly portrayed as 'Thick. Violent. Criminal'.[49]

The application of Sartre's framework of the imaginary to oppressive social identities involves three key elements. First, the imaginaries are produced by the dominant group. Second they are adopted by the oppressed group. For Sartre, this makes the experience of oppression that of *alienation*. The alienated self conducts itself according to an imaginary dictated by the gaze of others, without being in a position to challenge and reciprocate that gaze.[50] Third, the imaginaries are in play, not only in the affective associations attached to social groups, but in the *formation* of these social categories. What constitutes membership of the category is that you are someone to whom that imaginary has been applied (by yourself or others). Sartre provides this account of both Jewish identity and Black identity.[51] He does not use it for class, which he considers an objective category fixed by positionality in an objective economic order. Fanon, with some caveats, utilises it for Black identity. Although Beauvoir adopts this view with regard to old age, she does not seem to accept the formative or productive claim for sexed difference. For her, imaginaries originating in the dominant male group provide the affective content of sexed difference, but as with Sartre on class, she views sexed categories as having objective anchorage. McClintock accepts the formative and productive claim for the ragbag of 'Irish, Jews, feminists, gays and lesbians, prostitutes, criminals, alcoholics, and the insane'; and Owen Jones, recently, for his category, 'chav'. To find an account of the formative role of the imaginary in relation to categories of sexed difference we must turn to the work of Judith Butler, and her reworking of the Sartrean imaginary within a poststructuralist framework.

Judith Butler: the performativity of identity

In the writings of Judith Butler on the workings of gendered identities[52] we find a modification of the Sartrean model of both individual and social identity. For Butler, as for Sartre, the self becomes constituted out of the performative acts of ourselves and others, governed by social ideals, images of – given her concern with gender – what it is to be male or female. The deeds or performances which serve to constitute our identities as gendered subjects range across the whole gamut of behaviour, decisions, desires and corporeal styles, which we associate with being male or female: clothes, ways of walking, occupations, reading, immersion in car or celebrity magazines, nights out with the 'girls' or 'lads'. The gendered performances in which we engage are performances in accordance with a *script*. This script derives from ideal images of masculinity and femininity pervasive within society. These are imaginary and unachievable, but nonetheless they form the reference points in relation to which we act. What counts as a performance of masculinity or femininity is highly contextual and the operative imaginaries can be very variable, socially, historically and for one person over the course of their life. Being governed by an imaginary of a good Irish Catholic mother will be different from that of a successful executive, or an attractive television presenter; although these may jostle within one person. Thus the performance of gender is interdependent with the performance of other aspects of our identity. As with Sartre the notion of performance invokes the actor on the stage. But if we think that invoking the actor on the stage suggests a distinction between the performed identity and the real identity of inner selves, this is not a distinction which either writer allows. The performance gives as much reality as selves contain. 'Gender', says Butler, 'is a kind of persistent impersonation that passes as the real.'[53] Our identities are formed from our performances and the performances of others towards us.

For Butler gendered performances are tied up with relations of power. As Beauvoir had clearly articulated, the imaginaries of male and female support the dominant position of men. Although there are a variety of ways in which gender can be performed, in different times and places, there are certain dominant ideals which reinforce the power of men, and heterosexual people, over others (for the imaginaries of gender are intertwined with the imaginaries of sexuality). Unlike Sartre and Beauvoir, for Butler, those privileged by certain imaginary forms are not viewed as those who form such imaginaries and then impose them on those less powerful. Butler shares with Foucault[54] a conception of power which is all pervasive, present in our everyday interactions as well as in institutional frameworks. The way in which imaginaries emerge is diffuse and variable. But they nonetheless enable the emergence and retention of social power relations.

Butler, crucially, sees the imaginary as being central to the *production* of our categories of sexed difference. The productivity which Sartre gives to the imaginary in relation to certain oppressive social identities anticipates the productivity of discourse in producing social categories which is explored in the work of Foucault,[55] and put to work by Butler in relation to sex and gender. For her the social categories of male and female, man and women, are not, as pervasively thought, a consequence of objective biological or other structures.[56] They derive from the attachment of imaginaries of masculinity and femininity to certain people. Being a girl or a boy, a man or a woman, is a matter of our own performances, and those of others towards us, being governed by imaginaries of masculinity or femininity. It is not a matter of biological shape. For our binary cultural imaginaries of the male and female govern our classification of biological bodies. The divisions into just two sexes is for Butler driven by a set of heterosexual imaginaries (imaginaries which privilege heterosexuality) which lead us to divide people into male and female.[57]

If it is imaginary significations that form our sexed categories, then it remains possible that we can extend the categories of male and female to bodies that currently would not be included,[58] the imaginaries transferable beyond their current usage. (This has clear application in the discussion of transgendering.) And indeed if our imaginaries are productive of binary sexed difference then imaginary significations might be changed so that there are not simply two sexed/gendered categories. These categories could disappear or be extended to multiple others. We will discuss the mechanism for such changes below, for they are envisaged not just for sex and gender but for other social identities whose formation rests on the imaginary in this way.

Conversions in social identities

In our discussions above we have seen that Sartre left open the possibilities of conversions in the imaginaries governing our individual sense of self; the past and future reconfigured to yield a new imaginary informing our everyday performances. What possibilities are left open at the level of the social identities he describes, identities which are imposed rather than chosen? In the previous chapter we discussed ways in which social imaginaries, often operating at a pre-reflective level, can be made evident and subject to change. Here we want to re-address this question in relation to oppressive social identities.

For Sartre, being Jewish is described as a situation. For Jewish people, recognising their Jewishness (which means their classification as Jewish with its accompanying social imaginary) is a recognition of a facticity, which cannot be ignored without bad faith. An inauthentic response to the situation, Sartre suggests, would be to flee from this identification and attempt to pass as non-Semitic. The authentic response is both to surpass these categorisations towards individual imaginaries not determined by them, and to work within these classifications, recognising the social divisions they engender, and defending the interests of Jewish people, either as French Jews or within the context of Zionism. That is to recognise that, although anchored in the imaginary, these social classifications exist, and the interests of those so classified need to be defended. Ultimately, he suggested, with the creation of a classless society, material social divisions will pass and with that the capacity of one group to impose its imaginary onto a constructed Other. Then both the anti-Semite, and the Jew they have created, will disappear. Changing imaginaries then requires changing the objective power relations which allowed such 'othering' to persist.

In his discussion of the oppressive social imaginary attached to 'the negro', which he discusses in 'Black Orpheus'[59] (an introduction to a collection of writings of black poetry in the French language, from the *négritude*[60] movement), Sartre also explores another mode of response. He also sees the 'the negro' as a construction of white European colonialism. However, the negative imaginaries attached to the category can, he acknowledges, be collectively reworked to provide a *positive* imaginary. Thus Sartre saw the poets whose work he was introducing as becoming conscious of themselves as black and invoking an *alternative* imaginary of such blackness, and often of Africa and other lands imagined as an origin of such identity: 'Africa, out of reach, an imaginary continent'.[61] Such consciousness he saw as a necessary step in countering the racist imaginaries of the white colonisers 'to present to them an exemplary image of their negritude'.[62] In this poetry the negative values attached to blackness are reversed:

> A poem by Césaire ... bursts and wheels around like a rocket, suns turning and exploding into new suns come out of it; it is a perpetual surpassing. The density of these words thrown into the air like stones from a volcano, is found in négritude, which is defined as being against Europe and civilisation.[63]

But it is important to note what, for him, the source of such a reversal can be. Although Sartre exhorts black people to turn inward to find the positive images they create, this is not the appeal to a deep inner self to counter the objectifying gaze of the white community. For him there is no such deep self, either at an individual or social level. At the social level the identity category is created, for Sartre, by the gaze of others. Although there is an appeal back to characteristics of the cultures of Africa for the process of re-imagining, these cultures are themselves imagined. The reworking of the imaginaries which have been used to delineate the group then derive from an *appropriation* and *improvisation* of (some of) the characteristics negatively assigned to them (irrationality, closeness to nature, childlikeness), a reversal of their negative value. But this mode of response, this 'anti racist racism',[64] as he calls it, like that of the authentic Jew above, is but a step in a movement towards a society in which, with the disappearance of power differentials, different types of human beings will also go. It is a dialectic move, required by the colonising gaze, but itself to be surpassed.

Fanon, in response to Sartre, describes his own embrace of the images offered by the négritude movement, what he terms 'a fairy like Negro culture' saluting him: 'At last I was being recognised. I was no longer nothing.'[65]

> My negritude is not a drop of lifeless water
> over the dead eye of the earth
> My negritude is neither a tower nor a cathedral
> It dives into the red flesh of the soil
> It dives into the scorching flesh of the sky.[66]

> *Yet there are some values that are mine alone ... the essence of the world was my asset. A relation of coexistence was being established between the world and me.*[67]

But he also recognised the dangers of the moves he had initially embraced. For, as Sartre had claimed, the positive imaginary being offered was, in many respects, a reversal in value of the clichés and stereotypes which had accompanied the racist gaze. It worked within categories created by that gaze. Irrationality, emotion, closeness to nature, childlikeness, naivety, good heartedness, 'a series of destructive cliches'. Fanon criticised Sartre for making this moment of re-imagining simply a necessary move in a dialectic set up by the white gaze. For as such it robbed black people of agency on their own behalf: 'there you have it. I am not the one who creates meaning for myself, but the meaning was already there, pre-existing'.[68] Sartre, he complains, makes négritude 'a mere minor moment',[69] a merely subjective countermove as we wait for the objective conditions which will enable the creation of a society without differences of power.

Beauvoir in *The Second Sex* suggests a different kind of response. Although she recognises that women are most commonly in social and material conditions that make this difficult, she nonetheless insists that, in certain circumstances, they can be brought to a reflective recognition that being 'woman' is a situation not a destiny. (A destiny is an acceptance of the imaginary of the dominant group so that it appears to us as our nature.) We do not have to pursue projects within the confines of the imaginary of what it is to be female. An alternative personage (in Sartre's term) can be adopted for the conduct of our lives: writer, political activist, etc. In her discussion in *Old Age*, escape from damaging imaginaries is again considered in terms of the adoption of alternative personages, independent of one's positioning as 'aged'. Here, though, there is a clearer recognition by Beauvoir that such resistance is possible only for a privileged few. Her anger now is directed at a society for failing to provide material conditions and respect for its old by means of which the damaging imaginaries attached to aging can be surpassed. For most can only adopt the personas of the elderly which are on offer, and like Genet playing at being a thief, make them their own only in the way they play the part.

Later commentators have noted, however, that the acceptance of social imaginaries often has the consequence that these other personages did not present themselves as possible *for women*, or for *the old*, for these other identities were imagined, socially, as *male*, or as *youthful*. To counter these damaging effects requires intervention at the level of the imaginary itself, to provide positive images of femaleness, of aging. This is the intervention which Sartre recognises for 'the negro'. And it has been adopted by many feminist writers, who not only make explicit damaging imaginaries of the female, as we saw with Virginia Woolf in the previous chapter, but are engaged in the creation of positive imaginaries to take their place.

For Sartre, as we have seen, though strategically important, the effectiveness of such moves was only possible with a change in relations of power, and with changes of power the coherence of the groupings, united by the dominant gaze, would dissolve. Jews and black people were united under the anti-Semitic or white gaze, and re-imaginings can be in danger of overlooking the diversity in these lives. Once the unity of the othering gaze has been removed it is not clear what is left to justify a collective grouping and collective imaginary. As Fanon says: 'Negro experience is ambiguous, for there is not *one* Negro, but *several* Negroes.'[70] Similar points have been made regarding the diversity within women's lives, which put any collective re-imaginings in danger of creating new hierarchies of 'the One' and 'the other'. Moreover, as both Sartre and, unwillingly, Fanon, pointed out, the positive identities offered by the négritude movement echo some of the stereotypes they were responding to. And similarly the positive versions of femininity offered by some strands of feminism can be in danger of echoing binary stereo typical differences between the male and the female. And this as a consequence of the groupings which are to be re-imagined being initially unified by the dominant gaze.

In these circumstances it is not clear that it is appropriate to seek for re-imaginings of these categories, rather than their dissolution and destabilisation. Judith Butler takes this latter path. As we noted above, Butler sees sexed categories as working in much the way that Sartre sees the working of raced social identities. The categories rest on imaginaries projected onto certain bodily characteristics; and given the variability of those bodily characteristics, what unifies the categories is that those bodies have certain imaginary content attached to them. She was alert to the difficulties, sketched above, which made the re-imagining of such categories, outside of the imaginaries which served to constitute the groupings, problematic. Butler's goal is therefore to destabilise the dominant imaginaries which shape our categories of male and female (and hetero- and homosexual) and thereby undermine the binary categorisation of sex and sexuality which she sees as resting on them.

For her, the opportunities for destabilisation rest on the *iterability* of meaning, which poststructuralist accounts have brought to our attention. Central to Derrida's[71] discussion of meaning is its temporal dimension. Whenever we use a word we are engaged in an act of citation. We are repeating a term and echoing its previous usages. Moreover, those previous usages carried within them the possibility of such repetition. This repeatability, *iterability*, does not produce stability of meaning; for repetition takes place at different times/places and contexts and these render the meanings of terms underdetermined and to some extent unpredictable. (There is much to consider here which lies outside the scope of this discussion.) Butler exploits this account in describing the operation of gender norms: 'the action of gender requires a performance that is repeated. This repetition is at once a re-enactment ... and re-experiencing',[72] but 'the norms are never stable ... let us remember that reiterations are never simply replicas of the same',[73] and in this lies the chance for dominant imaginaries to be subverted. Her most famous example here is that of the drag artist. Via a parodic or exaggerated form of gender enactment, ordinary gender identity is itself exposed as an effect of performance, and the apparently natural package of gender/sex/sexuality is pulled apart. The audience, aware that they are watching a body with certain physical characteristics, watch as an imaginary gender is produced which is at variance with it. Here we are reminded of Sartre's discussion of Franconay. As in that example, what is made evident in the theatrical performance illuminates the everyday one. What is made evident is the imaginary constitution of categories that have come to appear natural. Butler, however, recognises the unpredictability of such subversions. While the performance of drag may serve to unsettle naturalising views of gender, it may also involve a process of reinforcing and reconsolidating the imaginaries attached to the norms of masculinity and femininity. The indeterminacy renders the outcomes unpredictable.

'Wilful misrepresentation'

For neither Butler nor Sartre is it possible to counter the damaging nature of imaginary significations by reference to a real which they fail to capture. For there is no deep truth about the self or about social identities which such imaginaries are intended to capture. For Sartre the imaginaries in terms of which others respond to us are to be countered by imaginaries which we posit for ourselves. Where these concern social groupings constituted via the imaginary, the very coherence of the groupings dissolves when the imaginary gaze is removed, leaving no base for alternative collective positing. For Butler resistance rests on the destabilising of the imaginaries and thereby the destabilisation of the social groupings to whose formation they are central.

There are, however, certain kinds of responses to the existence of damaging social imaginaries, which have been found in the political movements which resist them, which claim that such imaginaries are *misrepresentations*; that the history/culture/social relations of the groups concerned simply cannot be made sense of within the imaginary forms which are offered for them. Fanon himself relates how he started his resistance by pointing out: 'I knew ... these claims were false. There was a myth of the negro which had to be destroyed at all cost. It was some time since a negro priest was a surprise. We had doctors, professors, statesmen.'[74] Memmi and Walzer[75] have both problematised an account of Jewish identity which views it as entirely composed of the projected imaginary of the anti-Semite. For them this ignores the distinctive social material and cultural histories of people, with ties which are more than, and distinct from, being the object of the anti-Semitic gaze; people with a sense of Jewishness deriving from 'a cultural and religious tradition ... collective habits of thought and behaviour'.[76] In the case of Jewish identity, Walzer argues that the imaginary projections of the anti-Semite are a manifestation of bad faith because they ignore/cannot make sense of, 'wilfully misrepresent' the world/history/culture of those they categorise. These arguments are also made by those opposing a range of imaginaries imposed on colonial subjects by colonising groups and by African-Americans responding to imaginaries bearing the legacy of slavery.[77] Similar moves have also been made in relation to sexed identities. The characteristics of both women and men, it has been argued, fail to fit into the myths of both masculinity and femininity which haunt our social arrangements. Actual characteristics of men and women reveal a diversity of features/abilities which reveal the myths concerned to also be wilful misrepresentations. Feminist groups began by stressing the achievements of women, the history of women writers, stateswomen, sportswomen, artists. They provided examples of women displaying physical and mental robustness. These lives are invoked to show up that the imaginaries concerned are fantasies, projections from the dominant groups to justify social exclusions.

How do such claims of misrepresentation relate to the approach to the imaginary found in the writers addressed in this chapter? The claim that imaginaries misrepresent the character of social groupings seems to require that these groups have an anchorage over and above their constituents being the bearers of the imaginary of the dominant group. So Jewishness is not simply co-instituted with the anti-Semite and their imaginary. In the discussion between Sartre and Merleau-Ponty considered above, Sartre responds to the requirement that imaginaries have a grounding, make sense of our situations, by requiring imaginaries to accommodate the facticities of the situation. Otherwise they are a manifestation of one kind of bad faith. It is just such facticities that are being drawn attention to in the accusations of 'wilful misrepresentation' above. But nonetheless, for Sartre, the dominant imaginary will only be changed by changes in power relations, and not by drawing attention to such facticities. And once this has happened then the category, based on the dominant imaginary, will dissolve. For Memmi and Walzer, however, the category has the kind of objective base which Sartre gives to class and is not dependent on the projections of the dominant group. The dissolution of that imaginary will not therefore lead to the dissolution of the category, but to a reconfiguraton of its imaginary content.

For Butler it is not possible to access 'facticities' outside of some imaginary formation. So the apparently 'factive' claims rehearsed above are not countering illusory imaginaries with facts, but competing imaginaries put in play within the social arena. She rejects Sartre's account in which imaginaries are the outcome of the activities of imagining consciousness. They are encountered and offered as scripts within the social world; but their existence and continuation rest on their ongoing performative enactment. Challenges can then come by alternative or destabilising performance (someone performatively enacting part of the script of femaleness while heading up a government, for example). But Butler has been subject to criticism for failing to allow cultural imaginaries to be constrained by a materiality with which they are in conversation.[78] For her the world, including the social world, appears to be a canvas for performative constitution, its externality recognised only in the infinite re-significations to which it remains open.[79]

Merleau-Ponty also insists that the real is only available to us in terms of its imaginary. And his position is that endorsed within the present work. In its application to the social this problematises a view in which social groupings are simply given objectively, with characteristics to be discovered. What are offered as facts only carry significance within the context of an imaginary shaping. So social groupings, class or Jewishness are not simply objective facts. Nonetheless he sees such shapes as ones which we creatively uncover, rather than posit, as in Sartre's picture, or simply performatively enact, as in Butler's. Imaginaries are latent within a public world, the imaginary shape of which has to *make sense of* our situations and invoke recognition from different positions within it. So to modify his quote from above: there are not 'workers' and the 'bourgeoisie' because people in fact sell work, or, in fact, show solidarity to the capitalist machine; and nor do 'workers' or 'a bourgeoisie' emerge the day that history becomes imagined through the lens of class warfare. Such imaginaries are legitimate if they 'crystallise *what is latent in the life* to all producers'.[80] So his position is one which has room for the kind of criticisms which opened this section, the claim that certain imaginaries are ones which the social world simply cannot support. And here he is in line with both Castoriadis and Gatens and Lloyd, discussed in the previous chapter, for whom imaginaries could be dismissed as fantasies, debilitating illusions. For Merleau-Ponty, nonetheless, the imaginaries of our world, including the social world, have an openness of the kind stressed in the writings of Butler and other poststructuralists. They are open to the play of difference which is at the heart of that account. So currently instituted social groupings are not fixed but open to alternative imaginary formation.

Re-imaginings

The circumstances invoked to criticise the 'wilful misrepresentation' of oppressive social imaginaries can also be used to provide an anchorage for different ways of imagining Jewish/black/female/aging identities. These, it is claimed, contra Sartre, are not simply reactive reversals of the damaging imaginaries projected from the 'One'. The social identities invoked are not, then, seen simply as reactive stepping stones to an ultimate humanism in which there will be no such social distinctions (as Sartre suggests). Fanon stresses, here in opposition to Sartre, that blackness will *not simply dissolve*, and therefore the question of how to live this blackness will remain an urgent one. For contemporary post-colonial writers such as Kathryn Gines, 'Race has come to represent a more positive category that encompasses a sense of membership and belonging, remembrance of struggle ... and endeavour towards new ideals'.[81] For her, 'collective memory' provides a way in which for black people or Jewish people 'their situation could be defined from within their community ... rather than externally'.[82] For bell hooks, for example, the skin of the man lying next to her, 'soot black like my granddaddy's skin', can evoke 'a world where we had a history ... a world where ... something wonderful might be a ripe tomato, found as we walked through the rows of daddy Jerry's garden'.[83] This attention to the historical roots of black Americans in a Southern rural world is not an act of 'passive nostalgia ... but a recognition that there were habits of being ... which we can re-enact'[84] to provide ways of re-imagining blackness in positive ways.

A sophisticated discussion of such re-imagining is found in the work of Luce Irigaray. She argues that 'the human race is divided into *two genres* ... What is important ... is defining the values of belonging to a sex specific genre'.[85] Irigaray, though locating much of her writing in conversation with psychoanalysis, employs a concept of the imaginary which differs from both Freud and Lacan. The imaginary, for her, is not always an unconscious structure, nor can it be disentangled from the symbolic. Her notion has similarities with that of Castoriadis in its interweaving of the cognitive and affective, and the conscious and the unconscious.[86] But her writing also has commonalities with Merleau-Ponty's discussion of the visible and the invisible, in the way she suggests that the imaginary framing of our modes of being in the world is sometimes not evident, but is latent in the public symbolic, in myth, in works of art and literature. And in her writings she aims to make this latent imaginary explicit en route to a re-imagining, particularly of the feminine. She makes a distinction between male and female imaginaries. The dominant imaginaries, for her, are masculine; they are anchored in typically male experiences of the world. Because of the pervasiveness of this male imaginary, women often experience themselves and the world in terms of it. She criticises dominant cultural imaginaries for being *phallogocentric*, for presenting women as the 'other' to the rational man of western thought, as the lack which forms the necessary and negative opposite to the plenitude of masculinity, matched with imaginary associations in which female bodies are experienced as chaotic, formless and threatening. For Irigaray 'the feminine finds itself defined as lack, deficiency. She functions as a hole, in the elaboration of imaginary and symbolic processes'.[87] Thus far she is in agreement with the account of the imaginaries attached to 'woman' offered by Beauvoir.

For Beauvoir our response to this situation is to posit imaginaries for ourselves which are independent of our status as women, to make our lives in spite of this formation. However, Irigaray offers the possibility of the development of new imaginaries *of* women which would not have this source. This, however, as we have noted, is not an easy or straightforward project. Changing imaginary salience is not subject simply to will or argument. As the imaginary remains the domain of affect, the modification of it requires the devising of alternative images which can be affectively engaging. As Margaret Whitford comments:

> There is no simple manageable way to leap to the outside, nor any possible way to situate oneself there that would result from the simple fact of being a woman ... she deliberately attempts to speak as a woman, from a non-existent place, which has to be created or invented as she goes along.[88]

It is in this context that she employs one of her most famous metaphors. If we look at women's bodies through the flat mirror of the male gaze and consequent masculine theorising, the distinctiveness of their sex can be viewed only as a hole, as an absence. But if we look at female bodies with the speculum (the curved mirror which can be used by women for self-examination), we detect the specificity of their sexuality and the plenitude of their sexual organs.[89]

Irigaray recognises what both Sartre and Merleau-Ponty had made clear. Transformation of the imaginary cannot come solely from correcting misrepresentations. Damaging imaginaries can be countered only with alternative imaginaries (here the imaginary of the hole replaced with that of plenitude). But we do not reach this alternative by simply invoking a real of women's bodies outside of imaginary formation. For her, as for both Sartre and Merleau-Ponty, the imaginary involves creativity. But her picture is much closer to that of Merleau-Ponty than to that of the positing consciousness of Sartre. The creative reworking of the category is anchored in our corporeal anchorage in a world; an interrelated body and world which is being brought to expression in alternative ways; but ways which remain accountable to a 'nature' which is being both discovered and invented. The plenitude of female sexuality was an imaginary which was created, but one which, for her, was latent within that body. Merleau-Ponty made clear that such creations are themselves only possible in the context of *previously instituted imaginaries* which they both echo and displace, and it is this picture which also informs Irigaray's practice.

But there are the dangers to re-imaginings of the kind exemplified by both hooks and Irigaray which both Sartre and Butler have articulated. One concern is that as such re-imaginings take place in the context of those they seek to displace, there is always the danger that they are simply a reversal, and thereby partial re-enactment, of these images (as discussed above). Second, both Sartre and Butler saw the content of the dominant imaginings as providing the boundaries for (in Sartre's case, at least some of) the categories. How then can the categories be retained and their content re-imagined independently of this oppressive structuring? Fanon insists 'blackness will *not simply dissolve*'; Irigaray that 'The human race is divided into *two genres*'. Both must view such categories as *required* if the complexity of the material and social world is to be expressed; and not view them as artefacts of imaginaries intertwined with power relations. But there is nothing in the picture which Merleau-Ponty offers us which would legitimise such confidence. And in this he seems right. What imaginary forms come to expression, and are found publicly recognisable and liveable, is left open by him. So there may be ways of imagining inter-subjective living which do not make use of binary sex differences; or which pay no attention to skin colour. But they will be reached by an engagement with, and displacement of, those instituted identities we currently encounter.

This chapter has explored the role of the imaginary in the formation of both individual and social identity. It has also considered how such identities are capable of reflective evaluation and change. As has been evident here, in the discussion of both raced and sexed identities, both individual and social identities work through imaginaries of the body. So it is that which our next and final chapter will address.

Notes

1 Sartre, J.-P., 1981, *The Family Idiot: Gustave Flaubert*, vols 1–3, trans. Carol Cosman, University of Chicago Press. I am indebted here to the discussion in Cumming, R. Denoon, 1992, *Phenomenology and Deconstruction, Volume Two: Method and Imagination*, University of Chicago Press, Chicago and London.

2 Sartre, J.-P., 2004, *The Imaginary: A Phenomenological Psychology of the Imagination*, trans. J. Webber, Routledge, London.

3 Sartre, J.-P., 1963, *Saint Genet, Actor and Martyr*, trans. B. Frechtman, Pantheon, New York.

4 *Personnage*, Sartre's word, is used to convey persona/role. See the discussion by Cumming, R. D., 1992, 'Role Playing: Sartre's Transformation of Husserl's Phenomenology', in C. Howells, ed., *The Cambridge Companion to Sartre*, Cambridge University Press. It is distinct from the person, the *ipse*, the subjective sense of self as immersed in its projects. For an instructive discussion of Sartre's developing conceptions of the self and the distinction between 'ipse' and 'ego' see: Goldthorpe, R., 1996, 'Sartre and the Self: Discontinuity or Continuity?' *American Catholic Philosophical Quarterly* LXX, no. 4, pp. 519–536.

5 Ibid.

6 *The Imaginary* 191.

7 Sartre J.-P., 1954, *Kean*, Schoenhof's Foreign Books, Cambridge MA.
8 Sartre J.-P., 1969, *Being and Nothingness*, trans. H. Barnes, Routledge, London, pp. 59–60.
9 *Saint Genet* and *The Family Idiot*.
10 *Being and Nothingness* 59.
11 *Being and Nothingness* 60. There is a complexity here. For Sartre I am a waiter only in the eyes of others, and for the *ipse* this is an unrealisable state (see 527). Between myself as *ipse* and myself as *ego* there is an irreconcilable gap. Nonetheless I can posit an imaginary self as waiter, an imaginary ideal towards which I direct my performance.
12 *Being and Nothingness* 60.
13 *Being and Nothingness* 61.
14 *Being and Nothingness* 61.
15 *Saint Genet* 10.
16 *Saint Genet* 18.
17 *Being and Nothingness* 277.
18 Sartre was writing this at the same time that Beauvoir was writing *The Second Sex* and offering such a pattern of acceptance in the lives of women.
19 The subject, in its mode as *for itself*, cannot integrate a sense of itself for others.
20 *Saint Genet* 49.
21 *Saint Genet* 69.
22 See the discussion in *Being and Nothingness*, 'The Existence of Others', and in *Saint Genet* 29–30.
23 *Saint Genet* 489.
24 Sartre, J.-P., 1969, 'Itinerary of a Thought', interview, *New Left Review*, no. 58 (November/December), pp. 52–53. See discussion in Barnes, H., 1981, *Sartre and Flaubert*, University of Chicago Press, Chicago and London.
25 Barnes, *Sartre and Flaubert*, ch. 4, 'The Turning Point'.
26 *Being and Nothingness* 564.
27 *Being and Nothingness* part 4, ch. 2.1, 'Existential Psychoanalysis'.
28 *Phenomenology of Perception* 468–469.
29 Ibid., 470–471.
30 '[The] motivated presence of the world [is] dismissed by Sartre'; Merleau-Ponty, M., 2010, *Institution and Passivity*, trans. L. Lawlor and H. Massey, Northwestern University Press, Evanston IL, p. 146.
31 Thanks to Paul Gilbert for this thought.
32 For an instructive discussion of this play see Goldthorpe, R., 1984, *Sartre: Literature and Theory*, Cambridge University Press, ch. 5.
33 *Being and Nothingness* 497–478.
34 *War Diaries*, discussed in Goldthorpe, 'Sartre and the Self', p. 532.
35 For a discussion of the way in which Sartre provides an account which gives an intelligible interweaving of these objective conditions with Flaubert's subjective lived experiences and imaginary projects, see Goldthorpe, R., 1992, 'Understanding the Committed Writer', in C. Howells, ed., *The Cambridge Companion to Sartre*, Cambridge University Press.
36 'Sartre and the Self' 533–534.
37 Ibid.
38 'Understanding the Committed Writer'.
39 Sartre, J.-P., 1948, *Anti-Semite and Jew*, trans. G. J. Becker, Schocken Books, New York.
40 *Anti-Semite and Jew* 78–79.
41 *The Second Sex*.
42 *The Second Sex* 166.
43 *The Second Sex* 6.

44 Beauvoir, S. de, 1972, *Old Age*, trans. P. O'Brian, Andre Deutsch, London.

45 *Old Age* 283.

46 Fanon, F., 2001, 'The Lived Experience of the Black', reprinted in R. Bernasconi, ed., *Race*, Blackwell, Oxford, pp. 185–186.

47 Ibid., 187–188.

48 McClintock, A., 1995, *Imperial Leather: Race, Gender, and Sexuality in the Colonial Contest*, Routledge, London and New York, pp. 42–43.

49 Jones, Owen, 2012, *Chavs: The Demonization of the Working Class*, Verso, London.

50 *Being and Nothingness* 523–528.

51 In recent work on slavery it has also been pointed out that the practices of slavery themselves produced a category of people grouped together by their supposed suitability for enslavement, a suitability derived from the imaginary of the slave-masters. As argued in the paper 'What Is Wrong with [R. M. Hare's Arguments Against] Slavery?' by Dr Nathaniel Coleman, Wednesday 16 October 2013, University of Hull, Institute of Applied Ethics.

52 Butler, J., 1990, *Gender Trouble: Feminism and the Subversion of Identity*, Routledge, New York and London.

53 *Gender Trouble* viii.

54 Foucault, M., 1980, *Power/Knowledge*, ed. C. Gordon, Harvester, London.

55 Foucault, M., 1978, *The History of Sexuality, Vol. 1: An Introduction*, Penguin, London.

56 *Gender Trouble* 16–25.

57 Fausto-Sterling, A., 1993, 'The Five Sexes: Why Male and Female Are Not Enough', *The Sciences* 33, no. 2, pp. 20–25.

58 Butler, J., 1993, 'The Lesbian Phallus and the Morphological Imaginary', *Bodies That Matter: On the Discursive Limits of Sex*, Routledge, London and New York, ch. 2. For Butler, then, the imaginary phallic position (masculinity) which carries with it authority and power is a position which bears no necessary relation to any particular bodily shape. It can be contested and appropriated by those whose bodies have not previously been thought of as able to carry its significance. The consequences follow not only for the phallic position, but for all imaginary significances which bodies carry. For further discussion see Chapter 7.

59 Sartre, J.-P., 2001, 'Black Orpheus', reprinted in R. Bernasconi, ed., *Race*, Blackwell, Oxford.

60 *Négritude* was a literary and political movement, developed by francophone black intellectuals, writers and politicians in France in the 1930s. It included the future Senegalese president Léopold Sédar Senghor, Martinican poet Aimé Césaire, and the Guianan Léon Damas. These writers endorsed a common black identity as a rejection of French colonial racism.

61 Sartre, 'Black Orpheus' 120.

62 Ibid., 119.

63 Ibid., 127.

64 Ibid., 137.

65 Fanon, 'The Lived Experience of the Black' 191.

66 Ibid., 191.

67 Ibid., 193.

68 Ibid., 196.

69 Ibid., 199.

70 Ibid., 198.

71 Derrida, J., 1979, *Writing and Difference*, trans. A. Bass, Routledge, London.

72 *Gender Trouble* 140.

73 Butler, J., 1993, *Bodies that Matter: On the Discursive Limits of Sex*, Routledge, London and New York, p. 226.

74 Ibid., 188.

75 Memmi, A., 1966, *The Liberation of the Jew*, trans. J. Hyun, Orion Press, New York; M. Walzer, preface to Sartre, *Anti-Semite and Jew*, 1995 edn, Schocken, New York.
76 Memmi quoted in Walzer, preface to Sartre, *Anti-Semite and Jew*, xxii.
77 Gines, K. T., 2003, 'Fanon and Sartre 50 Years Later: To Retain or Reject the Concept of Race', *Sartre Studies International* 9, no. 2, pp. 55–67.
78 Alaimo, S. and Hekman, S., eds, 2008, *Material Feminisms*, Indiana University Press, Bloomington.
79 Butler, *Bodies That Matter* 'Introduction'.
80 *Phenomenology of Perception* 468–469.
81 Gines, 'Fanon and Sartre 50 Years Later' 56.
82 Ibid., 58.
83 hooks, b., 1990, *Yearning: Race, Gender and Cultural Politics*, South End Press, Boston, p. 33.
84 Ibid.
85 Whitford, M., ed., 1992, *The Irigaray Reader*, Blackwell, Oxford, p. 32.
86 Whitford, M., 1991, *Luce Irigaray: Philosophy in the Feminine*, Routledge, London and New York.
87 Ibid., 66–67.
88 Ibid., 124–125.
89 Irigaray, Luce, 1985, *Speculum of the Other Woman*, trans. G. Gill, Cornell University Press, Ithaca NY.

7 Bodily imaginaries and the flesh of existence

In the discussion of imaginary selves in the previous chapter, remarkably little was said about the body. Sartre's picture starts with Franconay impersonating Chevalier, the body the vehicle of the imaginary, surpassed by the imagined persona. And, for Sartre, so it appears to remain. For both individual and social identities the body seems to serve only as the analogon on which consciousness bases its imagining. Yet, as Fanon pointed out, the blackness of the black body in the context of white society was not something that could be surpassed. And central to Beauvoir's account in *The Second Sex* was the impact the social imaginary of 'woman' had on the way individual women experienced/lived the particular contours and features of their *bodies*:

> Around the age of twelve or thirteen ... the crisis begins ... as her breasts and body hair develop ... she inspects herself ... with surprise mixed with horror ... the swelling of this ... hard core, appearing under each nipple ... this new growth under her arms, beneath her belly, metamorphoses her into an animal or alga.[1]

Contrasting that experience with those of many western young women today makes evident the way in which the imaginary informs our sense of our body. Beauvoir's description would not capture the way young western women experience their bodies now, although their experiences are often governed by imaginaries of an equally problematic sort. In contrast it is not so clear that the imaginaries of aging have shifted in a parallel way since Beauvoir wrote: 'we are obliged to live this old age we are incapable of realising. And in the first place we have to live it, experience it, in our bodies.'[2] And this is the experience of the body which she characterises:

> I loathe my appearance now: the eyebrows slipping down towards the eyes, the bags underneath, the excessive fullness of the cheeks, and that air of sadness around the mouth that wrinkles always bring ... when I look, I see my face as it was, attacked by the pox of time.[3]

> ... with horror I see the copper coloured blotches of old age appear upon my hands.[4]

In this chapter we turn to consider the relation between the body and the imaginary. It addresses two distinct issues. The first will be addressed in Part I. It considers the imaginaries we have *of* the body and the role these bodily imaginaries play in yielding: our sense of our own body; the expressive shape of the bodies of others; and the social positioning of bodies. This discussion is linked to that of the previous chapter. Our sense of our individual and social selves is a sense of those selves as embodied; imaginary selves involving imaginary bodies. In the second part of the chapter we consider the way in which our bodily, or in Merleau-Ponty's term, carnal, existence is implicated in *all* imaginary formations. Such carnal existence is both a condition of possibility of our imaginary world and itself has an imaginary co-instituted with the imaginary of the world.

Part I: bodily imaginaries

Sartre and the body

Sartre does, of course, pay great attention to the embodied nature of the self.[5] Our being in the world as consciousness was being body; and there was no question of a separate mind which *had* a body. The *for itself* with its perceiving and imagining acts of consciousness was a mode of embodiment; though an embodiment, it was continually in the process of transcending towards an imagined future. Nonetheless, there is an unease in Sartre's account, because the body which constitutes our self as *ego* is nonetheless a body to which we stand in an *alienated* relation. He draws a distinction between the *body as being-for-itself* and the *body as being-for-others*. The body as being-for-itself is not encountered as an object, but as that *by which* the subject senses, perceives and acts. Our eyes are *what see*, and any change in them is experienced as a disturbance in that seeing. This body is a point of view onto the world; a point of view onto which, from the subjectivity it enables, it is not possible to take a point of view. It is qua object, invisible to us. There is, also, however, our body as being-for-others. When we encounter the body of others it is an object for us. But it is not normally a thing (under the surgeon's knife it may approach this). We encounter the body as having a set of psychological characteristics. Bodies are expressive, they display anger or sadness, irritation or pride. And these expressive characteristics are not a sign of a hidden interiority, but are objective features open to view:

> These emotional manifestations or, more generally, the phenomena erroneously called the phenomena of expression, by no means indicate to us a hidden affection lived by some psychism which would be the immaterial object of the research of the psychologist. These frowns, this redness, this stammering, this slight trembling of the hands, these downcast looks ... these do not express anger; they are anger.[6]

But these characteristics are only detectable by taking the stance of the Other. For us to get a sense of our own bodies *as* objects, as having objective characteristics, as expressive, we have to imagine ourselves as a body-for-the-Other: 'the body-for-the-Other *is* the body-for-us, but inapprehensible and alienated'.[7] For Sartre between this objective view and the non-objective body for self there is an irreconcilable gap. They are ontologically different. In adopting the objective view we are necessarily standing in an alienated relation to our body, as something which is both our self and stands outside our self, '*a thing outside my subjectivity*'.[8]

> The experience of my alienation is made in and through affective structures such as, for example, *shyness* ... the shy person ... is vividly and consciously aware of his body not as it is for him, but as it is for the Other. This constant uneasiness, which is the apprehension of my body's alienation, is irremediable.[9]

It is instructive here to compare Sartre's account to that of Lacan. For Lacan also there is a radical disjuncture between the subjective sense of the body, with scraps of perceptions and sensations, and the body as a unified object, that we see reflected back in the mirror or in the gaze of others upon us. This reflected body is essential for Lacan if we are to have a sense of ourselves as a unified and coherent entity; but this unified body is an imaginary one; and for Lacan, as we have seen, the imaginary is necessarily illusory.[10] As we have seen (Chapter 4), the mirror stage is the stage of development in which a baby first sees itself in a mirror and becomes fixated with that image. For Lacan, however, the image with which the child identifies is something *outside itself*, an image or a reflection of itself back from another. This external object then becomes internalised as a sense of self. The *imaginary self*, which the child develops in this way, is, however, in a key sense fictional. It sits in tension with the body yielded by sensations, which is still fragmentary, in 'bits and pieces'.[11] In Butler's terms: 'Through the dynamics of projection and misrecognition ... Lacan establishes the morphology of the body as a psychically invested projection, an idealisation or "fiction" of the body'.[12] 'Imaginary relations locate the centre of the ego outside itself, in the externalised imago which confers and produces bodily contours.'[13] This recognition of our body as object, which, for Lacan, is a *misrecognition*, is not contrasted with a 'real' or inner self. For Lacan, as for Sartre, the subjective sense of the body yields no sense of it as a coherent unified object. Moreover, for Lacan, we can only move from the *imaginary*, illusory self, by embracing the symbolic order, which assigns us a public subject position. But this is never wholly successful. The imaginary stays in play and we remain in thrall to it.

Sartre mentions Lacan's account of the imaginary with approval (without endorsing the structuralism informing Lacan's account of the symbolic). The subjective sense of our body as a unified entity in the world is the body from the point of view of the Other. But it is not illusory. It is one of the features of our situation, and as with other aspects of facticity, to be recognised but surpassed in our projects. He says:

> even this disability from which I suffer ... I surpass towards my own projects ... I cannot be crippled without choosing myself as crippled. This means that I choose the way in which I constitute my disability (as 'unbearable', 'humiliating', 'to be hidden', ... 'an object of pride', 'the justification for my failures' etc.)[14]

Thus, for Sartre, the body which constitutes oneself as an object in the world is a body imagined from the point of view of others. It is a body from which we necessarily experience alienation. And it is a body which is to be accommodated but surpassed by our own imaginings as we project ourselves towards our future.

Corporeal schemas and body image

Sartre's account of our living our relation to our bodies, *as alienated*, can be viewed as one of the imaginaries which can inform our way of experiencing our body. As he pointed out it is revealed in shyness and embarrassment, and Katherine Morris has recently used it to illuminate awkwardness and clumsiness.[15] It can also be invoked in discussions of bodily objectification in the context of such things as cosmetic surgery.[16] But the only route out of alienation he offers is a *surpassing* of the body. What he does not seem to be able to offer, within his ontology, is the possibility of a non-alienated relation to the body, as a corporeality in the world. Is it possible to have a sense of ourselves as sensing and active which is also a sense of ourselves as a spatial-temporal object, available to the gaze of others, without that object being something from which our sensing and spontaneous self is separated by an irreconcilable gap? Here we will explore this possibility and consider how the imaginary might be involved.

For Freud 'the ego is first and foremost a bodily ego'.[17] Our sense of ourselves is a sense of a body and involves an awareness of that body as having a certain shape or form. In the sense of image that has emerged in the process of this book, it requires a body image. For Freud, as for Lacan, the contours of the body emerge by means of emotion and desire; the body takes shape for us by being invested with affect. For Freud, this has its root initially in proprioception, rather than in an encounter with an external reflection, but it also involves the touches of others, and their responses to us. Butler[18] gives a certain picture of what the imaginary body consists in and how it gets constituted, beginning with the work of Freud. She suggests that the materiality of our bodies only becomes available to us, through its psychic investment. It is not that an already structured anatomical body is invested with affective significance. Rather the body as experienced becomes formed or structured by being invested with affect. As Butler points out, in her discussion of Freud's account in 'On

Narcissism',[19] for Freud, the contours of the body are yielded by sensations of pain and pleasure. In a discussion of toothache he characterises the way in which the aching tooth is experienced as the phenomenologically dominant aspect of the body. 'Concentrated is his soul … in his molar's aching hole'. As Butler comments, libido is lavished on that bodily part: 'But in a significant sense, that body part does not exist for consciousness prior to that investiture.'[20] Later in *The Ego and the Id*[21] Freud points out both that the ego is formed as a bodily ego and that

> pain seems to play a part in the process … the way in which we gain new knowledge of our organs during painful illness is perhaps a model of the way by which, in general, we arrive at the idea of our own body.[22]

And Butler, in her discussions of Freud, stresses the way in which imaginary salience gives us access to bodily shape:

> what is meant by the imaginary construction of body parts? … it would not be possible to speak about a body part that precedes and gives rise to an idea, for it is the idea that emerges simultaneously with the phenomenologically accessible body.[23]
>
> It is no longer possible to take anatomy as a stable referent that is somehow valorised or signified by being subject to an imaginary schema. On the contrary *the very accessibility of the anatomy is in some sense dependent on this schema and coincident with it.*[24]

The body image, structured by affect (and thereby in the terms of our discussion in this book a bodily imaginary) is not simply coincident with the anatomical body, for certain aspects of the body have a salience, and other anatomical parts do not show up, in our body image. Some parts are more significant than others, linked to experiences of pleasure and pain, for example, or to the possibility of effective agency, and these determine the overall shape or form which the body is experienced as having. But the body image has not, in this Freudian account, derived from an *external* image, from which we experience alienation, although its formation is mediated through our encounters with others. Later psychoanalysts stress that this sense of bodily shape and form, the *corporeal or bodily schema*[25] as it is often called, is facilitated by the affective interactions we have with others. Schilder points out that 'The touches of others, the interest others take in the different parts of the body, will be of enormous importance in the development of the postural schema [as he calls it] of the body.'[26] (And this can have both positive and negative consequences, in a way we will return to below.) The interest which others take in different bits of our body, the bits which get named and pointed out and the bits which are never mentioned, all contribute to our sense of our bodily contours and the emotional significance which is invested in them. Schilder also points out the multiplicity of such body images/schemas:

> It is one of the inherent characteristics of our psychic life that we con-
> tinually change our images; we multiply them and make them appear dif-
> ferent ... We let [the postural model of the body] shrink playfully ... or we
> transform it into giants.

Each individual has 'an almost unlimited number of body images'.[27]

In these psychoanalytic accounts the bodily imaginary is that by which our
sense of embodiment emerges, the way in which it takes shape for us. Merleau-
Ponty also makes the notion of body image and corporeal schema central to the
account he offers of the lived experience of embodiment. His account of the
body has parallels with Sartre's, in stressing that the body for the subject is
intentional, directed, engaged. This body in the world is an intentional body,
apt for or engaged in projects, expressive of emotion and desire. The mode in
which our bodies inhabit the world is shown in habitual action. The body
simply responds appropriately to the world by means of activity, e.g. opening
doors, picking up objects, scratching our nose, typing, playing an instrument.[28]
However, for Merleau-Ponty, the awareness of our body as that by which our
projects are enacted *requires* some kind of awareness of our bodies as objects in
the world, not as a brute materiality, but as having a certain shape or form.
This *corporeal or postural schema* or *body image* is implicit in our habitual
actions and responses and makes them possible. For Merleau-Ponty body image
is a 'global awareness of my posture in the inter-sensory world, a form in
gestalt psychology's sense of the word'.[29] Such a schema is 'neither the simple
copy nor even the global awareness of the existing parts of the body',[30] but the
integration of these in relation to the organism's projects. What he has in mind
here is well illustrated in a passage from Iris Marion Young, citing one of Tillie
Olsen's short stories: 'describing a kitchen dance in which a farm woman cans
her tomatoes while mindful of the colicky baby she holds between her arm and
her hip'.[31] In order to draw a distinction between the body image for the subject and the anatomical or biological body, Merleau-Ponty focuses on cases of
phantom limbs, where a subject retains a body image and consequent habitual
dispositions even when the body as characterised by biology lacks the appropriate limb. (Having a breast removed, for example, can leave one repeatedly
attempting to rest one's arm in an empty space.) A danger here is that the
concept of body image can suggest something like an inner mental map or picture which we have of our bodies. This separates the image from that which it
is supposed to be an image of. It makes the image a mental representation of
the body. This is not the picture. For Merleau-Ponty, our body images are the
shapes we experience our bodies as having (interdependent with the shape we
experience in the world).

For Merleau-Ponty others play a central role in this process of developing a
corporeal schema, but *not* as reflecting back to us an image of our body as
object, from which our subjective sense of self is necessarily alienated. In his
account of 'The Child's Relation to Others', in *The Primacy of Perception*,[32] he
emphasises the importance to early formation of the self of the phenomena of

imitation, copying the bodily gestures of others, returning a smile with a smile. In this *pairing of my body with other bodies* emerges the corporeal schema which enables my responsiveness to others and a shared world: 'the other's intentions somehow play across my body, while my intentions play across his'.[33] Such coupling remains in play in adult life as the way in which the world is experienced plays across the bodies of ourselves and others. Others are needed, then, for us to derive a schema of our own bodies, including a sense of their expressive qualities (to which we will return). But what we do not have is a necessary gap between the body-for-self and body-for-others, which for Sartre are irreconcilable. These are interdependent, the sense of myself for others interwoven into my subjective sense of my bodily corporeality. When Merleau-Ponty discusses Lacan's mirror stage he accepts that there is an initial disjuncture between the prior sense of self and the picture reflected back from the mirror. It is difficult to identify my body *here* with the image *over there*. But for Merleau-Ponty (here following the psychologist Wallon[34]), the child does not sacrifice their prior bodily engagement for an identification with an external fiction. Rather the two schemas of the body gradually become integrated. Nonetheless Merleau-Ponty accepts the *possibility* of the alienated relation, which is so central to Sartre's account, 'others can tear me away from my own immediate inwardness',[35] but when things go well, the resulting resolution allows the child an expanded sense of their own body and that of others, which enables their own bodily expressiveness and their responsiveness to the expressiveness of others.

As Schilder pointed out, there is not just one single, bodily imaginary at work in our corporeal sense of self. The imaginary body formed from individual engagement with an environment and personal histories jostles with images found in our social environment. Given that particular bodies have individual histories, even when lived within shared social space, we can understand both shared bodily imaginaries and individual differences. These differences will be the result of particular familial and other emotional and desiring engagements which particular bodies have undergone and which inform the way in which they are experienced as significant.

Bodily expressions

It is the affectively laden corporeal schemas (bodily imaginaries), which yield our integrated awareness of the bodies of ourselves and others, which give expressiveness to the body. For Merleau-Ponty, as for Wittgenstein whose work on expression is remarkably parallel in this respect,[36] the body is experienced as having a certain form which carries affective salience. As we discussed in Chapter 4, what is involved in the process of perceiving bodily gestures is grasp of a certain kind of *gestalt*,[37] recognition of a certain kind of patterning of the body as that of fear, or joy or grief, a pattern individuated interdependently with the response it invites.

Expressive content is not physiology, physical features as captured by scientific categorisation, but *physiognomy*, 'face or form as an index of character'.[38] In opposition to accounts of expression which retain a dualism of the expression and what is expressed, as if what is expressed somehow lies behind its expression, both writers emphasise the direct availability of expressive content. Thus Wittgenstein (as we noted):

> consciousness in the face of another. Look into someone else's face and see the consciousness in it, and also a particular shade of consciousness. You see on it, in it, joy, indifference, interest, excitement, dullness etc.; the light in the face of another.[39]

Merleau-Ponty writes:

> The operation of expression ... does not simply leave ... a reminder; it makes the signification exist.[40] Faced with an angry or threatening gesture, I have no need, in order to understand it, to recall the feelings which I myself experienced when I used those gestures on my own account ... I do not see anger or a threatening attitude as a psychic fact hidden behind the gesture, I read anger in it. The gesture does not make me think of anger, it is anger itself.[41]

Bodily expressions are therefore public and observable, not hidden, though there are circumstances in which we might find them difficult to read, or we might be mistaken about them. This allows us to perceive resemblances across faces which are physiologically very different, and differences in faces, in different contexts, which may be physiologically similar. David Cockburn remarks:

> two faces that, in most contexts, would strike me as utterly different, suddenly come together in a way such that I want to say that I saw, in each of them, *just the same* reaction to a humorous remark or to a dreadful piece of news ... the same emotion can find a grip on radically different facial features.[42]

'Similar expression' takes faces together in a quite different way from 'similar anatomy'. The emotional characterisations, here, which often find expression in patterns of behaviour over time, have autonomy from the physiological ones, though requiring that physiology to have an anchorage.[43] Nonetheless these characterisations are teachable, learnable and projectable to new cases. So Merleau-Ponty says: 'Behaviours create significations that are transcendent in relation to the anatomical structure, and yet immanent to the behaviour as such, since behaviour can be taught and can be understood.'[44] The expressive significance, which is seen in the behaviour and yet takes us beyond it, is here reflecting a characteristic which for Merleau-Ponty marked all our perceptual encounters.[45] An expressive gesture has a gestalt, a movement across time in which a visible or positive presence carries with it expressive depth. Joy is not on the face in the same way as its lines and crevices, but it is not elsewhere either. It is made manifest in those lines.

The account of expression offered by Merleau-Ponty and Wittgenstein shares with that of Sartre a recognition that expressive content is public and available; the anger in the gesture. It is less clear, however, how, for Sartre, the imaginary is involved in the expressive shaping of the body. We have noted that, for him (Chapter 6), when I express sadness I am aiming at an imaginary ideal of sadness which informs my performance. But he also claims that my body for others is an expressive body. In line with the account Sartre offers of the expressive content of works of art (see Chapter 3), this seems to suggest that the body of others is experienced in the light of an imaginary content posited by the imagining consciousness, surpassing a physiology which serves as an analogon for it. The analogon, however, is one which suggests such an imagining. For Merleau-Ponty no such additional act of imaging consciousness is required. The expressive content is encountered, as the bison in the pictures in the cave.

We have noted in Chapter 4 that the expressiveness of the body is constituted by means of its requiring or suggesting responses from those who encounter it. What response is invited is part of the invisible which we perceive in the visible behaviour. So to grasp expressive content *as* expressive, we must be engaged. We cannot be detached, for our own responsiveness is required. Bodily expressions are acts of communication. Expression only takes place if it can be taken up, responded to by others. To see bodily gestures as expressions is to grasp them as invitations for a response. Consequently to recognise expressive content is to grasp how that expression is woven into a pattern of *inter-subjective* life. Expressions of pain or grief, for example, prompt responses of comfort and solicitude from others. Overgaard remarks: 'seeing another suffer ... is recognising ... something ought to be done'.[46] Without such recognition, the expressive content has not been perceived. As we have been at pains to point out, what is at issue here is a normative, rather than a causal, relation. Whether or not we do respond to the pain of another, in grasping that pain is what is being expressed, we grasp that certain kinds of responses are appropriate. Here, as in our previous discussions, the detection of the pattern, and the recognition of the responses it renders appropriate, are not two separate processes. Without grasp of responses which are appropriate, there would be no way in which the expressive shape could be grasped, for it is constituted interdependently with the responses it invites. For Merleau-Ponty the grasping of such bodily gestalts depends on just the reciprocity between other bodies and our own described above. My body takes a responsive shape during my interactions with others and the shape it takes reveals the expressive content the body I am encountering has for me. As he points out:

> I do not understand the gestures of others through an act of intellectual interpretation ... I join with it in a sort of blind recognition.[47] The sense of gestures is not given, but rather understood, which is to say taken up by an

act of the spectator. The entire difficulty is to understand this act properly and not confuse it with an epistemic operation. Communication or the understanding of gestures is achieved through the reciprocity between my intentions and the other person's gestures and between my gestures and the intentions which can be read in the other person's behaviour ... The gesture is in front of me like a question ... and invites me to join it.[48]

Grasping a gesture as expressive is therefore to be distinguished from a mere description of it in which we are not implicated. It is to immediately recognise the call to my own body.

The reciprocal nature of our expressive perception allows, nonetheless, for the possibility that we might recognise that someone is expressing something we cannot grasp. A central fact in our relations with others is the extent to which they can elude our comprehension, confront us with a subjectivity which is always other to our own.[49] There are times when others remain quite opaque to us. We are not able to read their expressions and consequently find our feet with them. Expressions can be ambiguous, and our perceptions of them open to revision and re-evaluation. There are situations in which our inter-subjective practices simply cannot get off the ground. However, inference to something supposedly lying behind the expressions will not help. What is necessary is to be able to *imagine* the gestures in a certain way; a way that makes their position in the life of the subject, and ourselves, clear. Failing to understand others is not, then, a failure to form mental images of their inner life. It is a failure of sensitivity to the forms their bodies and world bear for them.

Bodily imaginaries and social identities

What emerges from the account of corporeal schema/body image, derived both from psychoanalytic sources and from Merleau-Ponty, is a notion of body imaginaries as modes of experiencing our own bodies and those of others as having shape or form, marked by an affective texture. It is such bodily imaginaries which then inform and enable our expressive and intentional interactions with others and our environment. Such a framework also seems required if we are to provide an adequate phenomenological account of the social identities discussed in the previous chapter. For in Beauvoir's account of the lived experience of women, and of old age, and in Fanon's account of the 'Lived Experience of the Black',[50] the body plays a much more pivotal role than can be accommodated by regarding it as simply the surface onto which acts of imagining are projected and resisted (where power relations make this possible) by competing imaginaries projected back. The discussion of bodily expressiveness made clear that our lived experience of our bodies is in terms of the (myriad) imaginaries which they express for ourselves and others. These imaginaries yield the shape and significant features which our bodies are experienced as having. What is evident once we address issues of what Alcoff calls *visible social identities*[51] is that we experience our bodies and those of others *as expressive* of *social positionality*. We become aware of certain physiological features in terms of their social imaginary significance, in the same way that we become aware of our bodily physiognomies in terms of the emotions they express. We perceive/experience certain bodily shapes directly as requiring/suggesting responses of our own or others. The phenomenology here is crucial. There is no two-stage process by which we detect a materiality and infer to a salience or social significance, or go through a process of interpretation to assign such significance. Rather the significance is part of our *immediate experience* of the bodies of others and ourselves. These social relations give shape to our corporeality.

Fanon explicitly employs the notion of corporeal schemas when he describes arriving in France, to find his prior corporal schema (which had been developed as he grew up, and which facilitated his expressive and intentional engagement in his world and community) crumble, in the face of the overwhelming significance of his blackness. This bodily feature, as he points out to Sartre, could never, thereafter, in white society, not be a key part of his body image.[52] Audre Lorde recounts a childhood memory which has the same structure:

> The AA subway train to Harlem. I clutch my mother's sleeve, her arms full of shopping bags, Christmas heavy. The wet smell of winter clothes, the train's lurching. My mother spots an almost seat, pushes my little snow-suited body down. On one side of me a man reading a paper. On the other, a woman in a fur hat staring at me. Her mouth twitches as she stares and then her gaze drops down, pulling mine with it. Her leather gloved hand plucks at the line where my blue snow-pants and her sleek fur coat meet. She jerks her coat closer to her. I look. I do not see whatever terrible thing she is seeing on the seat between us – probably a roach. But she has communicated her horror to me. It must be something very bad from the way she is looking, so I pull my snowsuit away from it too. When I look up the woman is still staring at me, her nose holes and eyes huge. And suddenly I realise that there is nothing crawling up the seat between us; it is me she doesn't want her coat to touch.[53]

Here her comforting sense of her body, pressed up against her mother with Christmas-heavy bags, becomes transformed by the horror she invokes in the women next to her; engendering the severe disjuncture between prior body image and the social salience the body is taken to have.

For Alcoff, visible identities[54] are those in which our mode of experiencing the bodies of ourselves and others is as expressive bodily forms, in relation to which the position of those bodies within sets of social practices becomes immediately evident. This is true of sexed identities, 'raced' identities, which are anchored in material bodily features, identity categories surrounding many disabilities, and as Beauvoir has made clear, the identity category of old age. Alcoff quotes from Richard Rodriguez's book *Days of Obligation*:

> I used to stare at the Indian in the mirror. The wide nostrils ... the thick lips ... Such a long face – such a long nose – sculpted by indifferent, blunt thumbs, and of such common clay. No one in my family had a face as dark or as Indian as mine. *My face could not portray the ambition I brought to it.*[55]
>
> (my emphasis)

Ambition is something expressible in a body of a different kind, and the face he looks at points to a positioning at odds with what he desires. The horror which Beauvoir describes on encountering her old face in the mirror is a horror at what such features express in terms of social positionality; what is expressed again in tension with the position she desires to occupy. For the transsexual man the female body he finds himself with expresses a social positionality, to himself and others, which conflicts with the only one he feels able to occupy. It is important to remind ourselves of the multiplicity of expressive possibilities and of the way that expressive content is dependent on background and context. They are, nonetheless, possibilities which are carried by the way the body's imaginary form is found within our perception of it. And it is just this feature which makes such imaginaries difficult to dislodge.

In the Sartrean picture the imaginary selves projected by others onto our bodies are part of a facticity to be surpassed by the pursuit of our own imaginary personas. For Beauvoir we also transcend the apparent destiny which our body appears to express, in the pursuit of projects, as writers, as activists, as teachers, *in despite of* the imaginaries which our bodies carry as female, or as aging. But neither of these options provides the possibility of developing a sense of our corporeality with which we can make an accommodation. Yet living with a corporeality which expresses a social positionality which we find unliveable is an alienation of an additional order to the one Sartre sees as marking each of our relations to our body. For the pursuit of projects *despite* modes of social embodiment, in the context of an inter-corporeality in which our bodily features are experienced *also by ourselves* as laying out certain possibilities for us, is very difficult. As a transsexual man it is not sufficient to pursue the projects and sets of social interactions which men engage in, surpassing the female bodily form, for projects informed by an imaginary of oneself as male. For these projects and interactions commonly *require a body which expresses to oneself and others the positionality which is aspired to*. It is also this which explains the popularity of skin whitening creams and bodily surgery to modify visible bodily features structured by the imaginaries of race or age.

Reconfiguration is not a matter of simply separating a bodily form and imaginary salience. For, as has become clear from the discussion of bodily emotions, such bodily forms come into view as the bearers of such salience. (Could we prise off the joyfulness from the very physiology of a smile?) The imaginary form is the way the body has taken shape for us and not simply a projection we have associated with a body already shaped. It is hard to make sense, for example, of the transsexual demand for sexed *embodiment* and the widespread demand for surgical bodily modification of many kinds, if these kinds of bodily alienation could be resolved by an appropriation to the bodies we possess, of an imaginary sig-nification normally associated with a body of a different anatomical shape.[56] On the account offered here, embodied imaginary or expressive content is something to which we have a certain kind of perceptual sensitivity. It consists in our being able to experience others in certain ways, which immediately ground our responses to them and position them in social practices. Such pat-terns of sedimented and habitual perception commonly operate below the level of belief and are difficult to dislodge by explicit reflection. Our habits of per-ception, together with other embodied practices, are interwoven with the workings of power, a power that can be at its most insidious when conditioning the way we experience our own bodies. The basic problem seems to remain even while we recognise that there is no single imaginary that bodily contours yield, but a raft of intersecting, contrasting and sometimes conflicting ones.

Alcoff remarks that 'perceptual practices are dynamic even when congealed into habit'.[57] Given the damaging nature of many of our interwoven personal and social imaginaries it is important to consider how bodies can be experi-enced in different ways, so that we can return to that snow-suited body the sense of her bodily self comfortably integrated with her mother's Christmas-heavy form. Any such re-imagining will involve altering the perceptual sensi-tivity which we have to our own bodies and the bodies of others, a modification which goes hand in hand with change in the sets of inter-subjective interactions which it is possible for us to engage in. If we go back to bodily expressions, we cannot retain the bodily morphologies which are expressive of pain and simply re-imagine them as expressive of joy. We rather have to learn to perceive dif-ferent patterns of significance in the bodies we encounter. Living with someone whose facial muscles have suffered paralysis, we may at first be unable to detect emotion in this face; or may respond to it as though it is expressing some untold terror. Living closely alongside such a face, however, we come to grasp what range of movement there is, as expressive of pain or joy. We come to perceive a physiognomy which is continuous with our perception of joy in physically very diverse faces. Here it is not that we experience the very facial features initially experienced as expressing terror, and re-inscribe them. The way the face is experienced by us comes to take a different shape, one in which the flicker of the eyelashes or the movement of one side of the mouth becomes the salient feature. And this is what is needed for bodies presently expressing damaging imaginaries of sex, (dis)ability or age. It is partly what Irigaray (see the discussion in Chapter 6) was attempting with her re-articulations of the female body. This was to enable such a body to be experienced in terms of a different bodily schema which enabled different kinds of pleasure. In a parallel way we need to re-imagine bodies, currently marked as aging, as shaped for possibilities of interactions with the world and others, and not simply expres-sive of decline and dependence. (And consequently, as noted in the previous chapter, given that the boundaries of the categories are given with the imagin-ary, a unitary category of the old might dissolve.) As we pointed out in previous chapters, the changing of imaginaries is a creative act, requiring the instituted/

instituting structure which Merleau-Ponty outlined, the processes of destabilisation described by Butler, and the contagious recognition spelt out in Kant's third *Critique*. Our imaginaries of the body, of course, intersect with our imaginaries of the world in the ways which we have made clear, and to re-imagine our bodies is to re-imagine possibilities for our inter-subjective practices in relation to a shared social world.

Part II: the flesh

We now turn from the imaginaries *of* the body to consider ways in which our bodily existence is implicated in *all* imaginary formations.

For Kant the art of the imagination, the art hidden in the depths of the human soul, was seen as a transcendental condition of the possibility of synthesis and thereby of perceptual experience. As became clear in the schematism, this art of imagination involved both spontaneity and passivity, even for the application of the categories, in a way that became clarified in the *Critique of Judgement*. For Merleau-Ponty in the *Phenomenology of Perception* it is our bodily manipulations that give shape to the world. But in his later work he was critical of this notion of bodily synthesis for still carrying an implicit division between subject and world. In this later work the central feature of our being-in-the-world was the fact that we *can bring the world to expression*. Through our (collective) responses to the world we are able to both create and discover a shape to it which we can make manifest and communicate. And this possibility rests on our carnal presence in the world, a presence he articulates in his later work (in *Eye and Mind*, but most importantly in *The Visible and Invisible*) by the notion of *the flesh*. It is that notion which we will try to clarify here.

Sartre also discusses the flesh in *Being and Nothingness* when characterising the different modes of being of the body. For him, the flesh is the body in its mode of materiality, as a thing. In certain experiences – pain, the feeling of nausea – we are confronted with the fleshiness of our existence, its being-in-itself, which for Sartre is a level of being which is incompatible with our sense of ourselves as a consciousness being-for-itself. Flesh for Sartre is 'the pure contingency of presence',[58] the mere *thisness* of material existence, an isolated object 'having purely external relations with other thises'.[59] Nausea is 'the non-thetic apprehension of [this] contingency'.[60] This is a contingency which can be 'surpassed by a transcendence which does not have to exist it'.[61] There is both a phenomenological and ontological dimension to this discussion. The phenomenological account characterises our mode of awareness of our bodies in nausea and pain. For Sartre this experience signals the different ontological levels of the body, which for him cannot co-exist. These different ontological levels are also manifest in the phenomena of the double sensation, in the fact that we can both touch and be touched. But for Sartre the touched and the touching necessarily pass each other by, as revealing distinct modes of our being in the world.

Sartre also discusses the flesh in the context of the (initially erotic) caress. The caress is one of the dimensions of our sexual relations. Our awareness of the corporeality of our existence is brought about by the caress of another; and although Sartre describes this as our being brought back to a passive materiality, the discussion here is more complex. I am *shaped* by the other's body as I also shape it: 'my caresses cause my flesh to be born for me in so far as it is for the Other, flesh causing her to be born as flesh'.[62] Here the thought is very close to that of Schilder's account (considered above) of our bodily schema being born under the touches of others. It is a body as affectively shaped that the erotic caress engenders, rather than the brute contingency of presence which might be suggested by the previous quotes. For Sartre this mutual shaping is the expression of desire: 'Desire is expressed by the caress as thought is by language.'[63] This desiring relation is found also in our encounters with the world:

> [as] flesh ... I apprehend the objects in the world ... to perceive an object when I am in a desiring relation to it is to caress myself with it ... In my desiring perception I discover something like the flesh of objects. My shirt rubs against my skin and I feel it ... the warmth of air, the breath of wind, the rays of sunshine etc.; are all ... revealing my flesh by means of their flesh, ... the ensnarement of a body by the world.[64]

He points out in a footnote that, of course, the relations can be 'anti-caresses': objects can appear with 'a rudeness, a cacophony, a harshness, which is unbearable'.[65] For Sartre the desiring relation to Others is a primitive mode of relation and as desire it is doomed to failure. For the Other is not pure flesh but a surpassing consciousness and what ensues is conflict in which each tries to use the other instrumentally. (We will not discuss this here.) Nonetheless in his *phenomenology* of the caress he suggests an inter-corporeality, and a relation between bodies, and between body and world, of a different kind.

When Merleau-Ponty turns to a discussion of the flesh, the mutual shaping of body and body and body and world remains central. It is what makes possible the miracle of expression, and thereby the imaginaries of bodies and worlds which we have been unpacking. For him there is not a conflict of levels between sensing and being sensed, passivity and spontaneity. Rather the mutual shaping of body and world requires that we are, in his terms, *sensible-sentients*, that 'my eyes which see, my hands which touch, can also be seen and touched'.[66] And, indeed, it is just this which enables the body to take up the textures of the world and the world to have textures for it. I am capable of feeling the 'textures of the sleek and the rough' and am unable to answer whether such textures are commanded by things or by my touch. As with Sartre there are both phenomenological and ontological elements in Merleau-Ponty's account of the flesh. The reciprocity of the touch, so that we are aware both of touching and of being touched, is also carried, for him, by other sensory modalities; so that our seeing is phenomenologically haunted by the possibility of being seen. There is always a gap, the touch never coincident with the touching or the seeing with the being seen. They are nevertheless aspects of a mode of being in the world which necessarily encompasses both. Only something perceptible is able to perceive, making:

> a vibration of my skin become the sleek and the rough, ... [I] follow with my eyes the movements and contours of the things themselves ... this pact between them and me according to which I lend them my body in order that they inscribe upon it and give me their resemblance, this fold.[67]

(He approvingly quotes Heidegger: 'This velvet, this silk, are under my fingers a certain manner of resisting them, and of yielding to them, a rough sleek rasping power which respond for an X spot of my flesh, lend themselves to its movement of muscled flesh, or tempt it in its inertia'.[68])

Merleau-Ponty's ontology of the Flesh is an ontology which makes possible the phenomenology he describes. It provides him with the metaphysical underpinning whereby the affective relation between the world and our bodies, which we have been concerned with in this book, has the logic of internal relations. The Flesh is not that which we surpass by the spontaneity of consciousness, but is Being itself of which we are one of the differentiations. 'Flesh itself, the term at which Merleau-Ponty arrived to replace Substance, Matter, or Life as the name of Being.'[69] Our relation to the world is not as to a situation to which we respond, 'but as a kind of "chiasm", an "interweaving" or "interlacing" of threads in a single fabric'.[70] He says in a late note in *The Visible and the Invisible*:

> *Flesh of the world* ... we are already *in* the being thus described ... we *are of it*, ... between it and us there is *Einfuhlung*.[71] ... That means that my body is made of the same stuff of the world (it is perceived) and moreover that this flesh of my body is shared by the world, the world reflects it, encroaches on it and it encroaches on the world (the felt [*senti*] at the same time the culmination of subjectivity and the culmination of materiality), they are in a relation of transgression or of overlapping.[72]

This is not a reduction of the sensing and the sensible to a unitary sameness. It requires, rather than eliminates, difference and differentiation. It is rather that subjectivity, rather than a 'hole' in being, as suggested by Sartre, becomes a 'fold', a 'hollow', one of the differentiations of the anonymous being which is Flesh.

Notes

1 Beauvoir, S. de, 2010, *The Second Sex*, trans. C. Borde and S. Malovany-Chevallier, Vintage, London, p. 331.
2 Beauvoir, S. de, 1972, *Old Age*, trans. P. O'Brian, Andre Deutsch, London, p. 291.
3 Beauvoir, S. de, 1965, *The Force of Circumstances*, trans. R. Howard, Penguin, London, p. 669.

4 Beauvoir, *Old Age* 299.
5 Sartre, J.-P., 1969, *Being and Nothingness*, trans. H. Barnes, Routledge, London, part III, ch. 2.
6 Sartre, *Being and Nothingness* 346–347.
7 Ibid., 353.
8 Ibid., 353.
9 Ibid., 353.
10 Lacan's key ideas here were developed in the paper 'The Mirror Stage as Formative of the Function of the I as Revealed in Psychoanalytic Experience', in Lacan, Jacques, 2006 [1966], *Ecrits*, trans. Bruce Fink, Norton, New York.
11 Lacan, J., 1953, 'Some Reflections on the Ego', *International Journal of Psycho-Analysis* 34, no. 1, pp. 11–17.
12 Butler, J., 1993, *Bodies That Matter: On the Discursive Limits of 'Sex'*, Routledge, New York and London, p. 73.
13 Ibid., 75.
14 *Being and Nothingness* 328.
15 Morris, K., 2010, 'The Phenomenology of Clumsiness', in K. Morris, ed., *Sartre on the Body*, Palgrave Macmillan, London and New York.
16 Morris, P. S., 1996, 'Sartre on Objectification: A Feminist Perspective', in J. S. Murphy, ed., 1999, *Feminist Interpretations of Sartre*, Pennsylvania State University Press, University Park PA.
17 Freud, S., 1961 [1914], 'On Narcissism: An Introduction', in *The Standard Edition of the Complete Psychological Works of Sigmund Freud*, trans. James Strachey, Hogarth Press, London, vol. XIV, pp. 73–102.
18 Butler, 'The Lesbian Phallus and the Morphological Imaginary', *Bodies That Matter* ch. 2.
19 'On Narcissism'.
20 *Bodies That Matter* 58.
21 Freud, S., 1961 [1923], 'The Ego and the Id', in *The Standard Edition of the Complete Psychological Works of Sigmund Freud*, trans. James Strachey, Hogarth Press, London, vol. XIX, pp. 1–66.
22 Ibid., 25–26.
23 Ibid., 59.
24 Ibid., 65.
25 For further discussion see Weiss, G., 1999, *Body Images*, Routledge, London and New York.
26 Schilder, P., 1950, *The Image and the Appearance of the Human Body*, International Universities Press, New York, p. 126.
27 Ibid., 67.
28 Merleau-Ponty, M., 2012, *Phenomenology of Perception*, trans. Donald A. Landes, Routledge, London and New York, parts I and III.
29 *Phenomenology of Perception* 102.
30 Ibid., 102.
31 Marion Young, I., 1998, 'Throwing Like a Girl (Twenty Years Later)', in D. Welton, ed., *Body and Flesh: A Philosophical Reader*, Blackwell, Oxford, p. 21.
32 Merleau-Ponty, M., 1964, 'The Child's Relation to Others', in *The Primacy of Perception*, ed. J. M. Edie, Northwestern University Press, Evanston IL.
33 Ibid., 119.
34 Ibid., 140.
35 Weiss, *Body Images* 14.
36 Lennon, K., forthcoming, 'Wittgenstein and Merleau-Ponty on Expression', in Komarine Romdenh-Romluc, ed., *Wittgenstein and Merleau-Ponty*, Routledge, London.
37 Both writers were reading and responding to gestalt psychology. See chapter by Katherine Morris in Romdenh-Romluc, ed., *Wittgenstein and Merleau-Ponty*.

38 *Shorter Oxford English Dictionary*, 1970, Oxford University Press.
39 Wittgenstein, L., 1967, *Zettel*, Blackwell, Oxford, p. 225.
40 *Phenomenology of Perception* 188.
41 Ibid., 190.
42 Cockburn, D., 'Emotion, Expression and Conversation', available at: www.lamp. ac.uk/philosophy/expression.html, pp. 4–5.
43 The character is experienced through the physiology; in Merleau-Ponty's terms the invisible that is seen *in* the visible.
44 *Phenomenology of Perception* 195.
45 Merleau-Ponty, M., 1968, *The Visible and the Invisible*, Northwestern University Press, Evanston IL, p. 114.
46 Overgaard, S., 2007, *Wittgenstein and Other Minds: Rethinking Subjectivity and Intersubjectivity with Wittgenstein, Levinas, and Husserl*, Routledge, London, p. 146.
47 *Phenomenology of Perception* 191.
48 *Phenomenology of Perception* 190–191.
49 Cf. Overgaard, *Wittgenstein and Other Minds*.
50 Fanon, F., 2001, 'The Lived Experience of the Black', reprinted in R. Bernasconi, ed., *Race*, Blackwell, Oxford.
51 Alcoff, L., 2006, *Visible Identities: Race, Gender and the Self*, Oxford University Press, New York.
52 Fanon, 'The Lived Experience of the Black'.
53 Lorde, A., 1984, *Sister Outsider*, The Crossing Press, Freedom CA, pp. 147–148.
54 *Visible Identities*.
55 Ibid., 191.
56 Lennon, K., 2006, 'Making Life Livable: Transsexuality and Bodily Transformation', *Radical Philosophy* 140 (November), pp. 26–35.
57 *Visible Identities* 276.
58 *Being and Nothingness* 343.
59 Ibid., 344.
60 Ibid., 342.
61 Ibid., 343.
62 Ibid., 344.
63 Ibid., 390.
64 Ibid., 392.
65 Ibid., 392.
66 *The Visible and the Invisible* 23.
67 Ibid., 146.
68 Heidegger, M., 1963, *Introduction to Metaphysics*, trans. Ralph Manheim, Yale University Press, New Haven CT, pp. 27–28.
69 Johnson, G., 2010, *The Retrieval of the Beautiful: Thinking Through Merleau-Ponty's Aesthetics*, Northwestern University Press, Evanston IL, p. xvii.
70 Carman, T., 2008, *Merleau-Ponty*, Routledge, London and New York, p. 80.
71 Empathy, in the sense of the feeling between things.
72 *The Visible and the Invisible* 248.

Afterword

Throughout the course of this work we have uncovered the way in which the imagination is at work in perception, and thereby in our everyday experiences of ourselves, others and the world in which we are placed. The imaginary, in the sense we have been at pains to explore, is not a realm set up in opposition to the real. It is rather that which precedes a division into the actual and the fanciful, and is required for both. It is what is necessary for there to be a real for us, it is constituted by its organisational form and affective texture. So it is found in perception, as well as in dreams and fantasies, in works of art and mental conjurings.

The account of the imagination offered has been distilled from the work of the philosophers discussed, and incorporates several key elements. It requires Kant's concept of the productive imagination, in stressing that our perceptual encounters with the world grasp that world in terms of a shape or form, *an image*, in the broadest use of that term. (But the productive imagination is disentangled from a picture of a constituting transcendent subject.) Second, the account also incorporates aspects of the reproductive imagination, not as inner mental copies of previously perceived events, but in terms of the absent and the elsewhere being *alive* in the present. Here we have been guided, not by Hume, but by Merleau-Ponty in conversation with Sartre. The metaphor employed by both these writers, of the world pregnant with possibilities, then developed in Merleau-Ponty's conception of the imaginary as what is made available to us *in-the-visible* (sensible), has been the informing motif of the book.

The third key element is the recognition that the images in terms of which we experience the world express *our affective relation* to it. In Sartre's terms our experience of the world manifests an *affective–cognitive synthesis*. And the interrelations between images and affect are also central to the writings of psychoanalytic thinkers, and contemporary theorists utilising Spinoza. In Merleau-Ponty's terms, the affective dimension derives from the way the imaginary yields a shape to the world that is echoed by, mutually constituted with, the shape of our bodily responses. We find the world expressive, a state of affairs constituted by our ability to express it in our bodily, linguistic and artistic responses. These are responses which the world invites. A parallel thought is captured in McDowell's articulation of our experiences of the world as offering reasons (in a broad sense of this term, meaning something like normative grounding) for our responses to it.

The imaginary which we encounter in the world is *both disclosed and created*. There are, in Merleau-Ponty's terms, an infinite number of expressions to which the world is legitimately susceptible. But these are not imaginaries *imposed* on the world. They emerge in our interrelations with it. To bring the world to expression our imaginaries must be disclosive of it. The model here is derived from Kant's third *Critique*. We creatively produce forms, by encountering a world with which we find ourselves in harmony (harmony here simply means that we find we are able to bring to light aspects of the world, by means of our responses to it). The legitimacy of the forms we suggest requires the possibility of their being taken up and recognised by others.

The imaginaries in terms of which we encounter the world are anchored in our *bodily* presence within it but also on the *social* context in which we are placed. We are initiated into experiencing imaginary form by our social upbringing. These socially anchored imaginaries have, in the terms of Merleau-Ponty (here in conversation with Castoriadis), an *instituted and instituting structure*. To be open to the world at all we require already instituted imaginaries. But these do not have a fixed and stable meaning. They are open to re-signification and creative renewal, acts whereby imaginaries are instituted in alternative ways. This becomes particularly important in the light of the damaging and distorting imaginaries of the social, and groups positioned within it, that we encounter. As these operate commonly at the pre-reflective level, the question of the way in which they can be brought to reflective scrutiny and instituted in alternative ways becomes an urgent one. For the writers discussed here this is not a matter of assessing them in the light of non-imaginary facts. For on the picture outlined such facts are not available to us. Rather, imaginaries need to be countered by alternative (and multiple) imaginaries, which make both cognitive and affective sense to the different groups of people who share a social space. We have suggested that one of the tasks of writers, visual artists, musicians and, perhaps, political leaders is to offer us new imaginary structures. But this is also a task in which we all take some part, via our everyday *iteration* of everyday imaginaries.

The methods employed in this book are primarily phenomenological. The imaginary is offered as a way of drawing attention to the character of our lived experience of the world. The ontologies of both Kant and Sartre are rejected. There is no assumption of a noumenal subject confronting a noumenal world, and imposing form onto it. Nor is there an assumption of a *for itself*, a consciousness, marked only by spontaneity, positing imaginary content. But there are residual transcendental elements. The claim that the imaginary is required for there to be a real for us is a transcendental claim. The imaginary is offered as a condition of possibility for the real. And the claim that the imaginary of the world requires that our relation to the world is such that we *can* bring it to expression, in a way that invokes recognition in others (which Merleau-Ponty unpacks as resting on our carnal presence within it), is also a transcendental claim. As someone whose formative philosophical training was anchored in Kant, I find such transcendental elements unproblematic. But defending their legitimacy is not part of my project here.

This book has directed our attention to the imaginary of the experienced world, 'inscribed within it (in filigree)'.[1] We can think of imaginaries as the ways in which the world is lit up for us, ways which are open and infinite. To close, here is the Reverend John Ames, from the novel *Gilead* (describing what Merleau-Ponty would characterise as an *advent*):

> I was walking up to the church this morning, I passed that big row of oaks by the war memorial ... and I thought of another morning, fall a year or two ago, when they were dropping acorns thick as hail almost. There was all sorts of thrashing in the leaves and there were acorns hitting the pavement so hard they'd fly past my head ... I remember a slice of moon ... there was such energy in the things transpiring among those trees, like a storm, like travail ... and I thought: It is still all new to me. I have lived my life on the prairie and a line of oak trees can still astonish me.[2]

Notes

1 Merleau-Ponty, M., 1968, *The Visible and the Invisible*, Northwestern University Press, Evanston IL, p. 215.
2 Robinson, Marilynne, 2004, *Gilead*, Virago, London, p. 64.

Index